THE CULTIVATED MIND

THE
CULTIVATED
MIND

EDWARD HODNETT

———————————
———————————————
———————————

HARPER & ROW, PUBLISHERS
NEW YORK · EVANSTON · LONDON

001
H66

For
JONATHAN AND DAVID
when they grow up

CONTENTS

1

THE CULTIVATED MIND

In the unforgettable Overture to *Swann's Way*, Marcel Proust tells how, when he was a small boy, his family tried to ease his evening ordeal of separation from his mother by means of a magic lantern. As a boy, I never owned a magic lantern. Perhaps for this reason, on those rare occasions when I saw one at a friend's house, the images they cast on a wrinkled sheet on a wall seemed to me magic indeed, even more than they did to the boy Marcel Proust, who, after all, could have his lantern whenever he wished. For me, much of the magic doubtless came from the mysterious workings of the lantern and the eerie chiaroscuro of the room. What the subjects of the slides were, I have long since forgotten, but that the characters were of villainous and of heroic stuff I have no doubt, for I sat enchanted while they played through their limited repertory again and again.

I have thought of calling this book *The Magic Lantern*, because the experiences from which it has grown still affect me in much the same way that the lantern did long ago. I have no intention of neglecting the intellectual content of those experiences or the useful ends they serve. But here at the very beginning of our journey together, I would like to assure you that one justification for cultivating your mind is that it is pleasure of the highest order. You cannot find a more enjoyable way of spending your time.

One of the commonplaces of our time is the need for breadth of education on the part of each of us as a human being, no less than as a family member, a citizen, a productive worker, or a manager of others. Gilbert W. Chapman says that at the top level of management "the daily problems call for broad general knowledge, open-mindedness, an understanding of human nature, an insight into human frailties, a fairness of mind, a clarity of thought, all these beyond the ordinary knowledge of a complex business problem. There must be an intellectual cultivation through which an individual views the main current of the life around him."

Who has not this need? The engineer, the doctor, the lawyer, the secretary, the housewife, the teacher, the government official, the self-employed businessman, you and I—we all do. Despite our lengthening hours of leisure, our increase in years of formal education, and the accessibility of information on everything under the sun through books, magazines, television, and other mass media, a cultivated mind seems precisely what many of us feel we lack.

We know we need growth to reach our full potential. Some of us are discovering that we missed something important in the school and college curricula that trained us to fit job descriptions as snug as a drill in a chuck. Some of us have had our opportunity for growth delayed by hard necessity. And others—I count myself a deplorable example—have failed to make the most of the wonderful opportunities we have had. We have a sharp sense of inadequacy in relation to whole provinces of knowledge and accomplishment in which others spend their careers or leisure. During the past hundred years a division has come about, not only between the "two cultures"—the literary intellectuals and the scientists—but between one specialist and another. It is not at all unusual for a musician and a metallurgist, say, to feel equally cut off from modern poetry and biochemistry.

The great schism, however, lies between "practical people"— farmers, lawyers, doctors, businessmen, engineers, journalists, politicians, and housewives—on the one hand, and "intellectuals"

—scientists, scholars, writers, and creative artists of all sorts— on the other. This division has become more acute in recent years, not merely because of increased specialization in employment and increased satisfaction with material comforts, but also because modern science is much closer to the arts and philosophy in its essential nature than it is to the practical arts. Theoretical science also has become the shaping force in human affairs, indeed in human destiny. Yet the great disturbing questions that the vast powers of science have raised in our time press us back to the two age-old considerations of civilized man: What is right? and What is good? These are the questions that have perplexed man since he lifted himself above savagery. These are the two questions that perplex us most in the governance of our private lives.

THE LIBERAL ARTS

What help for us there is lies in the wisdom of the past, in the noblest and most comprehensive statements of man's role in the universe and in the complex vision of order and peace that is our legacy from the greatest souls that have worn human flesh. This wisdom and inspiration is readily available to us in those manifestations that we signify by the phrase "liberal arts." Very simply, these are man's efforts to explain the principles that control his environment and his relationships with it and with his fellow men, and to establish meaning and goals for his existence. These are not the concerns of the technologies for husbanding raw materials, making and distributing goods, teaching arithmetic, sending astronauts into space, writing sermons, or playing sonatas.

In academic terms liberal arts embrace the sciences, social sciences, and humanities. The pathetic part of the effort of schools of business, education, and engineering to balance the diet of their students by prescribing courses in humanities is that a professor of Restoration drama or modern art is often governed by considerations just as technical as those that guide a professor of marketing, pedagogy, or thermodynamics. Yet there resides at the heart of science, philosophy, literature, and the fine arts certain apprehensions of truth that are basic in any program of growth which you or I may wish to inaugurate.

With ample awareness of my temerity, therefore, I propose in this book to examine the liberal arts with you—at least to live over with you my experience of some of the major figures and major works and to try to isolate for both of us what seem some of the concrete values of this meeting with greatness for the cultivation of our minds.

But first let us ask: What is the cultivated mind? And, What are its uses?

WHAT IS THE CULTIVATED MIND?

The cultivated mind can be distinguished by three qualities. *First,* it seeks understanding. It is not content with being merely well informed or knowing how to do things. It wants to know why. It acts in accordance with reason; it abhors the subjugation of reason to custom and prejudice. It conceptualizes, that is, it is speculative; it formulates ideas about experience. It is creative; it solves problems in fresh ways. *Second,* it is discriminating. It is aware, sensitive to value. It finds life infinitely interesting in many manifestations, some of which seem more meaningful than others. *Third,* the central concern of the cultivated mind is mankind. The trivial preoccupations of self and the busy affairs of the world cannot dull a pervasive sense of the beauty and dignity, the folly and sadness of human existence. Strength in one or two of these qualities or in others may make a mind able, talented, or attractive. But all three of these qualities meet in the minds of men and women we call truly cultivated.

I make this bald statement of what I think constitutes the cultivated mind because I know that the word "cultivated" may have for some a flavor of dilettantism, stuffiness, or even snobbism. It is curious that we have no more exact word for the positive state we have described. "Cultured" is tarnished. "Educated" embraces professional and other forms of practical training. "Civilized" sounds condescending. Perhaps the word "mind" in the title offsets the suspicion of dilettantism. It is a reminder that there can be no true cultivation without rigorous intellectual activity. One can be good, useful, popular, and successful with modest intellectual effort. But a mind that is conceptual, discriminating, and humane must draw its sustenance from study of the greatest achievements in many fields.

THE SEARCH TO UNDERSTAND

The cultivated mind, we have said, seeks understanding. This search is carried on in many ways. The most fundamental method is through speculating about experience and arriving at concepts about it. There are persons who have sailed the seven seas, built businesses, gone to the opera for years, raised families, fought in battle, or suffered grave misfortune, and yet have formulated only superficial concepts about their experiences. Except in a crude way, they have not added up what has happened to them. They have been involved physically and emotionally, but not intellectually. In its search to understand, the cultivated mind has a compulsion to find the meaning even in slight experiences, as illustrated by Robert Frost's poems, for instance.

Perhaps because so much of our education is crude memory-testing, and so much of our work even at the professional level is routine manipulation of data and procedures, we are a fact-bound nation. Yet the problems that confound us politically, economically, and socially demand decisions based on judgments too complex for the poor wits of a computer: how to take care of our less fortunate citizens without becoming a welfare state, how to raise the standard of living throughout the world without lowering our own, how to encourage freedom and noninterference in the affairs of all peoples without encouraging anarchy and dictatorship, and how to be peace loving and yet keep communism in check. Ill-starred marriages and business failures, like wars, are memorials to men and women who lack understanding, whose vanity, greed, or gullibility are greater than their wisdom. Our value to ourselves and to society depends to a considerable degree upon the nature of the ideas we have.

The mind that delights in formulating ideas about experience and in solving problems in fresh ways is creative. It is flexible. Like a well-trained dog, the uncreative mind stays behind invisible fences. The creative mind is not fenced in by practice or authority. It is not dominated by assumptions about what cannot be done, what the right answer is, what seems good enough, or what will please the boss or the critics. It tends not to be envious, jealous, overcritical, or deferential. It is not dismayed that life is untidy, that so many problems clamor to be solved. The mind that habitually accepts the routine and orthodox, at work, in leisure time, or in thinking about the universe, ceases to grow and turns dry and sere. The mind that takes pleasure in asking questions, formulating hypotheses, inventing imaginative solutions to hard problems, stays green and growing, creative, cultivated.

DISCRIMINATING AMONG EXPERIENCES

The cultivated mind is open to life. It enjoys a childlike enthusiasm for varieties of experience—a second naïveté, Santayana calls it. The difference between being alive, savoring experience and seeming interesting to others, and being dull, bored, and commonplace depends not a little on this range of awareness. An aware mind reacts acutely to color and texture and sound, whether it be in a flower, a piece of driftwood, a bird's song, or in a painting, a poem, a chorale. It responds appreciatively to those crafts and usages by which man makes his brief stay oh this planet more agreeable, such as those which shape Cape Cod cottages, sailboats, bridges, language, manners, weddings, laws. For as Yeats says, "How but in custom and ceremony are innocence and beauty bred?"

In addition to this response to the amenities of existence, the cultivated mind is discriminating. It makes qualitative distinctions among its experiences. The difference in pleasure afforded by a flashing double-play in baseball and the deft brush strokes of a Chinese screen is a matter of taste. But that taste is pointless unless it is founded on an appreciation of both kinds of skill and includes distinctions in the meaningfulness of the two experiences. This habit of distinguishing among values is what allows a cultivated mind to keep a proper perspective. Sensitivity to the psychological and ethical nuances of human behavior, including admiration for human excellence, is a critical part of this discrimination. Thus the awareness of a cultivated mind effects a sharp sense of reality—a sense at once akin to a child's zest for touching things, a poet's intimation of the relatedness of disparate experiences, and the scientist's passion to penetrate the secrets of the structure of matter.

A CONCERN FOR MANKIND

A profound concern for mankind is the third characteristic of the cultivated mind. Without this, awareness and understanding are sterile. It supplies the secret of the mystery of why some persons are so successful in their relations with other human beings and manage to employ their lives so constructively. It provides a sense of identity with others that clothes them with perpetual interest. This interest is intrinsic, not peripheral to a responsibility for what others do, an urge to be liked by them, or a compulsion to control their behavior. This enlargement of a sense of humanity places the cultivated mind above the press of worldly affairs with its collateral envy, fear, and dislike of others. This concern for mankind leads the cultivated mind to respect the priceless integrity of individuals, to show a generous regard for their accomplishments and aspirations, and to have a decent forbearance for their differences and shortcomings.

WHAT ARE THE USES OF THE CULTIVATED MIND?

If we go back to Mr. Chapman's statement, we have the basic reason for believing that the cultivated mind is the most useful mind in the world. "Broad general knowledge, an understanding of human nature, an insight into human frailties, a fairness of mind, a clarity of thought"—these are the results of wide cultivation. They are not the results of narrow specialization in philosophy or art any more than in dentistry or patent law. The imperative need for the conceptualizing, discriminating, humane mind among executives arises from the problems that give them the most trouble. How do you decide among several candidates for an important post? What can industry do to offset unemployment caused by automation and other technological improvements? Does a company have any obligation to keep a plant running if it is losing money? These are common problems facing business executives. Yet statesmanlike decisions must be based on considerations not included in technical training. To deal wisely with such problems in any professional field, or with the momentous problems that challenge us as wielders of public opinion, or with those personal problems that trouble our own small worlds so grievously, then in truth "There must be an intellectual cultivation through which an individual views the main current of the life around him."

The practical uses of the cultivated mind are apparent. The seemingly unpractical uses are equally valuable. John Donne's "No man is an island" is a brilliant aphorism, but it is a half-truth. At times the seas of life wash over the causeways that connect us with the mainland of our fellows. Then in our loneliness we have dire need of resources beyond those we drain from family and friends, of joys less transient than those manufactured to fill our idle hours. When we think of a Charles Lamb writing the charming *Essays of Elia* while he faces his sister's periodic insanity, or the imprisoned Sir Walter Raleigh writing poems as noble as "Even Such Is Time" and "Give Me My Scallop-Shell of Quiet" in the expectancy of being beheaded, we have a glimpse of what reserves the cultivated mind has to draw on. In these days, when most of us who are employed work only 40 of the 168 hours in a week and look ahead to several years of leisure after retirement, the occupations of the cultivated mind are the only steadfast defense against the perils of boredom and of frittering away the best portion of our lives in unsubstantial and unproductive pursuits.

TO BECOME AN INDIVIDUAL

The growth of a child leads to independence—the freedom to tie his own shoes, to roam the countryside or the city streets, to handle tools, to read whatever comes his way, to make friends, to criticize his parents. At the same time parents, relatives, teachers, older children, and sundry other helpful souls take a hand in educating him. In the end he is "educated" out of his marvelous sense of being a unique individual and of having discovered the world. William Wordsworth said it long ago: "Shades of the prison house begin to close upon the growing boy."

Our prison house today is social, intellectual, and psychological conformity. Somewhere along the line, we tend to make too successful an adjustment to society. We do the same things, we have the same thoughts, and we react the same way as our peers, our fellow prisoners in the several cells that make up our world of home, work, and community. The disabling part of much conformity lies not so much in what we conform to, as in our compulsive drive to conform. We are so eager to "relate," to "belong," in short to be liked by one another, that we end up being exactly like one another. Sameness, whether in the pattern of a linoleum floor-covering, of work tasks, or of our lives, is the enemy of individuality.

Individuality does not emerge from gestures of childish rebellion such as beards, turtle-neck sweaters, and irresponsibility. It must be won through constant cultivation of the mind. Once you have traveled the vast seas and continents of human knowledge, you no longer can truly belong to a parish. You will still have your commitments, but they are of your own choosing. Your disengagement is inward. Others may judge a house by its architecture; you by the quality of the life within it. Others may respect a man because of his money or power; you, because of his character and intelligence. Others may find cause for jubilation or for heartbreak in the shifts of fortune; your main concern is whether or not you are spending your time in a worthy manner. To the person who stops growing early, the immediate event, the material fact, and the competitive advantage loom large and are all-absorbing in their ego implications. If you keep growing, you achieve a detachment, a self-sufficiency that makes material advantage, status, and recognition seem not of the first importance. You have become an individual.

ON BEING CREATIVE

All truly cultivated minds are creative. To design a Brooklyn Bridge, to invent a chemical process for synthesizing chlorophyll, to write a *Playboy of the Western World*—these are creations of great individuals. Yet each of us in his own way can be creative; and the liberal arts are our best source of inspiration. Being creative does not mean only writing sonnets or inventing new chemical compounds. In its simplest sense creativeness means an habitual compulsion to find better than usual solutions for problems. The hostess who can make a dinner party sparkle by bringing guests together in fresh combinations, by having an original kind of entertainment, or by steering the conversation into interesting channels is creative. The college professor who spends his vacation working in a circus is creative. These problem-solving experiences have not the complexity or difficulty of, say, formulating a plan for an educational system in a new African country or of writing a novel about the emergence of such a country. In your own life your creativeness must be measured against the opportunities you have. What sort of problems might you be trying to solve? What sort of solutions are you usually satisfied with?

Creativeness implies something more than intelligent problem solving. It also implies a genuinely original solution. This requires a high degree of imagination. The imaginative working out of a difficult mathematics problem or the third act of a play transcends the obvious. In science or art a truly original action usually involves a fresh approach to a problem, even a restructuring of the problem, and it often requires putting together hitherto unrelated factors in a new synthesis. Something beyond intelligence, training, and experience is involved. But the indispensability of these three elements has been largely overlooked in recent writings on "creativity." Advertising executives, magazine writers, engineers, and business school professors have recently discovered that the brilliant inventions of science and art are arrived at by obscure processes that contain a strong dash of what they vaguely call intuition. They have then proceeded to throw reason and discipline out with the dishwater of problem solving by formula. There is a certain uncalculated drawing on the subconscious in the solving of our everyday problems, all the way from choosing what suit to wearing in the morning to what mate to marry in June. But the great imaginative constructions of the Newtons and Lavoisiers, the Goethes and Wagners have been based on something more substantial than the negative effort to create without using logic, experience, or critical faculties.

THE GREAT TEACHERS

Let us say that you agree with me that these are the characteristics of a cultivated mind and that the substance on which the cultivated mind is nourished is found in those works that make up the liberal arts. Who then will be our guide among the riches of science, philosophy, literature, and the arts? Who but the great minds that created them? The great creative minds are the great teachers. Ample association with them is our best hope to develop a cultivated mind. Many of us depend on magazines and newspapers ("papers of a day, the ephemerae of learning," Dr. Johnson called them), on radio and television, and on the prejudices of our peers for much of the most important part of our intellectual intake—our information, judgments, values, and even our motivation. How we cheat ourselves when a Sophocles or a Jefferson is willing to tutor us!

When we examine the life of Leonardo, Michelangelo, Rembrandt, Faraday, Bach, Beethoven, Shakespeare, Franklin, or Lincoln, we find that they were all students, hungrily drawing sustenance from the great minds before them. All of the aforementioned, incidentally, lacked university education. Aristotle, Dante, Erasmus, Newton, Milton, Goethe, Coleridge, Humboldt, and many more of the greatest creative minds rank among the world's greatest scholars. It is impossible to exaggerate the two related elements in the record of every great creative person— passionate learning from the achievements of the past and creative effort sustained with extraordinary intensity throughout a lifetime. When someone sought to probe the mystery of Johann Sebastian Bach's genius, Bach said in a tart understatement, "I worked hard." He might have meant that, driven by a bright vision of what music could express, he had engaged in a relentless, lonely struggle to master his craft, a process of learning too arduous for lesser souls to endure.

The act of creating myths, epics, poems, stories, and plays; biographies, histories, philosophies, and religions; songs, symphonies, chamber music, and operas; paintings, prints, sculptures, and buildings; scientific systems and inventions—all this, as I have said, is an act of magic. The imagination of the creative mind is a magic lantern that casts on the screen of our consciousness images of a reality truer than the one we know. When a Plutarch, a Cervantes, or a Pasteur operates the lantern, he casts a spell over the rest of us mortals so that we are as bewitched as figures in a fairy tale.

Great creative works evoke an excitement compounded of sharply heightened awareness and a sense of profound insight. They also bring delight. They do so partly because the creative act takes place in a mood of excitement and delight. There is something akin to play in all creation, whether it be the composition of a musical suite or the discovery of a new antibiotic. An element of the esthetic is always present. Chess is a game of great intellectual complexity. Yet it is play, and the keenest enjoyment it has to offer its devotees is delight in patterns of moves that they describe as "elegant." This is the same term mathematicians use for a brilliant solution of a difficult problem. So too in social relations—the inspired solution of a legal, labor, or international problem also has its esthetic aspect.

Who does not desire to taste a modest portion of the delight that a mathematician or a musician, a philosopher, or a poet derives from his creative life? Why do we not seek earnestly, zestfully, constantly to learn from the great teachers? It seems that we are intimidated by greatness, or rather by the reputation of greatness. Just as a celebrity often converses with almost no one at a reception in his honor because most of the guests shake hands and then stand at a distance from him, so most of us shy away from further acquaintance with Milton and Aristotle and other great minds we have met in a classroom or other transient circumstances. This is a pity. The great creators are not only great teachers; they are great companions, warm, lively, sympathetic, inspiring.

In this book, therefore, we shall try to become better acquainted with some of the great minds in some of their major works. We shall not pretend to deal more than casually with historical, technical, or other factual aspects of any subject. Our most urgent need today is not on the level of factual comprehension. It is on the level of human significance. Our physicists, congressmen, newspapermen, teachers, and housewives know their jobs in a technical sense. Our need is not to know more about how things are made or how they work, but what they are for. We do not need to know more about what is going on, but what it means. Man's greatest need today is humanity. For this we have to turn to the great conceptualizing, image-making, value-finding minds of the past. Theirs are the most inspired records of man's attempts to interpret the mysteries of existence —his relations with the universe, with other human beings, and with himself.

We must not be solemn. Reading history or listening to Bach in order to improve oneself is virtuous, but there is danger in this approach. The earnestness of the effort to benefit from experience . too often prevents it from having its full meaning and turns a person into a prig. The cultivated mind that results from continued education is one of the foremost necessities of our society. But at the moment an exciting idea is first met or the marvel of a cathedral is suddenly comprehended, the experience is not practical. It is an esthetic delight. The riches of arts and letters, philosophy and science are ours to possess. Let the magic work on us. Then perhaps we too may develop some of the insights, largeness of mind, and joyous response to experience that are characteristic of the great teachers.

In *The Cultivated Mind*, I try to share with you my adventures among the masterpieces, to appropriate Anatole France's phrase. If on occasion my modesty slips and I sound all-knowing or seem to imply that I have attained the enlightened state I celebrate, be charitable, reader. I am acutely aware of my ignorance; chiefly I wish to share my experiences, not my findings. My aim has been to explore, not to teach, to sample varieties of greatness with no concern about consistency of approach. In some instances a man receives the brunt of attention, sometimes his works. Sometimes the engagement with greatness seems best managed by fairly extensive consideration of a single work, sometimes by a survey of the high points of a career. The brief I file is simple: If I can consort with the masters with so much pleasure and some benefit, you can, too.

2

THE IMPACT OF IDEAS

"There is no adequate defense, except stupidity, against the impact of a new idea," the philosopher P. W. Bridgman once said. In man's slow ascent, thinking is his latest accomplishment. It is still his least natural activity. Even under the pressure of necessity most of us manage to get along artfully without thinking very much. We let other people think for us, or we use our prejudices for propellants. Few of us have discovered that thinking is not only crucial to our continued development; it is also a creative, liberating art.

Doing things is so vital a part of our society and so conspicuously rewarded that we tend to underestimate the extent to which men of action are controlled by men of ideas. Generals, prime ministers, and heads of industrial empires are rarely the initiators of the ideas that move them to deeds that affect millions. When a Moses, a Napoleon, or a Jefferson is both a man of ideas and a man of action, then we measure the impact of their lives in megatons.

In this chapter we shall get acquainted with five great creative thinkers. Not all of their ideas have withstood the siege of time, and not all of the consequences of their thinking have been beneficial. Yet in venturing into the vast reaches of philosophy, religion, economics, history, and psychology, we are bound to be stirred by the excitement of fresh ideas and to be moved to awe at the realization of how completely ideas shape civilization.

SOCRATES AND PLATO OF ATHENS

The death of Pericles in 428 B.C. marks the end of the greatest years of the little city-state of Athens, the most civilized political unit the world has yet known. During the fifth century B.C., Athens not only reached great heights in the arts of architecture, sculpture, drama, and oratory but also in the art of government. It was the first democracy, with each citizen taking active part in public affairs personally without intermediate representation. Athens had banded together with Sparta, the other leading city-state of Greece, to defeat the Persians by 479 B.C. But much as Russia and the Allies fell out after vanquishing the Nazis, so Sparta turned enemy of Athens, and in the "inevitable" Peloponnesian War (431–404 B.C.) Sparta humbled Athens decisively.

The lesson for us is grim: The citizens of Sparta were trained from childhood only to serve the state; the citizens of Athens sought to preserve the maximum of personal freedom for the individual within the framework of a government of law, much as Western democracies do today. The lesson is not merely that in war superior culture is not the match for superior force. It is also that a democracy weakens like an athlete with a virus as soon as the individual citizen puts his own self-interest and material comfort and pleasure before personal virtue and the welfare of the body politic. We have arrived at this stage without ever passing through any comparable to that of the Age of Pericles. The Greeks had to wait until an outlander, Philip of Macedon, and his son, Alexander the Great, united the city-states and tribes into a new kind of power, the national state.

In these dark years and a little later there walked in the public places of Athens the immortal trio of Socrates, Plato, and Aristotle, the first and third connected personally by the second. Plato may have been born the year of Pericles' death. About the age of twenty he became a follower of Socrates, when the latter was sixty—about 409 B.C. Socrates died in 399 B.C. at the age of seventy. Grief-stricken, Plato traveled for ten years and then returned to Athens to start the Academy, which became the first university in Europe and lasted 900 years. He died in 348 B.C. Aristotle (384–322 B.C.), his most famous pupil, is discussed in the next chapter.

The basis of the fame of Socrates is extraordinary. No writing of his exists; probably he wrote nothing. He talked, endlessly, and his talk lives in the writings of his devoted pupil, Plato. Miraculously, all of the writings of Plato are said to be preserved. What portion of the thought in them is essential Socrates, what is modied, and what is pure Plato is impossible to say. No doubt the earlier writings incorporate much of Socrates' characteristic speech; probably the middle ones and the later ones sometimes incorporate his ideas but use him more and more as a vehicle for expressing Plato's own thoughts. But throughout Plato's works are wonderful glimpses of Socrates as he must have been.

Socrates is one of the most beguiling, believable, and stimulating figures in the world, even if he did live 2,400 years ago. The son of a stone-cutter, he was poor, badly dressed, and famed for his ugliness—the purported likeness of him shows a bashed-in nose under a knobby forehead. He neglected his shrewish wife, Xanthippe, and his three children to haunt the streets, public buildings, and homes of the rich. The single mission of his life was the pursuit of wisdom. Except for his war service, one trip that he mentions, and walks in the countryside, he stuck as close to the streets of Athens as the sparrows. All he did was talk. He said that he went about seeking those who might be wiser than he was. Then he cross-examined them, invariably to their discomfiture. Or the sons of the aristocracy sought him out, egged him on with questions, suffered him to demolish their arguments, cherished his words, and made him their boon companion.

What did Socrates talk about? Love, friendship, piety, justice, death—the great universal themes underlying human existence and distinguishing it from animal existence. How did he talk about them? On short acquaintance you may think him a logic-chopper, badgering his antagonists with analogies and premises, drawing them by means of agreement with a series of seemingly self-evident truths to final admission of the invalidity of a belief stoutly held at the outset. But you have to meet Socrates in the various situations that are the occasions for Plato's dialogues to truly appreciate him.

You may be surprised to find philosophy taking wing in the form of drama. Yet Plato's works are a series of dialogues—scenes in which Socrates is the leading actor. Instead of the labyrinthine abstractions of German philosophers, Plato's characters use the conversational idiom of educated persons. Since they are highly articulate and deeply committed to what they are saying, their speech is often eloquent. Their dialogue is tense with the clash of subtly reasoned argument, though it is leavened with tolerance, humor, and affection. But in the midst of discourse about piety, justice, and such matters, the drama of ideas gives way to human drama when the life of Socrates himself becomes the paramount issue.

Plato presents this almost unbelievable biographical drama in four dialogues, *Euthyphro, Apology, Crito,* and *Phaedo.* In *Euthyphro,* Socrates meets a young man of that name at the place for initiating lawsuits. Euthyphro has come to charge his father with murder because he was responsible for the death of a serf who had killed a man. Socrates has a field day with this ambiguous situation. Self-righteous young Euthyphro becomes so entangled in contradictory statements of what piety is and is not that he cries: "I really do not know, Socrates, how to express what I mean. For somehow or other our arguments, on whatever ground we rest them, seem to turn round and walk away from us." In this dialogue Plato has Socrates announce casually that a beak-nosed young man named Meletus is bringing the charge against Socrates that he is corrupting the youth by inventing new gods and denying the existence of the old.

"A SORT OF GADFLY"

The *Apology*—the word here means defense—is sometimes called "The Trial of Socrates." But it is a monologue in three sections. In the first Socrates defends his way of life before the judges. He says:

If you say to me, Socrates, this time . . . you shall be let off but upon one condition, that you are not to inquire and speculate in this way any more, and that if you are caught doing so again you shall die—if this was the condition on which you let me go, I should reply: Men of Athens, I honor and love you; but I shall obey God rather than you, and while I have life and strength I shall never cease from the practice and teaching of philosophy, exhorting any one whom I meet and saying to him after my manner: You, my friend—a citizen of the great and mighty and wise city of Athens—are you not ashamed of heaping up the greatest amount of money and honor and reputation, and caring so little about wisdom and truth and the greatest improvement of the soul, which you never regard or heed at all?

The best reason Socrates can think of for their letting him off is this:

If you kill me, you will not easily find a successor to me, who, if I may use such a ludicrous figure of speech, am a sort of gadfly, given to the State by God; and the State is a great and noble steed who is tardy in his motions owing to his very size, and requires to be stirred into life. I am that gadfly which God has attached to the State, and all day long and in all places am always fastening upon you, arousing and persuading and reproaching you. You will not easily find another like me, and therefore I would advise you to spare me.

By a close vote the judges decide that he is guilty.

THE DEATH OF SOCRATES

In the second phase Socrates discusses what his penalty should be. This extraordinary procedure seems characteristic of Athenian enlightenment. Meletus has asked for death. Because he has neglected his own interests to teach the citizens virtue, Socrates says, he deserves a sort of Nobel Prize—the state should maintain him. But death, imprisonment, exile—these are unsuitable. So at the suggestion of four of his friends, including Plato, he proposes a fine that they will be surety for. By a larger vote the jury now votes for death.

In the third section Socrates, finally at bay, faces the enormous question of death. First he notes that he might have avoided the verdict by saying the right things. But "the difficulty, my friends, is not to avoid death, but to avoid unrighteousness; for that runs faster than death." He prophesies that there will be more accusers of the judges than of him. What he is really interested in, though, is the meaning of the experience to him. If death means sleep, good. If it means a new existence in the company of the illustrious dead, good: he has questions to ask them. In any case, he assures the judges, "Be of good cheer about death . . . no evil can happen to a good man." He asks a favor: When his sons are grown up, he asks that they be censured if they ever pretend to be something that they are not. He ends: "The hour of departure has arrived, and we go our ways—I to die, and you to live. Which is the better, God only knows."

The *Crito* takes place in prison. Crito, one of the rich young men, comes early to persuade Socrates to let him arrange for his escape. As leisurely as though he were strolling about the city with Crito, Socrates analyzes what is the right thing to do. He establishes that the good citizen, whose whole life takes its meaning from a government of law, cannot set the laws aside when he thinks they wrong him. Surely he, Socrates, must abide by the decision of the judges.

The *Phaedo* is the most dramatic of the dialogues, and it is one of the most moving scenes in all literature. Only remember that it is not fiction. It is often called the "Death of Socrates." Apparently Plato was too ill to be with his beloved master on his last day. He therefore uses the rehearsal device; Phaedo, one of the young men who was present, on a visit to Phlius tells Echecrates what happened. Also present in the prison were four other young men—Apollodorus, Simmias, Cebes, and Crito—and an attendant. Socrates has just been released from chains. In answer to a question, he explains why he has been turning Aesop's *Fables* into verse and composing a hymn in honor of Apollo. He was obeying a dream.

In the midst of tears and laughter Socrates discusses with the young men the nature of death for a true philosopher. Absolute justice, beauty, and good are never visible to the bodily senses, but through the mind alone. Wars and other evils come from the body. The souls of the good enjoy immortality. Therefore, he approaches his end contentedly. He takes a bath and says good-bye to his family. The jailer who has to give him the poison hemlock apologizes and bursts into tears. "How charming the man is," comments Socrates. He insists on not delaying as long as he might, drinks the hemlock, chides his young admirers as they all weep, and dies quietly. Such was the end, says Phaedo, of all men of his time the wisest and justest and best.

We have not space to account for the other dialogues of Plato. They are all conversational, discursive. They do not come to neat conclusions or add up to a systematic doctrine. His greatest influence on philosophy seems an extension of the logic of Socrates. Ultimate reality is made up of essences, ideas, forms, or universal truths. What we mistake for reality is only appearance. In his famous allegory of the cave in the *Republic*, Plato says we are like prisoners who have spent their lives chained in a cave facing the back wall. Behind them is a fire blazing and between them and the fire is a wall along which men walk carrying things. All that the prisoners ever see is the shadows, and these they take for reality. In the *Phaedrus* he illustrates the same point by having Socrates remind Phaedrus that the written word is only an image of the "living word of knowledge," a truth semanticists stress today as though they had discovered it. In the *Symposium* he argues that transcending physical love and beauty is a permanent, spiritual entity, an unchanging absolute. In the end moral goodness and esthetic beauty are one. This idea has had enormous influence on Western thought.

In the *Republic*, his longest dialogue, Plato applies his ideas to practical affairs. Since only the true philosopher can come to perceive the idea of beauty embodied in a flower or the idea of goodness in a man, states should be ruled by philosopher-kings. Though Plato's ideal state, projected against the disintegrating events of his time, strikes us as leaning toward dictatorship, it is fair to say Plato conceives of the perfect state only as the framework for the lives of men of wisdom. The *Republic* and all the other dialogues make up a wonderfully varied, poetic, tolerant, un-final examination of what the good life should be.

JEAN-JACQUES ROUSSEAU—
THE ROAD TO VINCENNES

Jean-Jacques Rousseau (1712–1778) is one of the least heroic, most exasperating, and most influential men who ever lived. *La Nouvelle Héloise* is one of the most significant of novels. *Émile* has had more influence on education than any other single book. *The Social Contract* and *A Discourse on Political Economy* were among the primers of the men who engineered the three greatest revolutions—the American, the French, and the Russian. Finally, Rousseau's *Confessions*, besides being the most famous of all autobiographies, contributed certain essentials to the image of the romantic personality, still unextinguished by the rising tide of science today.

His *Confessions* is Rousseau's masterpiece. He is too much infatuated with his subject to be ill at ease in telling the truth. Born in Geneva, Switzerland, but French in origins, motherless after nine days, apprenticed at twelve, adrift at fourteen, a temporary convert to Catholicism, at seventeen he entered the ménage of a remarkable twenty-nine year old divorcée, Mme. de Warens. This pretty, warm-hearted ash-blonde, who mixed pietism, herbary, hospitality, speculation, and political intrigue, tried hard to educate the talkative gossoon who walked on his heels because he had corns. He adored his *Maman,* as he called her, accepted her support without a qualm, but had difficulty later in shifting to the role of lover.

For some years Jean-Jacques' history is a succession of erratic episodes ending in ignominious failures. He tried his hand at twelve trades, including engraving, lackeying, tutoring, being a secretary, and teaching music without training. He either quit or was fired from every job he ever had. He was unstable; he lacked the minor talent of getting along with people. The only work he ever did with any appearance of responsibility was to copy music and, briefly at the end of his life, arrange portable herbaria for sale to amateur botanists like himself. Yet on more than one occasion he turned down sinecures. Mostly he lived on the bounty of friends.

TRUE CONFESSIONS

The title *Confessions* is not altogether unapt; *apologia* in the original sense might be better. Jean-Jacques does confess a few misdeeds, such as accusing an innocent serving girl of stealing a ribbon (they were both fired). Sometimes he doctors the facts to show himself to better advantage, but many times he reports misadventures with unvarnished candor and wry appreciation of the fool he had been. On the other hand he casts himself as the anguished hero in episodes that seem comic fantasies dreamt up by Da Ponte for *Figaro*—the one in which, for instance, at the age of forty-five he besieges with febrile passion the vivacious young Mme. d'Houdetot, who remains faithful to her lover far, far away, while her husband plays cards.

At this time Jean-Jacques had been living for a dozen years with Thérèse Levasseur, a charmless Paris peasant who never learned to tell time. Thérèse and her odious mother were the root of many of Rousseau's troubles. But the *Confessions,* so veined with criticism of others, traces no faults in the thirty-five year relationship with Thérèse. Anyone who could put up with Jean-Jacques that long deserved the accolade of respectability that he bestowed by marrying her in 1768. The most shameful act that Jean-Jacques brought himself to confess was that he cast into the Foundlings' Hospital all five of the children that he says blessed this union. In spite of his talent for squirming out from under the burden of guilt for his injuries to others, this cold-blooded cruelty haunted him ever after.

In 1748, Rousseau had the first attack of kidney trouble that caused him pain and embarrassment almost steadily the rest of his life and in its severe onsets was so excruciating that more than once he was sure that he was near death, possibly by his own hand. The uremic poisoning accompanying this condition is said to be the root of his increasingly violent persecution mania and the cause of his death. Coupled with the damage done to his nervous system by his motherless, cheerless childhood and the insecurity and turmoil of his existence, the disability of ill health makes his productivity amazing. For although Jean-Jacques was too undisciplined to hold any job, he had the iron will necessary to think through, write, and rewrite the thousands of pages in his collected works. Once when he was sick with pleurisy and fever while traveling in a stagecoach, he wrote the songs for an opera. What makes this volume of work even more remarkable, especially in political science, is that the only schooling he had that mattered was the reading he snatched by the way, beginning with Plutarch's *Lives* at eight. Jean-Jacques must have had a high I.Q., and he must have been one of those persons whose minds are highly absorbent to the random readings that interest them. He was unquestionably one of those rare persons to whom ideas are food and drink.

In the waning of his prolonged adolescence, Jean-Jacques had gone to Paris with the scheme of restoring *Maman's* fortune by selling his invention of a system of musical notation by numbers. He made no money, but he made friends with leaders of society and letters. One of these was Denis Diderot, the chief of the rationalistic *philosophes* and the brilliant editor of the great *Encyclopedia*. Just what Jean-Jacques had to offer Diderot and his friends then is not clear, but they remained his friends and enemies unto death. Resting by the side of the road on his way to visit Diderot in jail in Vincennes, Jean-Jacques had the first intimations of his destiny. He read the announcement of an essay contest on whether the progress of arts and sciences had tended to corrupt or elevate morals. Jean-Jacques' arguments for the negative view were weak, but his verve won him the prize and his first taste of notoriety. The concept that had come to him on the road to Vincennes was that the parlous state of man was the result of the misguided efforts that had produced the kind of civilization in which he found himself. Progress is really retrogression from a natural primitive society. The essay set the salons of the Continent a-buzz; Jean-Jacques had arrived. In essays, letters, and books he explored the implications of his paradox as long as he lived.

JULIE AND THE NEW SENSIBILITY

The reader of contemporary American rock-and-roll fiction has a hard time believing that *Julie, ou la Nouvelle Héloise* is one of

the most influential of novels. The story is silly. The parallel between the heroine, Julie, and the Paris girl who had the unfortunate affair with the medieval monk, Abelard, seems hardly
noticeable. Through letters—an annoying device Rousseau borrowed from Samuel Richardson, father of the English novel—the
reader follows the love of low-born hero, Saint-Preux, for eight-
een-year-old Julie d'Etange, whom he is tutoring together with
her cousin Claire. Julie's father wants to "sell" her to older baron
De Wolmar, but Julie gives herself to Saint-Preux. They feel
"married in the sight of God."

But Julie changes her mind, sends her lover away, and marries
the baron. Six years later, Saint-Preux returns from an expedition.
Julie is the happy mother of two boys. The baron, who knows
all, quenches any embers of the old passion by throwing the ex-
lovers together. Fatally ill, Julie makes a disingenuous effort to
bequeath Saint-Preux to Claire, then dies. The survivors decide
to dedicate their lives to her virtuous memory.

La Nouvelle Héloise seems to us to have all the suffocating
sentimentality of eighteenth-century French engravings. But it
was a best seller largely because of that sentimentality—or sensi-
bility, as they preferred to say. The "man of feeling" was something new in the age of reason. New also was the rhapsodic
response to nature, especially the trick of using it as a reflector
of moods. The low-born hero, his excessive emotionalism, the
focus on the woman's problems, the blend of eroticism, virtue,
and religious piety, and the tacit understanding that the characters are set apart from ordinary persons and not subject to the
usual rules of behavior—these, too, are Rousseauisms that have
rooted and spread like lilies of the valley.

THE EDUCATION OF ÉMILE

Émile (1762) traces the education of a boy from birth to manhood. More a tract than a novel, it has been called the "Magna
Carta of children." European education, Rousseau argued, rested
on unsound foundations. "Natural education" would spoil as little
as possible the essential goodness of the child and keep him from
being warped by the artificial pressures of society before they
had to be met. First, the young child should be nursed by its

mother—putting a baby out to a wet-nurse was the barbarous custom of the upper classes. Yet the child should not be coddled. It should wear loose clothing, exercise, breathe fresh air, and not be negatively conditioned to conformity, as we would say. In this stage of naturalness, Jean-Jacques admits, the child may be a *polisson,* a brat.

The child's curiosity should be satisfied by truthful answers to questions, but otherwise it should learn intuitively, discovering from actual situations the fundamentals of astronomy, geography, and dynamics. Knowing how to solve problems, not mere fact-piling, is important. With *Robinson Crusoe* as his one textbook, Émile learns that iron may be worth more than diamonds, a carpenter more valuable than an engraver. He begins to understand economics, but he also learns to handle tools—Jean-Jacques makes the admirable suggestion that every child should master one trade.

When he is about fifteen, Émile undergoes a "stormy upheaval" and the "second birth" of coming into a moral existence. Now he experiences sympathy for others less fortunate. Religious teaching begins at eighteen. Here Jean-Jacques introduces a profession of faith that reaches back to his illumination on the way to see Diderot. The doctrine of original sin is faulty; a man's life is good or evil as he wills it. Life in the hereafter will be good for the just man. Conscience, not reason or self-interest, is the source of morality. Émile's education ends in deliberately delayed romance, travel, and marriage. In spite of his indebtedness to enlightened women, Rosseau limited the education of girls to the preparation of family duties.

Modern school education would not be what it is without *Émile.* Pestalozzi, Froebel, Montessori, Horace Mann, John Dewey, and all builders of our elementary and secondary curricula and teaching methods have drawn much of their inspiration from the insights of a man who today could offer no qualifications for teaching even the third grade. From *Émile*—although, of course, there are other sources—comes the basic concept of the importance of the development of the individual child. The child is not just a small adult. The learning process must be adjusted to the child's capacities and interests at different ages. Learning is most meaningful when it proceeds inductively from firsthand investigation of realities, not from rote recitation of abstractions. Though education for citizenship is vital, the first aim of education is not to fit a child for service to the state or for an occupation but for meeting the obligations and opportunities of life as a human being.

THE STATE AS THE WILL OF THE PEOPLE

"Man is born free; and everywhere he is in chains" is the trenchant opening of *The Social Contract*. Again we are on the road to Vincennes. As early as 1750, Rousseau began to draft a comprehensive work on political institutions. It was too much for even his fertile mind, but that mind produced the essay *Political Economy* for Diderot's *Encyclopedia* of 1755 and *The Social Contract* in 1762, abiding contributions to man's efforts to govern himself in a civilized way. Jean-Jacques had renounced Catholicism and had regained his citizenship in Calvinist Geneva. His thinking about the proper organization of a state and the relation of the family and the individual to the state is strongly influenced by the Constitution of Geneva. He was thus able to imagine an ideal social organization in which the free citizen played a role not unlike the one he had in ancient Sparta. Rousseau's historic concept is that the state exists only as a pact among free men, as the will of the people. The individual obeys the laws for the general welfare but remains free, for he is in effect obeying himself. Jean-Jacques was no Communist; he believed in private property, religious faith, and natural rights. Indeed, his chief bequest to posterity is that the people are sovereign and must under no condition hand over their sovereignty to any person or group. But his ideas have helped light the fires of every revolution in the two hundred years since they were published.

Because so many of Jean-Jacques Rousseau's ideas are imbedded in our daily lives, it is hard to grasp how original they were and how influential they have been. He is the greatest single force in the creation of that way of looking at the world that we call romantic, which is essentially our own. Jean-Jacques taught us to subordinate reason to feeling, to look on nature as good, to believe in the nobility of savages and other simple people close to the soil, to imagine that children arrive "trailing clouds of glory" and that they, not the curriculum, are the reason for education, to accept the state as the servant of of the citizens, and to prize above all other considerations the freedom of the individual from tyranny in any form.

Jean-Jacques's writings antagonized the monarchists, the Catholics, the Calvinists, and the rationalists—a grand slam. He was forced to flee France and was given generous asylum in several places, including England. He quarreled bitterly with Diderot and his benefactor, the Scotch philosopher David Hume. In his last dozen years the poisons of uremia and paranoia drove him like a blind Lear about the heath of Europe until his death. Yet during this time he wrote his *Confessions*, which created the man of feeling as hero from Byron to Hemingway and Faulkner. Genius takes its residence in curious apartments. Hummingbird-like, Rousseau made his own quivering sensibilities an instrument for extracting from his messy existence concepts which started actions that are still changing the world today.

KARL MARX, THE BOURGEOIS THEORIST OF SOHO

The ideas of Karl Marx have probably had more impact on mankind than those of anyone else except Jesus Christ. He is a terrifying refutation of the practical person's contempt of theory. Men of action carry out social change, but without theories they are as aimless as toy bugs wound up and turned loose by a child. Mussolini was such a leader. Karl Marx provided the theories that Lenin, Trotsky, Stalin, Khrushchev, Tito, Mao Tse-tung, and their followers have invoked to bring half the earth under communism. He changed the course of history. How did this come about?

Karl Marx (1818–1883) was a completely bourgeois person. His father, a Jew turned Protestant, was a successful German lawyer who gave his son an aristocratic university education and encouraged his liberal thinking. Karl married Jenny von West-phalen, the daughter of a baron; she was related to the Duke of Argyll of Scotland. They were devoted to one another in the best tradition of the bourgeoisie. The only work Marx ever did for pay was journalistic, but his stints as an editor in Germany and France were brief and disastrous. In addition, incongruously, he was foreign correspondent for the now conservative *New York Tribune*. The closest Marx ever got to the proletariat was by liv-ing in Soho, then in the slums of London, where he took sanctu-ary after being chased from the Continent. He lies buried in the consecrated ground of a London cemetery, not within the walls of the Kremlin.

Even more bourgeois was Friedrich Engels (1820–1895), Marx's collaborator. Engels was the charming son of a German textile manufacturer. He managed one of his father's factories in grubby Manchester, England, and in his spare time teamed up with Marx in attacking the capitalist system. Constantly Engels gave Marx money that helped keep some of his large family alive; on occasion he wrote Marx's dispatches of the *Tribune* for him. When Engels came into an inheritance in 1869, he joyfully gave up making useful cloth to live on the profits of the infamous factories that he had condemned in his *The Condition of the Working Class in England in 1844*.

Marx and Engels began their association in 1844. That it lasted is a tribute to Engels' tact. Outside of his family Marx was a difficult person, suspicious, disputatious, intolerant. Squat, black-maned, bewhiskered, rumpled, he spent his days in the bleak circular reading room of the British Museum, reading voraciously and writing while his carbuncles ached. The rest of his time he spent in his Soho tenement in a fog of tobacco smoke and a welter of books and manuscript. In the 1840s he had been a leader of a socialist group called the Communist League. It expired and was followed by the International Workingmen's Association, which flourished briefly under his guidance and then foundered. What impact Karl Marx has had on history has been through the writ-ten word.

The hosts for the words of Marx that have been the bacilli in the spread of communism are the pamphlet-length *Communist Manifesto* and the 2,500-page *Capital*. For unknown reasons, in America the first is never referred to by its original German title, but the second usually is—*Das Kapital*. Both works were written for western Europeans against a background of the new industrial capitalism, an inhuman system by which a few owners grew rich from the work of poorly paid men, women, and children, who often slaved sixteen hours a day amid frightful conditions. That this barbaric type of capitalism still exists in many parts of the world is a great comfort to Moscow and Peiping.

THE TEN COMMANDMENTS OF COMMUNISM

The Communist Manifesto ends in the kind of blazing rhetoric we expect revolutionists to write:

The Communists disdain to conceal their views and aims. They openly declare that their ends can be attained only by the forcible overthrow of all existing social conditions. Let the ruling classes tremble at a Communist revolution. The proletarians have nothing to lose but their chains. They have a world to win.

Workingmen of all countries, unite!

The *Manifesto* was written for the international Communist League around Christmas 1847 and printed in London in February 1848. The times were seething with unrest. The lid blew off throughout Europe in 1848 and was roughly jammed back again. A good many American families proudly trace their lineage back to refugee revolutionists of 1848.

Only much later did the facts of world conspiracy match the implacable pronouncements of the *Manifesto*. But the fifty-page document is the tocsin that warned the world of that conspiracy and of the power to bring it about wielded by the brilliant young German partners. The two had absorbed economic theory from Ricardo, Malthus, and Mill, and socialism from Saint-Simon, Fourier, Owen, and other utopians. They did not discover either the ills of industrial society or the Communist cure. But they made historic contributions. First, they offered in the *Manifesto* for the first time a unified program of total social change. Second, their program was one of dynamic action promising progressive improvement. Third, it proposed ten concrete reforms that combine lucidity of statement with profound emotional appeal to the workers. Fourth, and most original, it presented a new theory of history as a struggle between those who command the means of production and the exploited workers who produce. And finally, for the first time it called on those workers to be the instruments of their own liberation through international revolution.

In the century since their writing, the ten plain proposals of the *Manifesto* have become the ten commandments of millions of Communists and the rationalization of the ruthless acts of their leaders. What ideas have caused more worldwide upheavals than "Abolition of landed property," "Abolition of all right of inheritance," "Confiscation of the property of all émigres and rebels," "Centralization of credit in the hands of the State," "National factories and means of production," "Centralization of of the means of communication and transport in the hands of the State," "Universal and equal obligation to work; organization of industrial armies, especially for agriculture"? These ideas are far from the abstractions of the German idealists, the plans of the liberals for ameliorating conditions without essentially changing the status quo, or the planless propaganda of the other revolutionists. Yet in this Communist credo are goals first realized in Western democracies: "A vigorously graded income tax," "Agriculture and urban industry to work hand in hand, in such a way as, by degrees, to obliterate the distinction between town and country," "Public and free education for all children. Abolition of factory work for children. . . ."

Most of the *Communist Manifesto* is not revolutionary rhetoric: It offers a vigorous, readable, sardonic presentation of what Marx and Engels considered the rationale for the overthrow of capitalism by industrial workers. A hundred years have destroyed the validity of many of the key assumptions and prophecies, but not the truth of the description of the emergence of modern industrial society, its anatomy, and its problems. We can hardly quarrel with a paragraph like this:

The bourgeoisie, during its rule of scarce one hundred years, has created more massive and more colossal productive forces than have all preceding generations together. Subjection of nature's forces to man, machinery, application of chemistry to industry and agriculture, steam-navigation, railways, electric telegraphs, clearing of whole continents for cultivation, canalization of rivers, whole populations conjured out of the ground—what earlier century had even a presentiment that such productive forces slumbered in the lap of social labor?

The pamphlet is full of arresting sentences: "The bourgeoisie has played a most revolutionary role in history. . . . The bourgeoisie cannot exist without constantly revolutionizing the instruments of production, and thereby the relations of production, and with them the whole relations of society. . . . The need of a constantly expanding market for its products chases the bourgeoisie over the whole surface of the globe. . . . [Old-established national industries] are dislodged by new industries, whose introduction becomes a life and death question for all civilized nations, by industries that no longer work up indigenous raw material, but raw material drawn from the remotest zones; industries whose products are consumed, not only at home, but in every quarter of the globe. . . . Owing to the extensive use of machinery and to division of labor, the work of the proletarians has lost all individual character and consequently all charm for the workman. . . . What the bourgeoisie therefore produces, above all, are its own grave-diggers. Its fall and the victory of the proletariat are equally inevitable."

THE MYTHS OF MARX

Capital is a monumental work in more ways than one. It appeared first in German in four sections, but with long delays punctuated by additional editions of single volumes and by a scattering of translations. Marx saw Volume I through the press in 1867. Engels brought out Volume II in 1885 and Volume III in 1894. The material that was to be Volume IV was reworked by Karl Kautsky and appeared in three volumes as *Theories of Surplus Value.* Thus Marx is fully responsible only for the first volume of his masterwork—over 800 pages, at that. In bringing order out of Marx's manuscript and notes, Engels made contributions beyond those of an ordinary editor. According to the preface of the American edition, "A large portion of the contents of *Capital* is as much a creation of Engels as though he had written it independently of Marx." The regrettable part of this blurring of authorship is that it allows Marx to get out of logical corners into which he painted himself.

It is important to note three things that are *not* true about Marx: He was *not* exclusively concerned with capitalism. He did *not* maintain that the economic motive is the mainspring of human activity. And he did *not* offer any concrete plan for the realization of his predictions and is, therefore, not the architect of the evils done in the name of "Marxism." The Communist party as we know it, and the Russian oligarchy with its Chinese and other copies, are the creations of Vladimir Ilyich Ulyanov, known as Lenin. To be sure, Marx preached revolution. He was neurotic and sometimes sadistic. He felt no shame about living off other people's money throughout his entire life, or about condemning his family to an existence almost as miserable and quite as tragic as any visited on the mill and mine workers by the most callous of capitalists. Yet he would surely have been horrified by the rule of murder and abrogation of individual rights in the police states of Stalin and Mao Tse-tung. No matter how opposed to his ideas we may be, he was a scholar, an economist and social historian, a publicist and satirist, and a humanitarian moved by a "holy anger" as deep as that of Swift, Rousseau, or Blake.

Capital is one of man's supreme intellectual efforts. Marx sought to devise and document an evolutionary theory of social history in which capitalism was only a phase, a better one than preceding epochs, a worse one than the two to come. Indeed, he wanted to dedicate the work to Darwin. He called his system "dialectical materialism." He was not using dialectic in the Socratic sense of a successive integration of differing views through discussion. He was borrowing the metaphysical jargon of the philosophy of Hegel, which had influenced him deeply at the University of Berlin. Hegel said that the beliefs and visions of man created the various patterns of civilization and that the interaction of one culture with another, like the modification of one argument by another, brought evolutionary change toward an ideal society. Change goes on ceaselessly in a cycle of three phases—thesis, antithesis, and synthesis. This, said Marx, is standing dialectic on its head. He did not deny that ideas are creative forces in themselves—as well he should not—but he argued that the thoughts, beliefs, and hopes of human beings arise primarily from the specific social environment that harbors them. So Marx substitutes his materialism for Hegel's mysticism.

Marx then adopts Hegel's fake scientific dialectic, but gives it a neat Messianic projection. Thesis is the existing bourgeois society; antithesis, the proletarian-dominated society, now in fictive existence in Russia and China; and synthesis, the harmonious classless, boss-less, anarchic society to come. Thus while pouring withering scorn on German idealism, all forms of supernaturalism, and utopianism, Marx invoked what was really a primitive faith in the magic number three to bring about a human society just as visionary as the noble ones of Plato and Sir Thomas More.

Marx squandered years of his life and of Engels' as well in a ponderous effort to establish "scientifically" two propositions basic to his entire case: First, every commodity is endowed with an abstract "value," labor alone produces "value," and profits come from the "surplus value" that the employer "steals" from the worker—the difference between the hours a worker needs to put in at "socially useful labor" and the much longer hours he is forced to work. Neither Marx nor Engels—left holding the bag after the master's death—ever nailed this absurd proposition down. The facts are too obdurate, the variables too flighty. No demonstration of its fallacy is needed beyond the simple overwhelming evidence of the misery of the backward nations teeming with millions of workers, often rich in natural resources, sometimes rich in cash and available credit, but lacking in the business trust underlying the broad voluntary investment that alone makes modern capitalism possible. Yet Communists, working for the state, a single monopolistic employer who decides what their work will be, what their hours, and what their pay and who steals their freedom as "surplus value," still muddle their wits making dogma of Marx's divagations. They have to, for the entire argument for communism collapses if the proletarian wage-earner is not the keel beam in the structure of modern society. Lenin made this myth even harder to uphold when he saw that the industrial worker was not as pliable as he should be and made the historic *rifacimento* by which Russia and the other capitalistically undeveloped countries became the chief target of communism.

Marx's second major proposition is more plausible. "Capitalistic production," he argues, "begets, with the inexorability of a law of Nature, its own negation" and carries within itself the seed of its own doom. Competition drives down prices. The employer has to become more efficient. He develops labor-saving machinery, invests in larger plants, and grows by mergers with other employers. For a period business is good. But the faster the machines produce goods, the more workers are idle, the less goods they can buy, and the more prices go down. The employer invents still more efficient machinery, throws more people out of work, and cuts wages. The only hope for the capitalist is the opening up of new markets. But in time, Marx says, bigness, greater efficiency, and expanding markets lose their effectiveness in offsetting what today corporation chairmen are calling the "profit squeeze." With amazing farsightedness Marx predicted cyclic depressions about every ten years, "inevitably" ending in one final bust. Then the proletariat would take over.

These dire prophecies have not come true. In the Great Depression of the 1930s some dispossessed intellectuals turned toward Moscow and the absolutes of Marx, but the American worker turned to Washington and the improvisations of Franklin Delano Roosevelt. Today, in Western capitalistic democracies the essential standard of living of the hourly-rated union worker equals that of his employer. The tight little family-owner-management circle has been exploded and is spread wide over salaried management, salaried office workers, professional workers, and millions of investor-owners, almost all of whom are "workers." Marx's insights also failed him in regard to the tremendous regenerative force that science would be in world economy—what entire industries with jobs for millions of workers would spring from the modest laboratories of the chemists of his generation, for instance. In the end Marx's blindest miscalculation seems to have been his misanthropic failure to imagine the role of conscience and education in the social transformation that occurs in the "ceaseless change" of human history.

THE RUSSIAN DILEMMA

With luck Karl Marx might have been the architect of "social revolution through peaceful and legal means," as Engels said Marx thought it might take place in England. Before he died, Marx is said to have cancelled his subscription to future development of communism in his name by declaring, "I am no Marxist." Terrorism, secrecy, hard-core control, and iron dicipline came from Russia as reciprocal reactions to czarist persecution. First the anarchist Bakunin, and then Lenin and his Bolsheviks, set the style that has made the Communist party an obscene international intrigue. After gaining power more or less by chance in 1917, Lenin led Russia into chaos by trying to put Marx's theories into literal practice. He had to turn back to private ownership, but he did not abandon Marx—he adjusted his teachings to reality. Lenin was the master of strategy and tactics who created the Communist party as the "vanguard of the proletariat" and thus the sole custodian of authority in the make-believe "dictatorship of the proletariat"—and in fact the rulers of the proletariat. At just the time that Marx might have become another nineteenth-century theorist, Lenin taught his followers to be political realists and to hold to the inflexible objective of world domination while being infinitely flexible as to means.

The paranoiac Stalin turned Russia into the first industrialized totalitarian state. And he added such refinements as heavy taxation on the workers, there being no other source of capital, incentive speed-up to increase production, police terror, forced service on collective farms, "liquidation" of several million of the more successful farmers, and subversion of free peoples—all in the name of Marx. Yet today under Khrushchev, Russia faces a dilemma that may prove Marxism no more durable than concrete with too much sand in it. In order to maintain its control over the vast non-Communist population, the Communist party must keep its members everlastingly busy recruiting, training, propagandizing, and doing other boring routine party tasks. But most party members also hold key positions in government, industry, agriculture, and education. To meet the staggering challenge of competing with the West, the party members must be better educated technically, more devoted to their regular jobs, and better rewarded. In this clash of interests, urgency is on the side of productivity at the expense of party. And after years of war and privation and promises, with better education and the capacity to match Western productivity, the rank-and-file Communist becomes indifferent to Marxist dialectic and yearns to enjoy Western materialism, as that bourgeois gentleman Friedrich Engels did.

In the light of conditions in the Western world a century ago and to a discreditable degree in Latin America, Africa, the Middle East, and the Far East today, Karl Marx's savage criticism of employers and landlords was justified. By giving pre-eminence to the social and economic forces that shape history, instead of making it seem only the record of dynasties, he contributed largely to scholarly research in the social sciences and to our modern view of human society. In his vision of a society free of exploitation, class distinctions, and discrimination, where work would be a creative cooperative enterprise, and the individual would be as free of interference from the state as possible, Karl Marx shared the great humanistic dream that has brought about most of the progress we call civilization. Compared to the selfish, hopeless existentialism of many intellectuals today, his philosophy shares with nineteenth-century liberalism the optimistic sense of going somewhere.

SIGMUND FREUD OF VIENNA

In this century of ours economic, political, and intellectual progress has given the individual an identity he did not own in the past. At the same time industrial and national competition has led to racial and class antagonisms, wars, and other dislocations. Heightened individual awareness and ambition in the midst of uncertainty and fear have substituted anxiety for the resignation that in past centuries has been the common posture of mankind in the presence of misfortune. It is inevitable, therefore, that in the rush of scientific progress since 1900 some of the most exciting discoveries have been concerned with the mysterious workings of man's mind and emotions. Among the leaders in these explorations no ideas have been more influential than those of Sigmund Freud.

For many years Sigmund Freud (1856–1939) suffered the multiple insecurities of lacking income, being a Jew, hungering for success, and having his theories ridiculed and rejected. It is idle to try to say here to what extent his ideas were anticipated by others, were corrected and fruitfully developed by others, or were unsound. It is clear that he advanced a number of original fundamental concepts, that over the years he hammered them into a comprehensive system, which he called psychoanalysis, and that this system has had a profound influence not only in psychology and medicine but in anthropology, sociology, literature, art, and education as well. Starting with the aim of helping neurotics, he contributed mightily to modern man's understanding of himself and his times. From his research and teaching stems a wholly new appreciation of what a complex thing a normal person is. Much of this contribution can be said to be a result of his stimulation, even when the response is contrary to his doctrine. The span of his interests can be guessed from a list of some of his publications: *Psychopathology of Everyday Life, The Interpretation of Dreams, Three Contributions to the Theory of Sex, Wit and Its Relation to the Unconscious,* and *Totem and Taboo.*

THE PSYCHOANALYTIC SYSTEM

Though as muddled in the popular mind as the contents of a boy's dresser drawer, Freud's ideas nevertheless have established themselves almost as commonplaces. First, he decided that the troubles of the neurotic—the person whose sickness is not organic in origin—arise from *repression*. What is repressed usually has a broad *sexual* basis, is related to *infantile* experiences, and is socially not approved. It is therefore hidden in the *unconscious*. The unconscious plays an important role in our lives; yet we cannot tell what lies in it without the help of a psychoanalyst. For example, in sons the rivalry with the father for the affection of the mother grows secretly into a father death-wish. Freud called this emotional tangle the "Oedipus complex." In the Greek myth Oedipus unknowingly kills his father and marries his mother. In women the rivalry is with the mother. This has been called the "Electra complex." Electra was the daughter of Agamemnon, who was murdered by his unfaithful wife Clytemnestra on his return from the Trojan War. Electra influenced her brother Orestes to avenge the death of their father.

The energy of the sexual instincts Freud called the "libido." It embraces self-love, love of parents and children, friendship, even love of beauty, as well as sexual love. An infant is born with a primitive self, the *Id*, whose only aim is fulfillment of basic needs. As the child grows, the adjustment to environment shapes the Id into the *Ego*, the conscious self. Neurosis may result when basic needs are thwarted, when the Ego suppresses the desires of the Id. Freud added another gallery to his mechanism of neurosis—the *Super-Ego*. This constitutes those rules of logic and morality, embodied in the conscience, that act as a form of censor higher even than the Ego.

The basic treatment that Freud adopted after discarding hypnosis was "free association"—prolonged recall by the patient of significant emotional experiences, dreams, obsessions, and other fantasies. The psychoanalyst helps the patient to discover what is being repressed, what unconscious drives are at the seat of the difficulty. Cure for the neurotic individual comes from bringing out into the open the true nature of his inner conflict and channeling the libido toward an acceptable object. This object might be an eligible person or, by what Freud called *sublimation*, a substitute activity such as teaching or community welfare. In this re-channeling the psychoanalyst plays an important role, for by the process of *transference* he takes the place of a person in the patient's life—his father, say—and becomes the object of hostility or affection.

Such success as psychoanalysis has had, it must be remembered, applies to neurotics, persons who though disturbed are still able to confront reality. They are often intelligent and competent. Psychotics—particularly schizophrenics and manic-depressives—do not usually respond to psychoanalysis.

Sigmund Freud's ideas may well be superseded. Two of his leading disciples, Carl Jung and Alfred Adler, left his ranks. Both felt that Freud put too much stress on sexuality. Jung, one of the earliest psychiatrists to embrace Freud's ideas, first used the term "complex" for a cluster of neurotic ideas and feelings about a central emotional disturbance. He also introduced "introvert" and "extrovert." Jung showed that these realities of the unconscious assume symbolic disguises, not only in personal dreams and fantasies but also in religion, customs, rituals, myth, and art—what might be called folk dreams and fantasies, or the "collective unconscious." This is broader than Freud's repressed conscious experience. Thus the search for revealing symbols during psychoanalysis has led to increased understanding of the importance of symbols in all human activity. Adler stressed the broad concept of desire for power and used the now universal term "inferiority complex" to describe what ails the neurasthenic personality. One new line of inquiry has drawn on anthropology to give the general cultural environment and group influences a greater role in the emotional life of the individual.

Many leading psychiatrists and psychologists still reject outright Freud's descriptions of what takes place in neurotic disturbances and his methods for dealing with them. But still there remains the simple truth that few men in history have ever opened the eyes of their contemporaries as Sigmund Freud has. In his insights lies hope that ultimately we may treat sick societies as well as sick persons.

MOHANDAS K. GANDHI, MAHATMA
OF SOUTH AFRICA AND INDIA

We know Mohandas K. Gandhi (1869–1948) as "Mahatma," a sage, and see him as a skinny brown man, bald and bespectacled, sitting on the floor with white yard goods wrapped around his middle. We know in an unclear way that he had a role in winning independence for India and hail him, together with Dr. Albert Schweitzer, as a symbol of sanity in a mad world. It is profitable to inquire how a brown man who never held public office, never commanded troops, and never even led a religious organization could challenge the might of the British Empire on two continents, warrant the respect and admiration of the very men he opposed, channel the course of history, and change the lives of hundreds of millions of people. For your purposes it may be more profitable to observe how in making himself the instrument of change of others, he first changed himself. This exhibition of what one man was able to do consciously to improve himself is in itself an inspiration to all of us who believe that growing is a lifelong process.

Gandhi's youth was singularly inauspicious for the training of a sage. As a boy in a village on the Arabian Sea, he had no motivating advantages, talents, or handicaps, unless marriage at thirteen is one of these. He complains in his autobiography that the forced use of English in school held back his education, and in fact he fled from a provincial Indian college after one term. But his older brother sent him to London at eighteen to study law at the famous Inns of Court. Strangely, he had no trouble passing his bar examinations before he was twenty-one.

The most noteworthy event of his London stay seems his "conversion" to vegetarianism. As a Hindu, he did not eat meat, but a shilling pamphlet by a man named Salt started him on his first mission—to convince others, by example and by testimony, of the virtues of vegetarianism, without salt. For sixty years he survived on sparse helpings of spinach leaves, baked potatoes, mangoes, raisins, marmalade, honey, goat's milk, and similar spartan fare.

But in London, Mohandas made up for the harrowing simplicity of his diet by dressing in the height of top-hatted, striped-trouser, stick-carrying elegance. Neither his Bond Street trousers nor his nearly three years at the Inner Temple helped build up a law practice when he returned to India. He seemed educated beyond his wits. Then by chance some Moslems sent him to South Africa in 1893 to keep an eye on their business interests. His first experience with brutal racial discrimination made a man of the phony English gentleman, but his legal training stood him in good stead, for M. K. Gandhi, Attorney, Durban, became both a champion of the Indian minorities and also the recipient of an income of $25,000 a year, an enormous amount around 1900.

In his law student days Gandhi had associated chiefly with faddists—indeed, he never lost a taste for their company. Among them in London, however, were Sir Edwin Arnold, Annie Besant, and other students of Indian culture. They led him to read the Bhagavad Gita. The Gita is a section of the world's largest epic, the Sanskrit Mahabharata. An allegorical poem, written about 300 B.C., it deals with the life of Krishna, the human embodiment of Vishnu, or God. Gandhi interpreted the ambiguous events to symbolize the struggle between good and evil within the individual with peace coming through personal purity and renunciation of all worldliness. He gradually made the Gita, or at least his interpretation of it, his daily guide.

NON-VIOLENCE AND CIVIL DISOBEDIENCE

Going to South Africa for one month, Gandhi stayed twenty years. The Indians had first come to Natal in post-slavery days as indentured servants to work on the tea, sugar, and coffee plantations for the English settlers. In time the industry, intelligence, and prosperity of some Indians brought down on all of them discriminatory regulations. Gandhi fought the English authorities with four forces not unique in the history of persecution but not previously marshaled with such skill, persistence, and success:

The major force then and throughout the rest of his life was *satayagraha,* non-violence and peaceful winning of opponents to truth.

With it he combined civil disobedience, whenever the legal authorities required an act contrary to conscience.

But since hate is a form of violence, and "all men are brothers," as Gandhi was never too discouraged to maintain, he punctiliously separated the man from the deed against him. He never used cunning in debate, he never took advantage of another's weakness, and he never wanted the success of his own cause to be the ruin of the other side. The quixotic courtesy and friendliness with which he dealt with opponents charmed a long line of government officials, police officers, and jailers.

Gandhi's fourth force was public opinion. Considering how little had been done before World War I to develop techniques of molding public opinion and how limited his resources were, Gandhi stands as one of the greatest publicists in history. Time after time, with little besides his naked will to sustain him, Gandhi directed world attention to his problems and used the moral pressure of world opinion to help solve them.

In Natal, Gandhi brought these four forces to bear on General Jan Smuts and the British government with such success that, when he finally returned to India in 1914, the restrictive measures against Indians had been repealed. That they have been restored by the independent Union of South Africa is a sad by-product of the *apartheid* laws against the movement for native rule in Africa. The inferior position of his people in South Africa first awoke the foppish young attorney to accept, without premeditation, the role of organizer and leader. Openly refusing to obey regulations and then welcoming a jail sentence without any show of resistance, no matter what the provocation, was a formula he improvised to offset the registration of Asians and the restriction of their immigration. By strange chance in a jail library he discovered Henry Thoreau's essay on "Civil Disobedience," an eloquent statement of what Gandhi was practicing.

Even earlier, one of his many white sympathizers had given Gandhi a book by John Ruskin. It preached the ennobling effect of simple living, high thinking, and manual labor. Taken with his reading of the Gita and Tolstoi's protests against "intolerable luxury," Ruskin's exhortations changed Gandhi's entire personal life, and he began an untiring effort to change that of others. He founded Phoenix Farm, the first of a series of ventures in communal living. There he and assorted disciples—they always included women and Westerners—shared the chores, carried on the usual unprofitable experiments in husbandry such as making "caramel coffee" from wheat, followed a vegetarian diet, and published a newspaper. Throughout the rest of his career Gandhi depended on his papers as his chief vehicle for publicizing his ideas in writing, including answering attacks, which he thoughtfully printed in full. Communal living at Phoenix Farm coincided with Gandhi's declaration of *bramacharya*, or subduing of the senses. In this celibacy his wife Katurbai and some of his disciples joined him. He was then thirty-six and the father of four boys. Gandhi's self-denial included denying his boys much affection or education.

Paradoxically, Gandhi's first action on his permanent return to India in 1914 was to help in recruiting for Britain in World War I. He had been decorated for organizing and leading an ambulance unit in the Boer War and the campaign against the Zulus. He always felt a lively sense of loyalty as a British subject and gratitude for the freedom the individual enjoys under the British system of government. Yet this feeling in no way prevented his becoming the leader—again almost inadvertently—in the struggle for liberation of India from British rule. But first he established an *ashram*, or communal hermitage, at Sabarmati across the river from the textile manufacturing city of Ahmedabad. And though his successful fight in South Africa was unknown to the masses in India, he soon earned the title *Mahatma* from the poet Rabindranath Tagore. He widened his theme of personal purity as prerequisite for social influence. He said publicly, privately, and persistently that India must purify herself before she could be worthy of greater freedom.

Two reforms filled his mind: village uplift and an end to untouchability among the Hindus. To improve the villages, where

THE IMPACT OF IDEAS 45

80 per cent of the Indians lived, Gandhi first induced the politicians to stop aping the English, to resume Indian dress, to use native speech, and to get out among the peasants. To the villagers he preached cleanliness and weaving—in fact, he made home weaving and the wearing of homespun clothes by all Indians a symbol of the rebirth of Indian self-sufficiency and self-respect. Home weaving also served to boycott foreign-made goods. With less success he blasted the rich for living in ostentatious luxury in the midst of the unutterable misery of the poor. The refusal of the rich to concern themselves with the poor turned Gandhi from a moderate, satisfied to achieve some betterment by voluntary action, to a believer in the necessity for state socialism.

FIFTY MILLION UNTOUCHABLES EMANCIPATED

The emancipation of the untouchables of India gives Mohandas K. Gandhi a place in history beside Abraham Lincoln. In 1915 about 50 million Indians were by birth condemned to a life of degradation from which they could never hope to escape except through reincarnation. Their fate had been decreed in that unrecorded dawn of civilization when the Aryans overran India and invented the system of four castes plus untouchables. The average Hindu—that is, the majority of Indians—piously observed the injunction not to touch an untouchable or a thing touched by one as one of the tenets of the Hindu religion. This religion is a tolerant accumulation of the centuries. Key aspects are reincarnation, renunciation, the sacredness of cows, and the prohibition of meat and alcohol. Gandhi, who was profoundly religious, though he added the teachings of the Bible, the Koran, and the Talmud to those of the Gita, never accepted the segregation of the untouchables as having religious sanction. To him, God was a force, an essence, and "search for Truth is search for God." In the clear light of truth, he remonstrated with the Hindus, "Inhuman ourselves, we may not plead before the Throne for deliverance from the inhumanity of others."

Gandhi as a boy and in the twenty South African years had

associated with untouchables. Now with his sure publicist's sense he dramatized his protest by renaming untouchables "Harijans," "Children of God," admitting a family of Harijans to live in the Sabarmati ashram, adopting their daughter, and living in the Harijan quarter during his endless travels throughout India. Gradually, in accordance with his teaching of the atomic power of individual action, Hindus began to eat with Harijans, to admit them to Hindu temples, even to intermarry with them, and to break down the other barriers that had lasted since Helen watched the Greeks besieging the walls of Troy. Today in India the liberation of the untouchables by personal conviction has progressed far, farther perhaps than the emancipation of the Negro by presidential proclamation has in the United States.

INDIA LIBERATED

In 1947, India became a full-fledged partner in the British Commonwealth. It reached this state of independence largely through the extraordinary efforts of Gandhi, extraordinary because he spent as much energy trying to reform the Indians as he did trying to persuade the English to get out. With both he depended first of all on face to face talk. Back in 1888 in an enlightened gesture Lord Dufferin, the British Viceroy, had founded the Indian National Congress as a means of open discussion of grievances. Under Gandhi's leadership the Congress became the semi-official voice of India, and in it he influenced directly the Hindu and Moslem leaders from the far-flung principalities. Even when he withdrew from Congress, Nehru and other leaders consulted him on every issue. To influence the Indian millions, mostly poor and illiterate, he criss-crossed the 1500-mile wide, 1900-mile long sub-continent, driving himself mercilessly, speaking to untouchables in mudhuts and to crowds as high as 600,000 in city squares. Since much of his speech-making came before public-address systems were invented and since he was no orator, his support by the masses must have been to a considerable degree based on faith, a relationship ironically uncongenial to Gandhi, who took a dim view of mysticism and the implications of his *Mahatma* title and who often stubbornly refused to ask people to follow the course of action he thought right because to do so would be a form of "violence."

In addition to the techniques he had used in battling General Smuts in South Africa—*satayagraha* (it worked with Smuts; he became a warm admirer of Gandhi) and courting jail sentences —Gandhi added "hartal," suspension of economic activity, and noncooperation, as by refusal to hold office. But his most famous means of applying moral pressure was to fast, or to threaten to— undeniably a kind of "violence." Again, quaintly, he used this device about as often against his friends as his opponents. His first fast, for instance, was designed to keep some strikers he was supporting from giving in, but he scared the employer, a good friend, into coming to terms! After a while fasting and the threat of fasting till he died became his last resort, and for years his several rendezvous with death became front-page news in the capitals of the world. Winston Churchill, who did not intend to preside over the dissolution of the Empire, refused to negotiate with a "half-naked fakir" or even to speak with him when he was in London. But after the fall of Singapore before the Japanese, pressure from Roosevelt and Chiang Kai-shek changed his mind. It is amazing how the fear of being held responsible for the death of this small brown man, adored by the downtrodden millions whom he had clothed in the invincibility of self-respect, shook the mighty in their chambers thousands of miles away.

INDIA DIVIDED

That the career of a man as good, as gay, as just, and as beloved as Mohandas Gandhi should end in the sort of defeat and death that came to him has the heroic and bitter quality of high tragedy. From 1924, when he went on a twenty-one day fast in a plea for better Hindu-Moslem relations, to no effect, more and more he equated the future of India with Hindu-Moslem unity. As early as 1926 he felt despair on this issue, but he fought on. With every passing year he moved the Hindus to be kinder to the Harijans and the British to be more responsive to the idea of Indian independence; yet he was powerless to check the rising Hindu-Moslem tension.

With the end of World War II and Churchill out of Downing Street, Britain offered India her long-sought freedom as a dominion of the British Commonwealth. The terms prescribed by Lord Mountbatten, the Viceroy, were acceptable to Gandhi, to Jawarhalal Nehru, head of the Congress, and to its Moslem members. But Mohammed Ali Jinnah, the fanatical lawyer leader of the Moslem League, torpedoed all efforts to have a transfer of authority to a unified Indian nation. He roused the Moslem peasants to murderous riots that brought on brutal Hindu retaliation. Fearing domination of the 100 million Moslems by the 300 million Hindus, he gave Nehru and Congress a hard choice between civil war or dismemberment of India on religious lines. Gandhi, who had wrung so many concessions from the English rulers with his charm and high-minded reasoning, got nowhere with his fellow countryman. The gentle Mahatma called Jinnah a maniac and threw himself into desperate pilgrimages to preach brotherly love to Moslems and Hindus, wherever terrorism was worst.

Nehru and other Hindu leaders reluctantly accepted partition because civil war was too terrible a price for unity. Jinnah wanted to divide India in two. The Moslem part, he insisted, should include the Punjab and Bengal, which had predominantly Hindu sections. Mountbatten, favoring unity, forced Jinnah to choose between one India and a partition by religious majorities with Moslem Pakistan on one side of India and Moslem East Pakistan 800 miles away on the other. Jinnah chose the latter, with hatred and the standing threat of war as his legacy to posterity. So Gandhi, who believed "Religions are different roads converging to the same point," had his dream of a free, purified, classless United India, so close to realization, shattered by the religious bigotry of a fellow Indian.

The death of Gandhi must have been to him a lesser defeat, almost an anticlimax. He had just ended a near-death fast in riot-scarred Delhi that had drawn a written pledge from the Congress of the new Indian Union that Hindus would "protect the life, property, and faith of the Moslems" and that Moslems who had fled to Pakistan as half of the greatest double migration in history would be welcomed back. Then, in the aftermath of this tremendous spiritual victory, as Gandhi arrived at afternoon prayers, the young editor of a Hindu nationalist magazine bowed to him in reverence, silently wished him well, and shot him dead. Gandhi's final effort to unite India had brought a death sentence from those who hated in the name of religion. But the fifty years of *ahimsa*, non-violence and the positive practice of love, made colonialism no longer respectable and will be forever one of the supreme demonstrations of the power of quite simple ideas to change the world.

The impact of ideas is personal as well as social. I remember well when I was first introduced to the subject of esthetics. One day, during my sophomore year in Columbia College, I was woolgathering in a class in German literature while the professor intoned nasally about Lessing's criticism of the late Hellenistic statue of Laocoön and his sons being destroyed by snakes. Lessing condemned it as bad art because sculpture and painting as space arts have no business to go in for story-telling, a time art. This revelation failed to ruffle the heavy-lidded boredom of the other barbarians from the fraternity houses who slouched beside me in the back rows of the drab classroom of Hamilton Hall. But to me it was as though a sunset had burst from the dusty blackboard and enveloped the bowed figure of the professor in its roseate glow. The idea bowled me over. Book illustration was —and still is—one of my cherished interests. But in spite of this shock, I suddenly realized that for me systematic thinking about art—esthetics—could be exciting, the kind of fun plane geometry had been in school. And probably for the first time I also realized that becoming educated meant fitting what you think you know into a coherent system of ideas.

The excitement of ideas is perhaps the least obvious of the pleasures open to the cultivated mind. Yet to share the thinking of great minds is exciting, as even my inadequate engagements with Plato, Rousseau, Marx, Freud, and Gandhi may suggest. From his probing of experience the original thinker arrives at perceptions of truth which, through the miracle of language, he puts into symbolic form and transmits to us as a fresh concept. One quality of true originality is that the freshness lasts. The mystical idea of personal faith in Jesus as the bridge to a life of righteousness that came to Saul the persecutor on the road to Damascus changed him to Paul the Apostle. It has changed the lives of millions since. Who knows what ideas, fresh as the day they sprang from the mind of a Plato or a Paul, may be lying just below the surface of a book, ready to fill your life with light and meaning and purpose?

3

THE SCIENTIFIC VISION

Science has had so much to do with the world you live in that clearly it is your duty to understand as much about science as you can. But this does not mean that you have to know how an atomic bomb is put together to have a keen interest in the role of nuclear energy in human affairs today, any more than you need to know the chemistry of paint or the history of Spain to enjoy El Greco's "Toledo" in the Metropolitan Museum in New York. Factual information is indispensable in understanding the significance of scientific events, but it does not guarantee such understanding. Indeed, I am not sure that preoccupation with fact does not deter the technically trained from thinking as much as they might about the nature and consequences of their activities. This seems as true in music and art as in accounting and engineering. If you do not have much background in the sciences, you still can look forward confidently to grasping the majesty and the significance of major scientific achievement.

THE YEAST OF CURIOSITY

Your growth is as dependent on intellectual curiosity as bread on yeast. Somewhere along the line—in school, at home, in front of a television set—children lose their wonderful eagerness to know for knowing's sake. They become adults in whom the desire to know anything flickers feebly or in whom curiosity has degenerated to inquisitiveness about trivial matters. How does true intellectual curiosity act? Here is a glimpse of a scientist, not at work but merely responding to the ordinary stimuli that impinge on our attention as well as his. The novelist, Naomi Mitchison, writes about her father, John Scott Haldane:

A year or two before my father's death we were walking through the Parks at Oxford, slowly, because rheumatism was gaining on him. He stopped at the pond to look at the water lilies, not the splendid full blooms, but the buds straining up towards the surface. He began to think about what gas was lifting them, pulling at the flaccid stems, how produced, how measurable: Was it, for example, being actively secreted? For, if so, it would tie up with certain aspects of animal physiology.

If you go over this simple statement, you will find the key to a great deal of the scientific spirit. First comes the identification of the problem buried in the common observation of floating lily buds, then the probing "how produced, how measurable," and finally the relation of the explanatory hypothesis to another branch of knowledge or area of interest. Something like this goes on in all productive inquiry. Curiosity is at the heart of all learning. In your intellectual development it should have a vital role.

Dr. James Bryant Conant says, "For most scientists, I think the justification of their work is to be found in the pure joy of its creativeness; the spirit which moves them is closely akin to the imaginative vision which inspires an artist." This emphasis on the kinship with art is echoed by Albert Einstein, who said: "The most beautiful thing we can experience is the mysterious. It is the source of all art and science." And Jules Henri Poincaré, the great French mathematician, said, "Scientific genius is the capacity to be surprised." The sense of wonder before the unknown evokes in the scientist a passionate curiosity that sustains him in concentrated and prolonged research. "I am on the verge of mysteries," the young Pasteur wrote a friend. "The nights are too long." On the other hand astronomers, it is said, are always sorry when the dawn comes.

Science has had a warp-and-woof history. Its roots dig back into the most ancient of human trial and error activities—cooking, weaving, making pottery, building boats, growing grain. Yet early in recorded history some of this empirical knowledge was generalized into theoretical knowledge. Separate and merged, these two ways of knowing help us to understand the nature of the physical universe and to control it to our purposes. In a rough sense the function of science is to understand and the function of technology is to control. In industry today the difference in aim is indicated by research on the one hand and development and production on the other. But in practice and in speech the distinctions blur. The layman and the journalist often put the making and operation of gadgets, such as X-ray machines, within the domain of science. The scientist is concerned primarily with the principles underlying materials, processes, and mechanisms, and for the past two centuries he has carried on his endless quest for more basic knowledge in experimental laboratories.

Apart from understanding the accomplishments of scientists, therefore, the chief value for you to gain from becoming acquainted with them is an improvement in your own thinking. There is no scientific method of thinking that you can pick up in ten easy lessons, but there are modes of thinking that scientists have used. These you can absorb and follow, so that your mind functions with something of the rigorousness and orderliness and possibly even the elegance of the mind of a Blaise Pascal, a Baron Jöns Berzelius, or a Josiah Gibbs. Thus you can in time come to possess a share of the scientific vision.

ARISTOTLE, "MASTER OF THOSE WHO KNOW"

In the incredible conjunction of three of the world's greatest thinkers in Athens, Aristotle's title to greatness is stunningly apparent. His life lacks the playlike quality of Socrates', and his writings the charm of Plato's. But his breadth, essentiality, originality, and influence on men's thinking make him a worthy anchor man on the famous trio. Perhaps the most rudimentary difference between Aristotle and his masters is that they are almost exclusively concerned with man and society; Aristotle is equally concerned with man the animal and his physical environment. Their methods of inquiry differ, too. They approach the truth by indirection, by suggestion, by figures of speech, in the spirit of art; his approach is systematic, analytic, in the spirit of science. He is, indeed, the father of science.

Aristotle (384–322 B.C.) spent his life studying, teaching, writing. A native of Stagira (therefore "the Stagirite," and not a citizen of Athens), he spent twenty years at Plato's Academy, left Athens for several years including two or three as tutor of Alexander, and returned for a dozen years as head of his own school, the Lyceum. His writings, almost all—over two thousand pages —miraculously saved, have the formidable bulk necessary to enfold the universal subjects that he painstakingly reduced to order. They can be squeezed under eight headings—philosophy, ethics, government, esthetics, logic, psychology, nonbiological science, and biology. To the vast scope of this inquiry must be added the fact that, while Aristotle set a model for scholars ever since by scrupulously reporting and analyzing earlier writings, much of the time he was sailing uncharted seas. He can be said to have invented logic and psychology. Putting him in this chapter instead of the previous one is merely an arbitrary way of emphasizing his scientific work.

It is easy to underrate Aristotle's contribution to science because experimental laboratories were two thousand years away and observation was not relied on as an indispensable tool but was used casually, as a watchmaker might occasionally reach for a hammer. But remember how little could be known in 350 B.C. about the earth, for instance, and how slowly we have gathered what information we possess. Then read Aristotle's chapter about the earth in his *De Caelo* [*On the Heavens*]. He opens with a typically lucid statement: "It remains to speak of the earth, of its position, of the question whether it is at rest or in motion, and of its shape." With the fairness, objectivity, and thoroughness that are the essence of the scientific spirit, he examines each of these questions in order. He says that most people believe the earth is in the center of the universe. Following Pythagoras, on the other hand, some think the sun is. Aristotle reports one explanation of the latter hypothesis that casts light on the Greek mind: Fire is more precious than earth and ought, therefore, to be central. These same Pythagoreans, he says, believe the earth and other bodies revolve around the sun and offer as evidence the observed greater frequency of eclipses of the moon than of the sun. Aristotle analyzes at length whether the earth is a sphere or a circular disk, the leading theories, and decides that it is spherical—because it was probably formed by centripetal force and because its shadow on the moon during an eclipse is always curved. Aristotle concludes that the earth lies at the center of the universe and "must necessarily be spherical"; he also states flatly, "It is clear that the earth does not move."

The greatness of Aristotle's contribution to science lies not in what he added to the substantive knowledge of biology, physics, and other fields. It lies in his stupendous effort to make a science of knowing, to invent a comprehensive system of scientific method. First, he takes long strides forward by means of the scope and basic nature of the subjects treated, by summarizing and analyzing what his scientifically minded predecessors had thought, and by tirelessly asking prescient questions that cut to the heart of many of the fundamental problems of science, such as "How can there be any time without the existence of motion?" and "What is place?"

"ALL MEN ARE MORTAL"

Aristotle called his book on logic *Organon*, an instrument. He sought a new scientific instrument for reasoning, one lacking the metaphysical element of Platonic dialectic. He saw that without a dependable system of proof, advance in knowledge would be slow—as it has been in the Orient—so he built one. The heart of his system is the deductive syllogism, the familiar "All men are mortal; Socrates is a man; therefore Socrates is mortal." It gives one pause to realize that not this brilliant man, nor any Greek follower or critic, nor any scholar for two thousand years saw how limited a use this tool has. It cannot be applied to relationships, that important area of scientific inquiry, as in "If A is greater than B, and B is greater than C, A is greater than C." A severe limitation, too, is that the initial generalization, the major premise, in a syllogism must be true. Without experimental research to prove the universality of the major premise—an absolute that science today rejects—Aristotle was driven back on axioms, self-evident truths—self-evident, that is, to everyone who accepts them. He recognized that a great deal of reasoning must be based on a modal proposition—"If A is true, B may be true." But the whole question of probability—a matter of much more relevance in human affairs than certainty—had to wait on the development of mathematics and experimental laboratories for scientific treatment.

Yet in the course of constructing his method of reasoning, in his discussion of the principles underlying proof, and in his analysis of the propositions that form the bulk of what he reasons about, Aristotle comes to grips with most of the critical issues involved in scientific method. Among these are definition and classification. Every science rests on these two cornerstones. Inevitably he gives his attention to the prickly question of language and the inherent danger of its ambiguities—"For as long as it is not clear in how many senses a term is used, it is possible that the answerer and the questioner are not directing their minds upon the same thing." He tackles the still mysterious problem of how we know, including the later much-investigated relation of sensation to knowing. He studies the distinction between form and matter and tries to impose order on the large questions of cause and change in the physical world. Aristotle reasons his way to many faulty answers to his own questions, but he gives an inspiring demonstration of the capacity of the human mind to reason.

The enormous irony of Aristotle's history is that his major contribution, scientific thought, was lost sight of for two thousand years. During this long night he was revered as "The Master of Those Who Know" by believers in closed systems of thought. This curious fate came about because Aristotle's writings were lost for two hundred years. (They were found in a cellar in a town where he had fled from the possibility of suffering the same fate as Socrates.) No one remembered the dynamic, tentative, questing aspects of Aristotle's thinking. What was remembered, the vise-like syllogism, came to dominate the thinking of medieval scholasticism. Therefore, when Francis Bacon and the other leaders of the Renaissance—literally the Rebirth of Learning—began to construct a modern view of the universe, instead of starting with Aristotle as their leader, they took him as their chief antagonist. Not until true scholarly research began in the nineteenth century did the dimensions of this great mind and his alignment with modern scientific thought become clear. The lectures to his students as he walked in the Peripatus of the Lyceum and the hundreds of pages of writings are still a fruitful part of our intellectual heritage, are still studied with respect by scholars in many fields. They put Aristotle with Plato and Socrates among the greatest of those who teach.

FRANCIS BACON, LORD CHANCELLOR, ESSAYIST, SCIENTIFIC THINKER

Francis Bacon (1561–1626) once suggested that his role was to "ring the bell that calls the wits together." This, rather than concrete advances in a specific field, was his great achievement. It is tempting to call him the first modern. Consciously, he sought to help Europe shed the cerements of medieval thought and to be reborn in the raiment of a wholly new scientific thinking. This remarkably ambitious program was the real goal of a career busy with great events of a quite different nature.

Talented and ambitious, lawyer Bacon had little luck at the court of Elizabeth Tudor. His powerful relative, Lord Burghley, some wit had said, was "more kin than kind." Bacon attached himself to Elizabeth's young favorite, the Earl of Essex, whose "fatal impatience" did Bacon no good. But under James I, Bacon's star rose. He became Lord Chancellor of England, chief of the entire political system; he was made Baron Verulam in 1618 and Viscount St. Albans in 1621. Then his enemies cut him down. He was charged with bribery, a common practice, admitted his guilt, and though the gifts he took apparently came after his decisions and never influenced his judgments, he was ruined. Yet, wonderfully, all of these events were external to what Bacon took to be his true profession, the reform of thought, particularly in what he called philosophy but which we would call science or perhaps scientific thinking.

By the time of his fall from power, Bacon had published his most significant ideas, though not all of his writings. He called his program the *Great Instauration*, or renewal of thinking, especially in science but also in logic, ethics, and politics. What he completed is generally known as the *Novum Organum* [*The New Instrument*]. His key idea, the foundation for modern science, is "Nature to be commanded, must be obeyed." More explicitly, he said that man "can do and understand so much and so much only as he observed in fact." This probably seems to you an unremarkable bit of common sense. But it helped bring about a major change in human thought; it helped end the tyranny of the old Aristotelian "instrument" of deduction.

Up to 1600, few men had bothered to study nature. The whole approach to thinking about the physical universe and the nature of existence began with generalization, with an assumption of what the truth ought to be. It usually took the form either of a guess as to what God intended or what was suitable for that perfect creature, man. For example, for centuries all learned persons "knew" that every human being was dominated by one of four "humors," or fluids—blood, phlegm, yellow bile, and black bile. Any individual, therefore, could be classified psychologically as sanguine, phlegmatic, choleric, or melancholy according to his respective humor. Aristotle's deductive system is bulletproof, if the starting generalization, or major premise, is true, and if the individual is a member of the group about which the generalization is made. This system underlies the classification that gives order to science.

What was totally lacking was any dependable method for establishing a truth. Bacon's doctrine of building up general truths by impartial observation of specific data—inductive reasoning—and by classification of similarities has given reliability to scientific research ever since. Oddly enough, Bacon never did much to try out his own ideas or even to talk to someone who had, although he died from a chill he caught trying to preserve a chicken in snow. One of the true scientists that he might profitably have cultivated, his own physician, Dr. Harvey, said: "He writes philosophy [i.e., science] like a lord chancellor."

THE FALSE IDOLS

It is possible only to sample Bacon's provocative ideas, for, as he said, he took all knowledge for his province. Among his most famous, and still powerful, concepts is that of the four classes of idols—Idols of the Tribe, Idols of the Cave, Idols of the Market Place, and Idols of the Theater. These are the false notions, phantoms, that beset men's minds and prevent progress. Idols of the Tribe are errors based on the belief that "the sense of man is the measure of all things"—because it seems so to us, for instance, therefore the earth is the center of the universe, and the heavenly bodies rotate about it. Idols of the Cave are the errors based on the limited experience of the individual—"For everyone has a cave or den of his own, which refracts and discolors the light of nature." Idols of the Market Place describes the errors imposed by improper communication because of the control over behavior exerted by words. Idols of the Theater is the label Bacon puts on the false doctrines that have fastened themselves on men's minds—"because in my judgment all the received systems are but so many stage-plays, representing worlds of their own creation after an unreal and scenic fashion."

The largeness of Bacon's effort commands respect. "The divisions of knowledge are like the branches of a tree that meet in one stem." "Men have been kept back as by a kind of enchantment from progress in the sciences by reverence for antiquity, by the men accounted great in philosophy"—a frontal attack on Aristotle—"and then by general consent." This he says is deplorable, "seeing that in the course of so many ages there has been so great a dearth and barrenness of arts and inventions."

It was unfortunate that Bacon did not know more about

science firsthand, particularly the work of Vesalius in anatomy and Kepler in astronomy. But in his *New Atlantis* he paralleled Sir Thomas More's *Utopia* with one of the earliest pieces of science fiction. In it Solomon's House is the prototype of the Royal Society and all other associations of learned men that exist to collect, preserve, and disseminate knowledge. Paradoxically, Roger Bacon (c. 1214?–1294) had attempted much the same "instauration" of scientific method and better than Francis had understood the importance of mathematics as the language of science. In 1600, William Gilbert (1540–1603), Queen Elizabeth's physician, published the first important work in English science, a treatise on magnetism, in which he gave us the word "electricity." Gilbert was a true scientist, and William Harvey (1578–1657), already mentioned, was also practising the scientific method while Bacon wrote about it. In 1616, the year Shakespeare died, Harvey announced the epochal proof of the circulation of the blood. Yet had Francis Bacon given his life to research in a limited field, his writings would hardly have ranged so widely, been so stimulating, or had so much influence. In his own seventeenth century the founding of the Royal Society is attributed to his inspiration. In the eighteenth century he inspired the preparation of Diderot's great French *Encyclopedia*. In the nineteenth century Darwin, in beginning his work on the origin of the species, said that he would proceed on "true Baconian principles."

An amazing mind was Francis Bacon's, capable of seizing the dimensions of problems generations away. "It is most unskillful," he said, "to investigate the nature of any thing in the thing itself"—thus foreshadowing the modern realization that basic knowledge of the structure of matter underlies all applied technology. Indeed, Bacon regretted that so little had been "produced by the industry of the chemists" because it had not been based on sound theory but accidentally "or else by a kind of variation of experiments, such as mechanics use." Many a modern industrial company has discovered belatedly that it has lost its markets because it put too small a part of its resources into basic research.

Bacon discovered nothing; he was mistaken or incomplete in some of his theories. The mathematics he lacked had not been invented. The discoveries of the great century of science that followed him could never have been made by following his system literally. He particularly failed to grasp the creative force of imaginative conceptualization in science—the very thing he was doing. But he saw the sorcery hidden in erroneous thinking. He saw the need of scientific objectivity in the study of nature and systematic accumulation of data from exhaustive experimentation. Beyond this, though, he had a vision of man mastering nature, controlling his environment, and improving himself, the vision on which all modern progress is founded.

ISAAC NEWTON AND THE OCEAN OF TRUTH

"I do not know what I may appear to the world; but to myself I seem to have been only like a boy playing on the seashore and diverting myself in now and then finding a smoother pebble or prettier shell than ordinary, whilst the great ocean of Truth lay all undiscovered before me." This famous remark reflects the modesty of the greatest figure in science. Isaac Newton (1642–1727) is an example of genius recognized, used to its full potential, and rewarded. A fatherless Lincolnshire country boy, he was encouraged to go to Cambridge by a discerning uncle. Independent studies pursued in 1665–1666 while away from the university during the Black Plague brought him the respect of older scholars, and at the age of twenty-seven he was Lucasian Professor of Mathematics at Cambridge, one of the highest academic posts in Europe.

A bachelor, he stayed on at Trinity College absorbed in single-minded research, until twenty-seven years later he was given first the lucrative position of Warden of the Mint and shortly after that of Master of the Mint. He had been elected to the Royal Society at thirty and was for twenty-four years its president. In 1705 he was knighted, the first English scientist so honored. He was considered the foremost scientist of his time; today he is rated by fellow scientists the foremost scientist of all time. With the growing volume, complexity, specialization, and interdependence of scientific research, it seems unlikely that one man will ever again be able to make contributions to knowledge that match Newton's in brilliance and grandeur.

Science in Newton's day belonged to amateurs. In England the interests and influence of these men came into focus at the Royal Society. Beginning about 1645 as an informal group, by 1663 it was functioning under a warrant from King Charles II as "the Royal Society for the improving of natural knowledge by experiments." But the desire to exchange information with Continental scientists led to correspondence and then to publication. Today one of the great repositories of scientific knowledge is still the *Transactions of the Royal Society*. Without such scholarly publications science—and thus industry—would wither. The foremost scientific work ever published is written in Latin, until this century the international language of scholars. It is Newton's *Philosophiae Naturalis Principia Mathematica* printed in 1687. Astonishingly, on the title page is also the name of Samuel Pepys, author of the most famous of all diaries. Mr. Pepys was at the time president of the Royal Society.

In English, Newton's title reads, *The Mathematical Principles of Natural Philosophy*—natural philosophy, or philosophy, at that time meaning science. The work is generally referred to as the *Principia*. His other great work, the *Optics,* was published in English in 1704. In the years of his prime Newton worked unmindful of food and sleep, so absorbed in his research that the *Principia* and *Optics* were published years after he had made most of his discoveries. He wrote notes on his experiments, tossed them into drawers, and went on to the next of the endless problems that fascinated him. Only the wheedling of his friend Edmund Halley of comet fame dragged his works into print.

The *Principia* and the *Optics* sum up most of what was known about the physical world at the time of their publication. Newton explained his own contributions by saying that he "stood on the shoulders of giants." But his achievements are overwhelming in their magnitude, both in themselves and as shoulders for later scientists to stand on. In mathematics alone he profoundly extended the binomial theorem and then invented the differential and the integral calculus. The claim of his great German contemporary, Leibnitz, to priority in inventing the calculus was one of several disagreeable incidents of the sort that upset Newton. The differential calculus solves the problem of computing *instantaneous rate of change* of a function with respect to a variable upon which it depends—for instance, the change of velocity of a projectile with time. Because change is one of the chief preoccupations of science and technology and control of irregular change one of its principal problems, the calculus is indispensable.

The iris of Newton's *Optics* is his discovery that sunlight can be broken down into a spectrum of red, orange, yellow, green, blue, and violet light, as it is in a rainbow. This was the first step toward spectroscopy, the most precise and powerful means the modern scientist has for penetrating the mysteries of the structure of matter. By means of X-ray, infrared, nuclear magnetic resonance, and other subtle forms of spectrum analysis, the spectroscopist can describe the composition of a competitor's chemical compounds or measure the heat of a star.

NEWTON'S LAWS

Newton's mightiest achievement is his three Laws of Motion. He had to invent the calculus in order to carry out his elaborately detailed experimental proof of his theories. The great system is set forth in the *Principia*. First Law: "Every body remains in a state of rest or of uniform motion in a straight line, when it is compelled by impressed forces to change that state." (A mule, for instance.) Second Law: "Change of motion [acceleration] is proportional to the impressed force, and takes place in the direction of the straight line in which that force is impressed." (What happens when you step on the gas to pass another car.) Third Law: "Action and reaction are equal and opposite." (Head-on collision.)

From these laws Newton deduced his Law of Gravitation. This says that every pair of particles in the universe attract each other: "Masses are attracted to each other with a force varying directly as the product of the masses and inversely proportional to the square of the distance between." Newton not only turned a faint surmise of scientists into a certainty; he united celestial and terrestrial physical behavior. The earth obeyed the same laws as the sun, and it pulled the moon toward it, no less than the airborne apple. The action of tides, of planets, of comets, of sound, of all the phenomena of nature, so long a mystery or so obscurely understood, began for the first time to fall into a harmonious, verifiable master plan.

Newton's "laws" are like the axioms of Euclid's geometry, in strict logic incapable of proof. He postulated certain truths and then made them part of the proof—circular reasoning. But this hardly matters. Under ordinary conditions scientific experience is consistent with Newton's "Laws of Motion." Today they are the foundation of all dynamics, that essential discipline in our technological civilization. Whenever an engineer measures mass or force in order to deal with the problems of motors, missiles, or molecules, he puts his faith in the validity of Newton's theories, and the mathematics he uses is the calculus.

THE *PRINCIPIA* AND THE *OPTICS*

For the person who knows mathematics and physics, reading the several hundred pages of the *Principia* and the *Optics* must be a tremendous adventure. In them it is possible, as it is in only a few other instances, to follow precisely the discourse of a great mind step by step in the creation of a massive intellectual structure. Even the mathematically deficient cannot fail to be moved by turning these historic pages. Newton not only built up his mathematical proof with fastidious care; he recorded his experiments with a teacher's concreteness and often with engaging personal accent. How disarming it is to find the first theorem of the *Optics*—the famous "Lights which differ in color, differ also in degrees of refrangibility"—opening with the homely words:

Experiment 1. I took a black oblong stiff paper terminated by parallel sides, and, with a perpendicular right line drawn across from one side to the other, distinguished it into two equal parts. One of these parts I painted with a red colour and the other with a blue. The paper was very black, and the colours intense and thickly laid on, that the phenomenon might be more conspicuous. This paper I viewed through a prism of solid glass.

He had first performed this experiment thirty-eight years before in a tiny upstairs room in his mother's farmhouse in Woolsthorpe, Lincolnshire, during the bubonic plague. The prism he had bought at a country fair.

Whatever your mathematical background, you will find highly readable in the *Principia* Newton's brief prefaces, the introductory note and Rules of Reasoning in Philosophy [Science] at the beginning of Book Three, and the General Scholium [Commentary] at the end; in the *Optics*, the last four pages or so. Book Three of the *Principia* has the title "The System of the World," a reminder that Newton was constructing nothing less than a new model of the universe. In the few pages of the General Scholium at the end of Book Three, he points out that, while he has proved the laws of gravity, he has discovered no cause of this power. "It is enough," he says, "that gravity does really exist and act according to the laws which we have explained, and abundantly serves to account for all the motions of the celestial bodies and of our sea." "I frame no hypotheses; for whatever is not deduced from the phenomena is to be called an hypothesis; and hypotheses, whether metaphysical or physical, whether of occult qualities or mechanical, have no place in experimental philosophy [science]."

Newton uses hypothesis in the sense of an assumption accepted as true, not as we do, of a working theory to guide investigation. Yet he also offers as self-evident: "This most beautiful system of the sun, planets, and comets could only proceed from the counsel and dominion of an intelligent and powerful Being." After an Aristotelian argument—"for all our notions of God are taken from the ways of mankind by a certain similitude"—he concludes, "And thus much concerning God; to discourse of whom from the appearances of things, does certainly belong to natural philosophy [science]."

Still carrying on Bacon's war with Greek and medieval deductive rationalism, Newton is much more insistent about the virtues of the empirical method for reaching the truth than he is about the finality of his discoveries. He summarizes his credo in the next to the last paragraph of the *Optics:*

As in mathematics, so in natural philosophy, the investigation of difficult things by the method of analysis ought ever to precede the method of composition. This analysis consists in making experiments and observations, and in drawing general conclusions from them by induction, and admitting of no objections against the conclusions but such as are taken from experiments, or other certain truths. For hypotheses are not to be regarded in experimental philosophy. And although the arguing from experiments and observations by induction be no demonstration of general conclusions, yet it is the best way of arguing which the nature of things admits of, and may be looked upon as so much the stronger, by how much the induction is more general. And if no exception occur from phenomena, the conclusion may be pronounced generally. But if at any time afterwards any exceptions shall occur from experiments, it may then begin to be pronounced with such exceptions as occur. By this way of analysis we may proceed from compounds to ingredients, and from motions to the forces producing them; and, in general, from effects to their causes, and from particular causes to more general ones, till the argument end in the most general. This is the method of analysis; and the synthesis consists in assuming the causes discovered, and established as principles, and by them explaining the phenomena proceeding from them, and proving the explanations.

Again it is necessary to make the reservation that in his strictures against hypotheses Newton is attacking the Greek and medieval habit of reasoning abstractly from premise to conclusion without evidence. But notice that like Bacon he seems unaware of the crucial role of the fruitful working hypothesis, without which all experimenting is nothing but random trial and error. Newton's neglect of this point is strange. When he says about his Woolsthorpe experiments, "In the same year [1666] I began to think of gravity extending to the orb of the moon," he enunciates what is probably the greatest scientific hypothesis yet conceived. As we noted in the first chapter, how these transforming hypotheses occur to great creative spirits is a mystery. But we do know that, as in the case of twenty-four year old Isaac Newton, they come only to the "prepared mind."

Look back at the last sentence of the paragraph from the *Optics*. The clause beginning "and the synthesis" announces an advance of the deepest significance in scientific methods, an all-important step beyond Bacon, really a harmonizing of the contributions of Aristotle and Bacon. In other words, the goal of all empirical observation and experiment is to establish by induction principles or laws that can be dependably applied deductively to specific phenomena without further experiment. Thus, Sir Isaac Newton is one of the Great Teachers. He contributed more than any other man to our knowledge of the universe, and he contributed almost as much to our understanding of how to go about gathering knowledge of any kind. What he apparently did not realize is the importance, actually the necessity, of the inductive inference that establishes the sort of probability short of certainty on which fruitful action in science, as well as in human affairs, must often be based.

In his verse autobiography, *The Prelude*, William Wordsworth records how as a Cambridge undergraduate he could see from his window Newton's statue

> The marble index of a mind for ever
> Voyaging through strange seas of Thought, alone.

Hundreds of other lonely voyagers have charted their way to the horizons of the "great ocean of Truth" by the *Principia* and the *Optics*, and Max Planck, Albert Einstein, and a few others have penciled important changes on the chart. That is what Isaac Newton expected. The man whose majestic system can be compacted into the seedlike parsimonious part-Leibnitz notation

$$f = m \frac{d^2s}{dt^2}$$

would be delighted by the elegance of Einstein's $E = mc^2$ for relativity.

Newton was a proud man, but he ends the Preface to the first edition of the *Principia* with the humble, "I heartily beg that what I have here done may be read with forbearance; and that my labors in a subject so difficult may be examined, not so much with the view to censure, as to remedy the defects." Humility, forbearance, acknowledgment of difficulty, constructive building on other men's efforts—these, too, are elements that the scientific spirit contributes to the cultivated mind.

THE EVOLUTION OF DARWINISM

Every schoolboy presumably knows that Charles Darwin made his name a synonym for evolution. Every adult is aware of the earth-shaking impact that the theory of evolution had on the modern world and the bitter controversy it engendered among religious fundamentalists. The absurdities of the 1925 Scopes trial in Tennessee have not disappeared entirely. But we are inclined to imagine that Darwin invented a theory called evolution, which at once cleared up much of the mystery of life on earth. Even in a few paragraphs, the story of the evolution of Darwin's ideas is worth review. How do scientific ideas that rock the world come about, how are they received, and how are they established?

Darwin championed two main ideas—evolution and its mechanism, natural selection. Neither idea was wholly original, and Darwin was never wholly sure how his mechanism worked. Nor is the matter settled yet. His ideas were bitterly assailed by such eminent scientists as Louis Agassiz, the Swiss-American zoologist and geologist, and Lord Kelvin, great nineteenth-century mathematician and physicist. Lacking the specialized knowledge to counter his attackers, Darwin, a reasonable and uncontentious man, wavered and compromised and retreated through the twenty-three years that followed the publishing of *Origin of Species* in 1859.

Charles Darwin was born on the same day as Abraham Lincoln, February 12, 1809, and died in 1882. In his modest *Autobiography*, written at the end of his life, Darwin tells how after failing in a classical schooling, he then failed in the study of medicine, and as a last resort went to Cambridge to study for the ministry. His hobby of collecting beetles and the friendly interest of a science professor got him a berth as a naturalist on the "Beagle," a Royal Navy ship that sailed in 1831 for a five-year scientific expedition around the coast of South America. More important than the fascinating book, *The Voyage of the "Beagle,"* that resulted, Darwin found his career in science and his destiny in trying to answer the riddle of the origin and continuation of the various forms of life.

Chronic illness put him on a four-hour workday for the remaining forty years of his life. Luckily he did not have to work for a living. During those years he published his *Origin of Species* and in 1871 his *Descent of Man,* two of the world's most significant books. In addition, he published numerous other works and carried on serious correspondence with scientists. He never answered directly the attacks on his theories, and he never discussed their religious or philosophic implications. Thomas Henry Huxley and Herbert Spencer in England and Ernst Haeckel in Germany popularized and defended his theories. Spencer gave currency to the phrase "survival of the fittest" and the term "evolution." Darwin seldom used the latter word.

THE FINCHES OF THE GALÁPAGOS

During the voyage of the "Beagle," Darwin combined observation of plants and animals with shrewd hypotheses in a way that has rarely been matched by any scientist, let alone by a lad in his twenties with practically no formal scientific training. The apogee of his experience came when he reached the Galápagos Islands, several hundred miles off the coast of Ecuador. There, cut off from the rest of the world, was a perfect laboratory for the study of species of flora and fauna. Particularly puzzling to young Darwin were the fourteen species of finches. In all the world the only species they resembled was one on the mainland of Ecuador. How had such variation come about in the first place, and then why so much in the same limited environment? Darwin was sure these finches were variants from an earlier form, though he had no explanation as to how the changes happened. Yet from this limited improvised hypothesis he leaped to the grand one that all living organisms are variants of earlier forms. But it was not until 1839, he says, that he got his cue to this great generalization from reading a book by Thomas Robert Malthus.

Malthus worried because population grows at a faster rate than food production. War, famine, plagues, cataclysms, and birth control are the only deterrents. (This nightmare haunts us still.) Darwin says it occurred to him then that in the struggle for existence "favorable variations would tend to be preserved and unfavorable ones destroyed." From this process would come new species. His finches, that is, would originally be the same as those in Ecuador. The main differences in the fourteen species were their bills and eating habits. As the Galápagos colony grew crowded and the competition for food acute, those individual birds that *by chance* had bigger, narrower, or otherwise deviant beaks would be able to feed where others could not. They would tend to survive, to mate with others with similar advantages, and thus in time to create new species. When new food supplies were lacking, a species could not diversify. So Darwin at long last thought he knew how evolution worked. He called the method *natural selection.* But except for conversations and letters to his scientist friends—who, he said, never really understood him—he kept his ideas to himself and patiently experimented with plants and pigeons and gathered evidence from every possible source, including pigeon fanciers in ale houses. Much of the impact of Darwin's theories came from the amazing breadth and logical organization of his supporting evidence.

THE ORIGIN OF THE SPECIES
AND THE DESCENT OF MAN

Not until 1859 did the *Origin of Species,* like a great storm that had been building up, burst on the world. Ironically, Darwin's scrupulous gathering of evidence in all fields before presenting his full account nearly led to his giving up before the world heard about his labors. In 1858 he received from Alfred Russel Wallace, a biologist who was collecting animals in the Moluccas, an essay presenting much the same theories as his

own. The eminent geologist Lyell persuaded Darwin not to ef-
face himself but to share the announcement with Wallace by
making public one of his earlier private statements. Wallace
always generously recognized the priority and greater range of
Darwin's research. Lyell also persuaded Darwin to publish his
work in extended form in *Origin of Species* the following year.
The full title is *On the Origin of Species by Means of Natural
Selection, or the Preservation of Favored Races in the Struggle
for Life.*

In the *Origin,* Darwin said cryptically that "light would be
thrown on the origin of man and his history." Clearly if all other
species have descended by modifications from earlier forms,
man must have, too—unless man is an exception. In 1871, in
Descent of Man, Darwin turned on the light. Acknowledging
courteously and specifically where other scientists disagreed
with him and punctiliously giving credit to all who shared or
had anticipated his views in any respect, he stated in full the case
for man's existence being only a phase in the great continuum.
As he put it quaintly, an ape, "if he could take a dispassionate
view of his own case," would admit fundamental differences between himself and man, but Darwin found it impossible to
ignore the many similarities. So the international debate that
raged over evolution after 1859 was fired up again over whether
or not "man was descended from a monkey."

Before we look at the reception of Darwin's ideas, we must go
back to see from what thinking Darwinism evolved.

Aristotle was the first to differentiate species, or *phyla* as he
called them. But the study of nature languished until the eighteenth century. Then the awakening of scientific observation and
classification brought forward a number of predecessors of Darwin. Among these, oddly enough, his own grandfather is notable.
In 1794, in his *Zoonomia,* Erasmus Darwin discussed the variety
of changes in animals in normal growth, by cultivation, and by
adaptation to climate and other conditions, and he concluded:
"From thus meditating on the minute portion of time in which
many of the above changes have been produced, would it be too
bold to imagine, in the great length of time since the earth began

to exist, perhaps millions of years before the commencement of the history of mankind, that all warm-blooded animals have arisen from one living filament?" Erasmus Darwin even held that evolution worked by "the power of acquiring new parts . . . and . . . the faculty of continuing to improve by its own inherent activity, and of delivering down those improvements by generation to its posterity, world without end." In 1785, James Hutton read before the Royal Society of Edinburgh the results of his lonely meditations, and ten years later published his *Theory of the Earth.* He posited the earth as constantly wearing away and renewing itself, and for this endless change he said, "we find no vestige of a beginning—no prospect of an end."

Jean Baptiste de Lamarck, a Frenchman, came close to anticipating Darwin. He suggested daringly that man might have an origin analogous to that of the other animals. But Lamarck believed that evolution operated by inheritance of characteristics acquired from the environment. The giraffe, he thought, was once an antelope-like creature that developed a long neck by being forced to stretch when it could no longer graze otherwise. But he could not explain the giraffe's spotted coat. Lamarck missed the essential point in Darwinism—in a certain environment those members of the giraffe species with the longest necks and spotted coats were best adapted to survival. In Paris, Baron Georges Cuvier, one of the first comparative anatomists, was doing extraordinary things by using knowledge of existing animals to reconstruct extinct animals from fossil bones.

The man who most influenced Charles Darwin was Charles Lyell (1797–1875). The first volume of his *Principles of Geology* (1830) accompanied the young Darwin on the voyage of the "Beagle," and he eagerly picked up the second volume during the journey. On his return Lyell became his friend. The *Principles of Geology* provided the evidence for revising the age of the earth drastically and thus gave a time schedule necessary for evolution to be feasible. Strangely, Lyell arrived at belief in evolution belatedly by way of Darwin's work. But Darwin acknowledged his indebtedness to Lyell and dedicated his

THE SCIENTIFIC VISION 73

Origin of Species to him. Lyell was a biologist as well as a
geologist and contributed a good deal to Darwin's ideas of the
part played by environment in changing the species.

The resistance Darwinism met had a variety of causes. His
doctrine of evolution ran counter to the generally held notion of
"catastrophism"—the creation of the earth from the sea in successive upheavals. Current Christian theology found this theory
compatible, although where the water went no one seemed to
know. Hutton and Lamarck and others were "uniformitarians."
They viewed man at the top of a flight of steps reaching down in
ordered sequence of distinct species far beyond the Biblical span.
Darwin changed the steps to an escalator. The religious objection
to evolution was twofold: A seventeenth-century tidying up of
the Bible read Genesis to start six thousand years in the past. To
challenge this detail was to challenge whatever else anyone
cared to think the Bible said. More seriously, in place of the
once-and-for-all divine design of each species for its appointed
purpose, Darwin substituted chance endlessly working. When, in
the *Descent* in 1871, he presented the pious and sentimental
Victorians with anthropoid ancestors, he added insult to sacri-
lege. He also antagonized the fashionable school of German
philosophical metaphysics, who abhorred scientific materialism.
Yet in searching for physical causes instead of assuming divine
purposes, Darwin was reflecting the Baconian revolution in
thinking that marked the end of the Middle Ages.

The tide of popular interest as well as science was running in
Darwin's favor. The great advances in mathematics, physics, and
astronomy of the seventeenth century had led to extreme opti-
mism about science and the perfectibility of man and his institutions in the eighteenth century. Delightful books, such as Gilbert
White's *Natural History of Selborne*, Thomas Bewick's and Audubon's prints of birds, Tennyson's popular poetry, magazines and
books aimed at the new middle class created by the industrial
revolution, and the spread of educational opportunities—all
helped give Darwin an audience. The vogue of John Stuart Mill's
"utilitarianism" and the Manchester school of *laissez faire* eco-

nomics did a great deal to create a body of thought congenial to Darwinism. The doctrines of "The greatest good for the greatest number" and the survival of the fittest in free competition for markets seemed to be endorsements of Darwin's theories.

THE SURVIVAL OF THE
THEORY OF EVOLUTION

By the time of Darwin's death in 1882 the bulk of scientific and public opinion was on his side. Step by step other scientists, bringing new techniques to bear, verified his hypotheses. He had reasoned without evidence that birds evolved from reptiles. The discovery of a fossilized Archaeopteryx, a bird with reptile teeth, confirmed his brilliant guess. But Lord Kelvin, the father of thermodynamics, used his great authority to raise doubts that Darwin and Huxley never laid to rest, for they could not meet him on his own grounds. Using what we now know were erroneous estimates of the rate of loss of energy by the sun, Kelvin estimated the age of the earth as 20 million years or so. Darwin needed 300 million even to take care of the infinitely slow change of organisms that was the cornerstone of his system. The present estimate is around 500 million. Pathetically, in successive editions of *Origin of the Species* he altered statements, until he was back with Lamarck and uniformitarianism.

Another key problem that bothered Darwin was heredity. Although it was crucial to his doctrine, neither he nor, to the best of his knowledge, anyone else knew much about it, and what he knew about domestic breeding was misleading. The irony was that the very evidence he needed was printed in 1866 but ignored, like its author, until 1900. It was the record of the monk Gregor Mendel (1822–1884), who in the monastery of Brünn, Moravia, working with common peas, established a predictable system by which organisms pass on their characteristics to their offspring and future generations. A truly great man, the monk Mendel, the founder of the science of genetics. Discouraged, he gave up his research, trusting that posterity would recognize the worth of what his own age failed even to notice.

Modern genetics, biochemistry, paleontology, physiology, geology, and other scientific disciplines have corrected some of the errors in Darwin's thinking. The methods by which evolution takes place are still not altogether certain. Darwin overlooked the vast interlocking system of cooperation in nature, notably the mutual dependency beween plants on the one hand and birds, animals, and insects on the other. And he failed to take into account that man controls his environment to an extent not covered by natural selection. Today scientists think of evolution as beginning with elementary particles and moving through atoms and molecules to the nucleic acids that may have formed the first living organism. From this crucial development may have followed genes, chromosomes, cells, and human life. They think of the earth as perhaps 4 billion years old. The first 2 billion years were necessary for the preliminary chemical evolution, and $1\frac{1}{2}$ billion years for the evolution of forms of life complex enough to leave fossils. That leaves 500 million years for the primates, including the missing link, Adam, and Charles Darwin, to evolve —that is, in a relatively short time, a few million years at the end of the accelerating sequence of algae, fish, amphibians, reptiles, birds and animals. But in the main, after all its vicissitudes, the grand conceptual scheme of Darwin, set forth with unprecedented comprehensiveness and supported by a lifetime of research, is now vindicated. It is one of the noblest manifestations of the scientific vision.

LOUIS PASTEUR, THE SCIENTIST AS HERO

Only Abraham Lincoln surpasses Louis Pasteur (1822–1895) as an indubitable hero of the past century. He discovered that infectious diseases were caused by microorganisms—germs, microbes, bacteria are the common terms—and could be identified and prevented by steps such as vaccination and pasteurization. The son of a poor provincial tanner, Louis Pasteur became the popular symbol of the beneficence and invincibility of science. Although he remained a faithful Roman Catholic, he did as much as any man to build up the faith in science that underlies the materialism of Main Street and Moscow and that makes the layman look on the scientist as the controller of forces that can unriddle the mysteries of life and make man captain of his destiny. Of the various centers of interest in Louis Pasteur's career, therefore, none is more relevant here than that career itself.

Until doctors stopped belittling Pasteur, they were little better armed to fight disease in the nineteenth century than they had been in the Middle Ages. Blood-letting, a few folk remedies, a solemn manner, and advice to stay in bed were their stock in trade. The plague that had terrified Europe at the time of Chaucer, Shakespeare, and Newton was still a ghastly visitor. In the presence of tuberculosis, syphilis, or any other contagious disease, the King's Physician knew little more than a jungle witch doctor—sometimes less, since quinine, for instance, as a specific for malaria, was known on the banks of the Orinoco before it reached the Seine. It is hard to grasp the extent of the changes Pasteur wrought or to guess the number of lives he saved.

At the age of twenty-five his doctoral dissertation made Pasteur famous overnight. He announced that the molecules of living matter, such substances as "sugars, starches, albumens, gelatine, fibrin, or cellulose, rotate the plane of polarized light, and in the process of crystallization they assume forms whose mirror-images cannot be superposed on them." This discovery was a major contribution to stereochemistry, the arrangement in space of the atoms in the molecules of which substances are composed. This step toward the elucidation of molecular structures was of enormous value in the advance of chemistry.

For a time Pasteur dreamt that he might be close to the secret of life. In a sense he was. Optical activity is one of the most distinctive chemical characteristics of living organisms. And Pasteur's conviction, "The universe is asymmetric," has recently been widely accepted. But in the last few years by means of stereo specific synthesis man has for the first time been able to arrange atoms as nature does. Through the polymerization of olefins, for instance, chemists are now able to duplicate natural rubber in a laboratory. They are able to make hormones that have the same effect as natural hormones, something man-made hormones have not had before. They have even elucidated the structure of the nucleic acid DNA, the key to heredity, the prime necessity for the reproduction of living organisms.

Had Pasteur followed this brilliant beginning in the study of molecular structure, he would certainly have made significant further discoveries and pushed the frontiers of science ahead by many years. Chance led him into the arena of practical technological problems, and he accommodated himself to the accidental. He always regretted that he did not continue his studies in crystallography in order to probe into the basic mysteries of chemistry. But in bridging the gulf between abstraction and application, he shaped his own career and the lay image of the scientist in an important way.

THE CAUSE OF FERMENTATION

As professor of chemistry and dean of science at the University of Lille, Pasteur had a duty to interest himself in fermentation in the local manufacture of alcohol from beets. The great German chemist Liebig had explained alcohol as the result of some sort of "sympathetic vibration" that affected the sugar molecule as a result of the decomposition of the yeast in reaction with oxygen. From his earlier research, as noted, Pasteur had concluded that only living organisms rotate the plane of polarized light. Since one of the by-products of the fermentation that he studied showed this reaction, he hypothesized, a life process was present in the yeast and this was the cause of the fermentation. This theory pushed aside the chemistry-only theory of Liebig and the other experts. Experiments and microscopic studies led Pasteur to the theory that all fermentation took place in this way and that the active agents were always microscopic living organisms that he called bacteria. Furthermore, Pasteur stated, this life process involved in fermentation took place in the absence of oxygen, an impossibility in the eyes of Liebig and most other chemists. In 1857, Pasteur characteristically had already made a full statement of his theories and his experimental methods for testing them in his first paper on fermentation, a study of the conversion of sugar into lactic acid as in the souring of milk.

Pasteur's interest in the problems of the workaday world led him to apply his theories of optical activity and fermentation to vinegar, wine, and beer. He improved the art in each case and taught the manufacturers some of the chemistry of their processes. He saved them from the heavy spoilage losses they were inflicting on themselves because generations of practical men had held unscientific beliefs, such as the usefulness of the ugly mess of worms generated in making vinegar and beer. The wine experts had always "known" that air was bad for wine. Pasteur showed how the complex process of wine-making takes place, including the action of the wild yeasts that are on the skin of the grapes and the beneficial role of oxygen in aging the wine. He also proved that the diseases plaguing the wine industry were caused by microorganisms. Even more important, he taught how they could be rendered harmless by partial sterilization through the application of the right amount of heat. So the incalculable blessing of pasteurization, by which milk and other foodstuffs may be kept wholesome over extended periods, had its birth in industrial technology.

DISEASES OF SILKWORMS

In 1865, Pasteur was appointed by the government to see what could be done to help the silkworm industry, nearly ruined by mysterious diseases. "*Pébrine,*" the worst, was so called because of spots like black pepper within the silkworm. Serving a government commission, Pasteur and his assistants had to work for four years in the public view and give periodical public reports. They demonstrated that the mind trained in scientific procedures can solve unfamiliar difficult practical problems—it can, that is, if the mind belongs to a Pasteur. Pasteur's attack on the silkworm mystery was characteristic. In two weeks after arriving at his field station, near Alais in the south of France, he recommended a method of egg selection that produced worms free of *pébrine*. A year later he had a method for avoiding *flacherie*, the other leading disease. With no previous experience in silkworm culture he had first learned how to tell the symptoms of disease. He taught the silkworm raisers to destroy the potentially sick at the

stage when the symptoms appeared, and thus to assure themselves of healthy worms. He saved the silk industry in Europe
and the Near East.

But he was far from knowing the causes of *pébrine* and
flacherie. This is hardly remarkable, because he was a chemist,
untrained in medicine, taking the first steps into the untraveled
darkness of infectious disease. Nevertheless, he soon began to
conceive of epidemics as transmitted by anerobic microorganisms. Moreover, many years ahead of his times, he thought
correctly that immunity was subject to complex individual
variability according to health and environmental conditions. His
silkworm campaign was interrupted for many months by a severe
stroke. The brilliant work for which Pasteur is most famous was
carried on during twenty-five years that he was partially para-
lyzed. He could not even perform his own microscopic studies
or write his own reports. But he could think.

Pasteur's career moved from chemistry to bacteriology to medicine. By mid-career he had reached certainty that microorganisms caused contagious diseases in plants, animals, and human
beings and that immunization against them was possible. In
1874 a young English surgeon, Joseph Lister, wrote him in
homage and reported how the germ theory had led him to
develop antiseptic techniques in surgery that are now historic.
In 1879 during a discussion of childbirth fever at the Paris
Academy of Medicine, Pasteur had interrupted a doctor who was
poo-poohing germs as a cause of childbirth fever, which he as-
cribed to a "puerperal miasm." "The cause of the epidemic,"
asserted Pasteur, "is nothing of the kind! It is the doctor and his
staff who carry the microbe from a sick woman to a healthy
woman!" And he drew on a blackboard an organism like a string
of beads, the picture of the evil streptococcus. Yet he had made
his only observation of a case of puerperal fever just a few days
before! Pasteur's fight for sterile conditions of surgery has saved
millions from slaughter in the operating room.

Pasteur's germ theory had been persistently attacked by the
believers in spontaneous generation, a theory of the beginning of
life held by Aristotle, Newton, and common-sense observers of

maggots appearing from nowhere in rotten meat. Pasteur battled in print and debate and by theatrical challenges and public demonstrations to prove that only life begets life, that alleged proofs of spontaneous generation were invalid, and that when substances are sterilized and sealed from bacteria in the air, no life appears. To argue the case, some of Pasteur's cultures still remain unchanged in their flasks to this day. To test his theories in the animal world, Pasteur chose to tackle anthrax, a scourge among sheep. Dr. Robert Koch, co-founder with Pasteur of medical bacteriology and famous for isolating the tubercle bacillus, had already done extensive research on anthrax bacilli. Pasteur corroborated Koch's work by growing anthrax bacilli and reproducing them in animals. But his goal was immunization.

IMMUNITY THROUGH VACCINATION

In 1769, Edward Jenner, an English doctor, had tested a folk belief that a person who had had cowpox was safe from the dreaded smallpox. He blithely inoculated a boy with cowpox and later with smallpox and proved the folklore true. In 1798 he published the results of his further research, and vaccination (*vacca* is cow in Latin) against smallpox became widespread. Pasteur admired Jenner's work, but in the true scientific spirit he sought to establish immunization against disease on a broad front. Brilliantly, he found his answer in a mistake in laboratory procedure, a forerunner of the serendipitous discovery of penicillin. In the course of his investigation of an epidemic of chicken cholera, his assistants inoculated a hen with a cholera culture that had stood in a cupboard while they went on a holiday for several weeks. Nothing happened. They then inoculated the same hen with a deadly fresh culture. Still nothing happened. With his habitual swiftness in seizing on the meaning hidden in a few skimpy facts, Pasteur saw that aging had weakened the first culture to the point where it was harmless to the fowl, yet potent enough to give immunity from the disease. He had an equivalent of Jenner's cowpox vaccine. After patient repeated experiments, he theorized that inoculation with "attenuated virus" should immunize sheep against anthrax. Then he vaulted to his broad hypothesis that the same basic method should protect man against infectious diseases.

With much difficulty Pasteur developed the anthrax vaccine in his laboratory and then in a blaze of publicity in April 1881 subjected it to a nerve-wracking field test. Pasteur's adversaries stood by ready to pounce on any evidence of failure. But the un-inoculated control sheep died, and the inoculated sheep lived. Not only had Pasteur vanquished anthrax with unending benefit to animal husbandry; he had proved the soundness of his grand hypothesis—vaccination could give immunity from infectious disease. He proved it over again the same year by developing a vaccine for swine erysipelas, which had carried off a million pigs in the United States in one year. Strangely enough, even then a bitter critic of vaccination was Dr. Koch himself. But Pasteur received the Grand Order of the Legion of Honor. He was a national hero.

His theory and his hero status were put to a cruel test. He had begun research on rabies. He had even more difficulty than he had had with anthrax because he could not isolate the responsible microorganism. It was a virus—a microorganism that can be seen only with an electron miscroscope, not then invented. But with his usual brilliant deductions from observation, Pasteur es-tablished the spinal cord as the site of the virus and developed a technique for making a vaccine. His experiments proved suc-cessful. Then in 1885 there appeared at his laboratory a nine-year-old Alsatian boy, Joseph Meister, badly bitten by a rabid dog. The doctors said he was doomed, but since rabies has a long incubation period, this was only an opinion. Pasteur agreed to treat the boy. The vaccine had never been used on a human being. It had to be administered in a series of inoculations, in-creasing to a final one of full virulence. Between July 4 and July 16 the boy received thirteen injections. He lived.

Rabies patients came to Pasteur from all over. Of 350 treated, all lived except one. The one was a girl brought to Pasteur thirty-seven days after being bitten. He had the courage not to turn her away to protect his reputation. Her father praised his humanity. Because of the terror that surrounded mad dogs, Pasteur was now an international hero. The scientist as miracle man had appeared. In 1888 he took possession of the research institute in Paris built by popular subscription in his honor. There his assistants developed the modern method of immunization by heat-killed bacteria. Antitoxins for diphtheria, tetanus, typhus, tuberculosis, whooping cough, and other diseases followed. As for Joseph Meister—he grew up and became a gatekeeper at the Pasteur Institute; there in 1940 he took his own life rather than open his benefactor's crypt to the Nazis.

PASTEUR'S SECRETS

The most depressing footnote to Pasteur's career is the energy and malice shown by respectable members of the scientific community in trying to discredit his work. Berzelius, Liebig, Wöhler, Helmholtz, Berthelot, Bernard, Koch, founding fathers of chemistry, were among his detractors. Their scientific discipline led few of his opponents, in the presence of overwhelming evidence, to put his theories to experimental test or to make cordial acknowledgment of Pasteur's achievements. Pasteur's certainty of his own rightness, his ready tongue, and his zest for public showdowns may have contributed, as he admitted, to the turbulence that followed in the wake of his discoveries. He was more often wrong than he ever realized. For instance, he was sure that he had swept spontaneous generation into the same dustbin into which Lavoisier had thrown the phlogiston theory. Yet recently a chemical version of spontaneous generation has gained acceptance as an explanation of the beginning of life on earth. But even when he was wrong, Pasteur made contributions to knowledge that had productive results.

When we look back over this great man's career, we see two secrets of his greatness. The first was the breathtaking speed with which he conceptualized. He set up comprehensive hypotheses so soon after beginning a new investigation that it is said that he arrived at the truth "by intuition without adequate evidence." This is misleading. Intuition means to obtain knowledge "without recourse to inference or reason." To say that Pasteur relied on intuition is to imply that he was more mystic than scientist. It is modish these days to belittle logic. But Pasteur, like Beethoven and other great creators, seems to me to have employed a logic superior to that used by most of us in that unrigorous activity we call thinking. He simply needed less data than duller minds need in order to draw fruitful inferences. As Beethoven built a symphony from a few notes, or as an astronomer sees Taurus and Gemini where I see only a random sprinkling of stars, Pasteur saw enough significance in a few facts to trace a pattern of converging evidence that yielded him his grand hypotheses. The initial evidence on which Pasteur went ahead was never sufficient to be conclusive, but it was adequate—for him.

To avoid talking nonsense, it is important to remember the obvious—just as Beethoven's notebooks are full of notations that did not grow into symphonies, not all of Pasteur's hypotheses proved right. He discarded many as soon as his reason told him they were unsound, and he modified many others. Prolific speculation and shrewd modification of a few productive concepts— these are characteristic of all great problem solvers. Pasteur had no illusions about working hypotheses, no matter how promising or how cherished:

Preconceived ideas are like searchlights which illumine the path of the experimenter and serve him as a guide to interrogate nature. They become a danger only if he transforms them into fixed ideas—this is why I should like to see these profound words inscribed on the threshold of all the temples of science: "The greatest derangement of the mind is to believe in something because one wishes it to be so." . . .

The great art consists in devising decisive experiments, leaving no place to the imagination of the observer. Imagination is needed to give wings to thought at the beginning of experimental investigations on any given subject. When, however, the time has come to conclude and to interpret the facts derived from observations, imagination must submit to the factual results of the experiments.

The second secret of Pasteur's greatness throws light on the first. "In experimental science," he liked to say, "chance favors only the prepared mind." His mind was better prepared than most. In common with all great minds, he had extraordinary powers of concentration. He said, "My only strength lies in my tenacity." And Roux, his chief assistant, declared, "How many times, in the presence of unforeseen difficulties, when he could not imagine how to get out of them, have I heard Pasteur tell us, 'Let us do the same experiment over again; the essential thing is not to leave the subject.'" Throughout his life, he never "left the subject." His assistants reported how he would stand as in a trance for hours observing the reactions of animals during experiments. He made intense observation and precise recording of minute changes the cornerstones of the experimental method. "In everything," he said to students, "the secret of success is in prolonged efforts. Through perseverance in one field of investigation, one succeeds in acquiring what I am inclined to call the instinct of truth."

When he was being received into the Académie Française, he did not praise intuition. Instead, he paid tribute to

this marvelous experimental method, of which one can say, in truth, not that it is sufficient for every purpose, but that it rarely leads astray, and then only those who do not use it well. It eliminates certain facts, brings forth others, interrogates nature, compels it to reply and stops only when the mind is fully satisfied. The charm of our studies, the enchantment of science, is that, everywhere and always, we can give the justification of our principles and the proof of our discoveries.

You do not have to be a Pasteur or even a Frenchman to be enchanted by science, moved by the grandeur of its great syntheses, charmed by the beauty of its inner harmonies, and illuminated by the revelation of logical order that the scientific vision evokes.

4

BIOGRAPHY AND OTHER
REVELATIONS

"The great and glorious masterpiece of man is to know how to live to purpose: all other things—to reign, to lay up treasure, to build—are at most but little appendices and props." So said the wise Montaigne. Nowhere can you discover how to "live to purpose" better than by reading biographies and other personal revelations—autobiographies, essays, letters, and diaries. Once you have cultivated a taste for biographical works, you will find them more irresistible than detective stories. Thrillers soon pall. Biographies grow in fascination. Inevitably they bear the stamp of authenticity: These are people who once lived; these are their dreams, problems, decisions, actions, failures, successes. Whether the record be one of an ancient Egyptian king, an eighteenth-century composer, or a Nobel prize scientist, you will gain perspective for your own career.

You are free to draw what you will from the rich garner of experience piled high in biographical works, like corn in wagons at harvest time. Since achievement is the usual justification for a biography, you will be alert to note how these men and women "programmed" their lives. For no matter how different their condition, they shared your urge to give design to your life, to overcome the limitations imposed on it, and to have it rise above mediocrity and take on some accent of distinction. The fact that genius lifted many of them to greatness gives your study a bonus.

PLUTARCH'S PERICLES

The most bountiful biographical reservoir is Plutarch's *Lives.* Shakespeare alone dipped into it for three of his plays—*Julius Caesar, Antony and Cleopatra,* and *Coriolanus.* It is sometimes called *Parallel Lives* because in his forty-six biographies Plutarch paired one Greek leader with one Roman. For centuries the book was read by schoolboy, prince, and scholar as an authentic account of how the ancient world was governed. It has done more than any other book, perhaps more than any other force, to carve the various images of the statesman to which kings, dictators, and presidents have sought to shape themselves ever since.

Plutarch lived about the time of Christ. He taught philosophy in Rome before retiring to his home town in Greece. Many centuries before such tools of research as printing and accurate records could give biography the semblance of reliability, Plutarch had a surprisingly sound grasp of his methods. The trustworthiness of his sources diminished as his subjects receded backward into the dim centuries of recorded history. Yet Plutarch consulted available authorities, showed a sober skepticism, and fitted his figures deftly into their backgrounds. The plum-pudding richness of his anecdotes accounts for the enduring popularity of the *Lives.* But Plutarch's grasp of political realities, his analyses of the motives and pressures determining the actions of leaders, and his judgments of the ethics and wisdom of their behavior make his book a manual for statesmen and business executives today, no matter how inaccurate some of the details may be.

Plutarch's life of Pericles (c. 490 B.C.–429 B.C.) is a fascinating case study. It has startling parallels in our own times. Pericles was a wealthy, well-educated young Athenian aristocrat. The philosopher Anaxagoras, who also taught the great dramatist Euripides, was his tutor. Ambitious, opportunistic, and somewhat stuffy, but intelligent, eloquent, and brave, Pericles found the road to the heights blocked by Cimon, a successful general and even wealthier aristocrat. Biding his time until Cimon was off fighting, Pericles moved into politics—on the popular democratic side. In place of the nickname "Onion-head" that his elongated skull had given him, the comic writers now sardonically called him "The Olympian" because of his high-flown speech and studied aloofness. Pericles could not match Cimon's private largesse to the poor, so he topped him by handing out state funds. He began pay for jury duty and other services that were formerly considered a privilege of citizenship, and he even doled out allowances for playgoing. He may not have invented the welfare state, but he made it work. So Pericles gained power and for a time banished Cimon.

Long before Machiavelli spelled out a prince's first obligation —to keep himself in power—many a ruler must have earnestly conned Plutarch's account of the stratagems Pericles used to balance his shifting fortunes. Among these were some constructive steps. He gave the citizens of maritime Greece extensive training in seamanship. He made land grants to the idle for colonization. And he spent lavishly for new public and sacred buildings. Through his public-works program, miners, carriers, suppliers, artisans, artists, and the whole economy of Athens benefited. Under the over-all supervision of the sculptor-architect Phidias, marvelous structures, such as the Parthenon on the Acropolis and the temple at Eleusis, came into being, adorned by some of the finest figures of the greatest period of sculpture the world has known. When his power seemed secure, Pericles no longer courted public favor. Keeping the interests of the country unswervingly in mind, "For the most part he was able to lead the people with their own consent by persuading and showing them what was to be done, and sometimes by forcing them to comply with what was to their advantage."

The rest of Pericles' rule brought severe challenges from within the state—such as charges against him and Phidias about the handling of public money and the trial of his mistress, the politically minded courtesan, Aspasia—and challenges from hostile forces without, which in the main he evaded. Once the citizens voted him out of power but soon recalled him. But all his ability to sway the people with the "thunder and lightning" of his speech had no potency over the plague. He lost his son, then fell before it himself.

An anecdote of Plutarch's gives insight into how Pericles' self-mastery made him master of others. He bore in silence the insults of a low fellow who followed him about all one day. "And as it was dark when he came to his own door, he ordered one of his servants to take a torch and light the man home." Pericles saw that the chief fault with fighting is that it is stupid. His last proud words were: "No Athenian through my means ever put on mourning." Plutarch says Pericles is chiefly to be admired because "amidst the distractions of business and the rage of his enemies . . . he never gratified his envy or his anger, or ever treated any enemy as irreconcilably opposed to him."

ALEXANDER'S GREATNESS

You may sometimes feel that you cannot learn much from the lives of great men because they are either extraordinarily gifted or incredibly lucky. Alexander the Great (356 B.C.–323 B.C.) is an example. He was both gifted and lucky, yet his life is as full of precepts as a *McGuffey Reader*. Alexander came to power at twenty and brought under his rule all the lands from Greece to India in a brief dozen years. He conquered the Persian Empire in a long series of great land battles and sieges that rank him among the half-dozen greatest military geniuses. The feat of marching an army seventeen thousand miles through Asia Minor, Egypt, and Persia to India and then bringing them back across the brutal wastes from the Indus to Babylon has never been matched.

Alexander was lucky. Although he was from Macedonia—the wild country directly north of Greece—he had one of the greatest Greek thinkers for teacher, Aristotle. Moreover, he was well trained for warfare and took over a superb army from one of the greatest of military organizers, his murdered father, Philip II.

It is always instructive to strike a balance on the achievements of a famous man. On the debit side for Alexander are a few items that show up on the ledger of many other generals of armies, chiefs of state, and captains of industry. He became a captive of his own success. He was conquered by the Persians he had defeated. In place of his remarkable personal self-denial, he adopted not only their oriental ease and splendor but their pernicious notion of deification of the person of the leader. Clearly, Alexander had extraordinary qualities of leadership just to hold his army together for a dozen years away from home in the face of great success and great hardships. Yet, although he assumed the role of a god on earth, his troops grew mutinous and refused to go farther East than the edge of India. The gallant, casual, magnanimous youth became distrustful, unapproachable, vindictive. For real and fancied treachery he had some of his leaders killed, and in a fit of rage he himself struck down Clitus, his closest friend. The master of a vast empire was no longer master of himself. Nor was he really master of the empire. His last days were spent in trying to unify and manage his vast disunited nations. For a man who since he was sixteen had known only the clash of swords and spears on armor, Alexander's last days, learning to govern amidst the clash of conflicting interests and personalities, must have been acutely annoying. In the short time before a fever cut him down at the age of thirty-two, he did not learn this difficult art. Alexander did not have time to organize and educate for orderly succession. So his empire quickly pulled apart, like a portable house when the key bolts are withdrawn.

What are Alexander's accomplishments? Some would say that all he did was to provide Caesars, Napoleons, Mussolinis, Hitlers, and Stalins with delusions of world conquest and lessons in mass slaughter. Three quiet accomplishments are notable. The ships he built and sent back from India left a valuable record for future commerce between the Mediterranean and the Orient. The uniform silver currency after the Greek model that Alexander introduced as he struggled to administer his empire brought lasting value in furthering East-West relations. Most important by far, the young warrior who campaigned with his copy of the *Iliad*, with Aristotle's corrections in it, always by him, the Macedonian who loved Greek culture, the restless wanderer who founded the ideal city of Alexandria in Egypt where Aristotle taught, the destroyer of cities who built scores of other cities also named Alexandria all the way to Samarkand and back—this battle-glorious youth merited the title of "Great" more through spreading the ideas, customs, and laws of the civilized Greeks than by his victories at Issus and Gaugamela over Darius III, king of kings, and his Persian hordes.

THE PARADOX OF HENRY TUDOR

Sometimes what the great build endures; sometimes it falls apart like a haycock in a hurricane. The desire to learn from the past has led to the scrutiny of the lives of all leaders who have any claim to greatness. Scholars spend years analyzing their personalities, their cultural environment, the events in which they figured, their acts, and the effect they have had on history. You will derive special value from becoming acquainted with a period by reading the biographies of a number of leaders of the time. Few periods in history respond to this approach more richly than Tudor England.

The greatest and most colorful of all the rulers of England are father and daughter—Henry VIII (1491–1547) and Elizabeth I (1533–1603). This simple fact is one of the ironies of history, for the great events that Henry Tudor set afoot began with the fear that Mary, his only heir by his first wife, Catherine of Aragon, would become the first queen of England. As a matter of fact, she did—for five years before her half-sister Elizabeth began her long and glorious rule. The lives of Henry VIII and Elizabeth I are full of ironies and paradoxes, but they also are astonishing exhibitions of the role of personality in state affairs. They are also case histories in the management of men.

Henry Tudor, who reigned from 1509 to 1547, was a bundle of contradictions. He was the son of the cautious negotiator, the first Tudor king, Henry VII. A lusty, sports-loving youth, he was pious, musical, quick of mind, and responsive to the fresh winds of Renaissance humanism. The young king who let Cardinal Wolsey govern his realm while he poured his tremendous vitality into hunting, games, and revelry became a violently egocentric ruler, who sought to turn the state into a mechanism to serve his wishes. The handsome lover of life grew fat, morose, and cruel. The young athlete who risked his neck in the jousts and boar hunts became quick to order the necks of others to the ax. This egotistic monster never had an army to enforce his wishes, and yet he had them granted, for he had a surer sense of the will of his people than any minister of the realm.

This burly, brutal man wrought great changes in the Western world. How some of them came about is edifying. It is true that he had no male heir of Catherine of Aragon, devout Catholic daughter of Columbus' patrons, Ferdinand and Isabella of Spain. Otherwise he might well have been satisfied to have Anne Boleyn as his mistress, as her sister had been. But England had never been ruled by a woman, and the people shared his desire for a prince to succeed him. So Henry asked the Pope for an annulment of his marriage to Catherine on the hypocritical pretext that the marriage had never been valid, since Catherine had been married earlier to Henry's dead brother, the boy prince Arthur.

The argument was belated, for Henry and Catherine had been married seven years. Pope Clement VII would doubtless have obliged had he not been just then under the thumb of Charles V of Germany and Spain, whose troops had sacked Rome in 1527. Catherine, who resolutely refused to be put aside, was Charles' aunt. Wolsey's failure to negotiate a satisfactory settlement brought about the fall of this proud cleric in 1530. The lust of Henry for the casual Anne Boleyn had turned into a question of male succession to the throne. Now this issue became submerged by the still larger one of the subjection of England to the will of Rome.

From this point on both Henry's ruthlessness and his political astuteness come into play. He sought within England to secure legal sanction for the annulment of his marriage. Because Catherine was respected and Anne was not, this would have been a hopeless quest had not other forces been at work. But ever since Wycliffe and Chaucer over a century before, there had been responsible criticism of abuses by monks and friars and others who held power and property apart from the local parish church. This criticism had taken a sharp new turn with the introduction of humanistic learning into England by Erasmus of Rotterdam, his close friend Sir Thomas More, and a number of other brilliant scholars, who, by making it possible for the layman to read the Bible in English and by their reforms in education, created a climate congenial to spiritual and intellectual independence of Rome.

Before Henry could have his way, however, much blood flowed. Many otherwise loyal subjects could not bring themselves to say that Henry's marriage to Catherine was invalid, and they died for their scruples. Chief among these was the learned, tolerant, and urbane chancellor, Sir Thomas More, the author of *Utopia,* who thoughtfully left a tip for his executioner. In the end Henry worked his will through Parliament. With its help in 1531 he secured from the clergy recognition of his authority as head of the Church of England. This large action was followed by the anticlimactic annulment of the marriage to Catherine and the marriage to Anne Boleyn in 1533. Anticlimactic, because Anne's only child was the girl Elizabeth. Henry's great passion chilled, and Anne was beheaded in 1536 on the charge of incest. She was followed by four more wives: Jane Seymour died bearing a boy who succeeded Henry at the age of nine as Edward VI and died at sixteen. The marriage with Anne of Cleves was annulled. Catherine Howard was convicted of immoral behavior and beheaded. Jane Parr outlived Henry.

Several aspects of this chronicle are worth noting further. They show how limited is the control even so mighty a man as Henry Tudor has over the outcome of the events he sets spinning. It is a truism of the history of science that great inventions lag until the scientific world is ready for them. Henry could not have set up a separate religious establishment had not the climate of religious opinion in England been just right. Henry did not embrace the Reformation of Luther, and thus he was able to secure the acquiescence of the bishops and other secular clergy. They thereby achieved new standing at the same time that the monasteries were confiscated and distributed among Henry's friends.

Henry's historic break with Rome resulted in the burning and beheading of both Papists and Protestants, but it avoided the religious wars that scourged the Continent. Then, too, in the process of getting support for what he wanted where he could get it, Henry allowed Parliament to sit for seven years. Thus it took a long step toward becoming the basic instrument of government of England, the master, not the servant, of the king, and the inspiration of free men everywhere.

ELIZABETH TUDOR, MANAGER OF MEN

The half-century following Henry Tudor's death was packed with drama, irony, and instructive lessons. On the death of his only son, the sick boy Edward VI, the lovely Lady Jane Grey was queen for nine days and then died under the ax with her conniving father-in-law Northumberland. Henry's first child, Mary, whom he had stigmatized as illegitimate, became Mary I. In a whiff of time she undid the passionate labor of her father's reign and made bootless his crimes and stratagems by placing England again under submission to Rome. She hardly deserved the grim title of "Bloody Mary," although in her reign beheading was still a nostrum for dissent. She had little reason to feel protective toward her half-sister, Elizabeth Tudor, sixteen years her junior. Elizabeth, like Mary made illegitimate at the divorce of her mother by Henry VIII, was still by act of Parliament in the line of succession. She was a clear threat to Mary, and when Wyatt's uprising in Elizabeth's behalf failed, but for Mary's clemency she would have left her head in the Tower of London, where her mother, Anne Boleyn, left hers.

Catholic Mary Tudor, lost in her devotions, stubbornly set her course farther away from English sentiment by marrying Philip of Spain and making England a Spanish pawn. But Fortune showed once more how outrageous she could be to the Tudor women. Pious Mary lacked the one means by which she might have given continuity to her Catholic rule—a child. She died in 1558, and Elizabeth Tudor, twenty-five and unwed, was her only heir.

The first act of Elizabeth's reign was her boldest. She disavowed Rome and re-established Henry's in-between Church of England, only now she had to let it move closer to Protestantism. Thereafter Elizabeth played a long canny game of keeping out of trouble. Patiently, adroitly, she gained time and kept peace with the great Catholic powers of Spain and France by pitting them against each other. Hampered by lack of funds, she brilliantly managed her greatest resources, the talents and devotion of statesmen like Walsingham, Burghley, Leicester, Gresham; adventurers like Raleigh, Drake, Grenville; and intellectuals like Bacon, Coke, and Hooker.

Two charming, unlucky persons shot star-bursts of melodrama across Elizabeth's sky. The first was the beautiful and intelligent Mary Stuart, Queen of Scots. Cousin of Elizabeth and heir apparent, Mary tried to impose Catholicism on Scotland when she succeeded to the throne there. The unpopularity of this course and her seeming complicity in the murder of her consort Darnley led to her overthrow and her fleeing to Elizabeth. But as long as Mary Stuart lived, plots to kill Elizabeth, place Mary on the throne, and reinstate Catholicism in England were an ever-present danger. Finally, the Star Chamber judged her guilty of being party to such a plot and Elizabeth reluctantly had her beheaded.

Then there was Robert Devereux, 2nd Earl of Essex. Charming, gallant, and impetuous, he became an influential favorite of Elizabeth, though forty years her junior. Essex had the poor judgment to think he could engage in what enterprises he liked in defiance of the Queen's wishes and still hold his place at court. When he pushed his luck as far as abortive armed rebellion, Elizabeth rather sadly took action. She never had her father's stomach for beheading friends and relatives.

The spacious reign of Elizabeth I cannot be squeezed into a paragraph or two. We can only round out the chronicle of the Tudors. We think of Elizabeth as we have seen her in the absurd portraits, a bony-skulled old woman propped up in a fantastic farthingale loaded with rich stuffs and jewels. We do not think of the young woman called on to govern a divided people with few assets besides her name, an excellent education, a wariness bred of a girlhood spent in the shadow of horror, and her tough

Tudor fiber. We think of the dangerous admirer of young men, the penny-pinching exhibitionist, the deceitful staller, the imperious Gloriana who brooked nothing short of absolute loyalty and obsequious adulation. We do not think of the lonely pain-wracked woman who every day for forty-five years faced without fear the threat of assassination, the routine burdens of office, the placating of powerful nobles, the cajoling of Parliament, and the making of momentous decisions.

The most remarkable achievement of Elizabeth Tudor's rule is that it lasted so long and was successful. At the beginning and toward the end of her tenure she was not popular; but she was the most respected, most powerful woman ruler who ever lived. She gave permanent form to the Church of England that Henry VIII had founded. She built up the Royal Navy that Henry had begun, and with the defeat of the Spanish Armada she inaugurated Britain's rule of the seas. She lent her support to the use of English as the official language of church and state. She ended the anarchical rule of the barons and brought unity of government through Parliament and the courts under the Crown. Though her harsh methods in Ireland yielded neither gain nor loyalty, she kept out of devastating land wars, encouraged manufacturing, trade, exploration and settlement in North America, and thus laid the groundwork for long prosperity. In the golden weather of the last dozen years of her reign, when Elizabeth's personal popularity was on the wane, the Tudor love of music and learning and letters burst into flower so that the term "Elizabethan" like a great seashell will forever echo the surging creativeness that crested in the songs and sonnets and plays of the man from Stratford, William Shakespeare, whose genius alone was mate to that of the Virgin Queen.

Elizabeth could not make her final exit without a last flourish of Tudor irony. For her entire reign she evaded the often pressed issues, first of marriage and then of naming an heir. At her death James VI of Scotland became James I of England and so united the two realms. His Tudor blood trickled down from Henry VII, but his father was the murdered Darnley and his mother was the unlucky Mary, Queen of Scots.

JAMES BOSWELL'S SAMUEL JOHNSON

The most famous of all biographies is Boswell's *Life of Dr. Johnson*. Samuel Johnson is an important eighteenth-century figure in the history of English letters and deserves a remarkable literary monument. Singlehanded he wrote the first English dictionary of any value. He was one of the most discerning of early English literary biographers and critics. And he did much to release the literary man from bondage to patrons; he helped make writing a respected profession. But in Boswell's pages Dr. Johnson lives, as no one else of the past ever has, as an extraordinary personality—for what he was, rather than for what he did.

The vividness with which Dr. Johnson has registered on the memory of generations of readers comes partly from Boswell's graphic record of his looks and habits. Who can forget the many candid-camera shots of the rolling, slovenly, scrofulous, one-eyed, head-shaking savant? Who can forget his endless cups of tea, his obsessive "singularities," his contrariness, his melancholia, his rudeness, his extraordinary kindness?

But the fame of Dr. Johnson rests on his talk. And this is almost the invention of James Boswell. Samuel Johnson was a great talker, but apparently like an old-fashioned pump he had to be primed. Boswell has been amply praised for recording Johnson's talk so diligently. He also deserves credit for deciding to record it in the first place, and much more for the skill he had in framing the questions that aroused Dr. Johnson to hold forth. You will never have a better demonstration of how the right questions contribute to good conversation.

"I was desirous to examine the question closely," says Boswell in one revealing passage. He does not write a life of Johnson in the ordinary sense, but rather an anecdotal record of the conversations that he heard during the 270 days that they were actually together during the twenty-one years of their acquaintance. The fascination of these conversations lies in their structure: Dr. Johnson, Boswell, and their distinguished friends are forever examining propositions. Their idea of entertainment is to use their minds in an endless game of true-or-false. The propositions they examine range from a good many trivial matters such as whether wine improves the mind to why respect for authority had diminished in their time. They sought diligently for causes, often with an insight we should think could come only from modern scholarship. For instance, Dr. Johnson thought one of the chief reasons for the decline in respect for authority was the wider distribution of money. "The shoe-black at the entry to my court does not depend on me," he said. Before economics and sociology were invented, Dr. Johnson put his finger on economic dependence as a prime buttress of the authority of heads of families, employers, and suppliers of goods.

Dr. Johnson was at his best in the arena of moral judgments. One of the most illuminating conversations took place in 1773, when Dr. Johnson was sixty-four. The subject was toleration. Though sharply harried by others in the group, Dr. Johnson expounded a conservative position in regard to the rights of an individual to hold doctrines and the duties of the "magistrate" in return. He summed it up: "If a man thinks erroneously, he may keep his thoughts to himself, and nobody will trouble him; if he preaches erroneous doctrine, society may expel him; if he acts in consequence of it, the law takes place, and he is hanged." One of those present gasped, "Sir, you have untwisted this difficult subject with great dexterity!" Boswell often slyly leaves it an open question as to how close to inspired truth his hero's pronouncements really are. You may on occasion have the impression that Dr. Johnson's opponents, especially Boswell himself, have the better of their debates. In the end, however, you come to respect this incongruous pair, the gross marred man of letters and the popinjay son of a Scottish lord, who had nothing in common but mutual affection and delight in the play of the mind. Their constant effort was to challenge, to analyze, to differentiate, to make up their minds where they did stand, and to express their thoughts with vigor and color. They are an enduring indictment of dullness.

THE STRACHEY MANNER

It is hardly an exaggeration to say that contemporary biography in English takes its pervasive tone from the writings of Lytton Strachey. There are still many studies, such as Freeman's lives of Washington and Lee that are in the best nineteenth-century tradition of Lockhart's *Scott* and Forster's *Dickens*. But Strachey, a Cambridge don, deliberately set out to improve on "Those two fat volumes, with which it is our custom to commemorate the dead," and which, he said, are so funereal in tone that they might be written by undertakers. He sought to correct "their ill-digested masses of material, their slipshod style, their tone of tedious panegyric, their lamentable lack of selection, of detachment, of design." So he introduced to English and American biography the "becoming brevity," dispassionateness, and wit that he admired in French practitioners. Hack writers hastened to pervert his intent by cobbling up rewrites of standard lives in order to debunk the subjects. But this cheap game has played out. The best biographies of today try to unite scholarly accuracy with Strachey's freshness of appraisal and burnished style. You will find examples in the often sparkling short lives in the *Dictionary of American Biography*.

Eminent Victorians (1918) emancipated English and American biography from stuffiness and flattery. Reading it for the first time now, you may be puzzled at its reputation. It is a short book of 350 pages dealing with four persons of modest fame—Cardinal Manning, Florence Nightingale, Dr. Thomas Arnold, and General Gordon. They had been eminent during Victoria's reign and had been fitted with solemn biographies. The novelty lay in doing them over in the manner Strachey described in his brief manifesto prefacing the book. In so doing, Strachey brought under scrutiny important episodes in the religious, medical, educational, and military history of England.

The seventy-two page study of Florence Nightingale illustrates Stracheys method. The mark of that method is selection of revealing detail. As he says, he rows out on the ocean of history, lowers a little bucket into the depths, and examines with careful curiosity the specimens he hauls up. So in introducing Florence Nightingale, Strachey wonders "Why, as a child in the nursery, when her sister had shown a healthy pleasure in tearing her dolls to pieces, had *she* shown an almost morbid one in sewing them up again?" Florence Nightingale, born into wealth and the inner

circle of English society, is known as the saintly founder of
modern nursing, the "Lady of the Lamp," who in the Crimean
War devotedly served the wounded and dying in hospitals at
Scutari and Balaklava. While this is true, it is only part of the
truth, and partial truth taking root as myth is dangerous. Strachey's strategy is to correct the astigmatism of hero worship.
Even her mother had a false image of Florence. She said, "We
are ducks who have hatched a wild swan." "But," says Strachey,
"the poor lady was wrong. . . . It was an eagle."

At the age of twenty-five Florence Nightingale finally prevailed on her parents to let her be a nurse. "A 'nurse' meant
then a coarse old woman, always ignorant, usually dirty, often
brutal, a Mrs. Gamp, in bunched-up sordid garments, tippling
at the brandy-bottle or indulging in worse irregularities," says
Strachey in the no-grey manner of the enormously popular nineteenth-century writer, Thomas Babington Macauley. Florence
Nightingale changed all that. Today nursing, the training of
nurses, and hospital administration rank higher than most other
women's careers in professional standards and *esprit de corps*.

At the age of thirty-four Florence Nightingale moved in on
her destiny. Britain was at war with Russia in the Crimean Penin-
sula. Her close friend Sidney Herbert, a member of the same
powerful family as Queen Elizabeth's Sir Philip Sidney, was a
cabinet member and head of the War Office. Backed by Herbert
and adequate private funds, Miss Nightingale and thirty-eight
nurses reached the military hospital at Scutari in November
1854, between the bloody battles of Balaklava and Inkerman.
The four miles of beds in the huge barracks held the sick,
wounded, and dying in the midst of unutterable misery, dirt,
stench, and neglect. Lacking soap, clothing, and the simplest
utensils, let alone drugs and equipment, the hospital was tragi-
cally inadequate. "The Bird," as the military sarcastically dubbed
her, at once sailed in to do battle with the incredible bureau-
cratic inefficiency. She pleaded, wheedled, browbeat, and out-
maneuvered the fuddy-duddies who, swaddled in red tape, had
long since lost their will to act. In time she brought order, cleanliness, adequate care, and better cheer to the soldiers—and even

persuaded them to send money home. When finally she returned to England, her reward was fame, honor by the Queen, and the idolatry of the public.

She was also ill and for years was supposed to be not far from death. Yet her real life had just begun. Although spending many years as an invalid, almost a recluse, she pressed for reform, first of military hospitals and all other aspects of army medicine and then of the War Office itself. She fought the bureaucrats, Colonel Blimps, and obstructionists with manic fury. Relentlessly she used and bullied the volunteers who served her causes without pay year after year. Strachey thinks that she harried the gentle devoted Sidney Herbert and her chore-boy, the poet Arthur Clough, into untimely graves. Her effort to clean up the red-tape jungle of the War Office failed, but her hospital reforms triumphed. Her 800-page *Notes on Hospitals* is the cornerstone of modern hospital construction and management.

Florence Nightingale was an amazing woman. Whether she, Manning, Arnold, and Gordon were extraordinary in precisely the ways they are said to be in *Eminent Victorians* is questionable. Scholars have charged that Strachey's bucket-dipping often misrepresents the facts, quite as much as popular myth does. But his effort to lift biographical writing out of the pit of pedantry to the level of art has had a salutary effect on all his followers. And modern biography, borrowing heavily from the advances in psychology, has become an indispensable adjunct to our understanding of our fellow human beings, particularly those who have been masters of their careers. This explains why biography rivals the novel as modern man's favorite reading.

PERSONAL TESTIMONY

How often have you wished that you might talk face to face with a famous man, be able to ask him frank questions, and get candid replies? A large number of fascinating, if not always famous, men and women have given their personal testimony about their journey through life and what they have learned on the way. You will find this testimony in autobiographies, diaries, letters, and essays. These statements vary in form and in accent, but for your purpose they bear a common stamp—the author is keenly interested in his own development, and he gives you a close-up of matters that biographers can only guess about, if they are aware of their significance at all. That these records are often as warped as a phonograph record left on top of a radiator may make the testimony questionable but yet not unenlightening.

Access to pen, ink, and paper, or to a ghost writer, has tempted saints, singers, and grandmothers to write autobiographies, and few, it would seem, have resisted. Among the autobiographies that endure are records of the pure and the evil, the wise and the foolish, but if they endure, they all have something to tell you. They vary from the spiritual histories of St. Augustine and Cardinal Newman to the raffish records of that observant pair, Benevenuto Cellini and Giacomo Casanova. They are explicit in telling what the authors did to prepare for their careers, as in the accounts of Benjamin Franklin and John Stuart Mill. And sometimes they are delightful, as is W. H. Hudson's *Far Away and Long Ago*. In addition, many of the best novels are auto-biographical—Samuel Butler's *Way of All Flesh*, Thomas Mann's *Buddenbrooks*, James Joyce's *Portrait of the Artist as a Young Man*, Somerset Maugham's *Of Human Bondage*, and Marcel Proust's *Swann's Way*, for instance.

THE FAILURE OF HENRY ADAMS

An autobiography that has special pertinency for you is *The Education of Henry Adams*. Henry Adams (1838–1918) was the great-grandson of President John Adams, the grandson of President John Quincy Adams, and the son of the able Civil War Minister to Britain. He himself never was called to public office, the cause no doubt of his tiresome refrain of "failure." Instead, he was a scholar-author, a professor, an editor, and a traveler. Besides his self-history, he wrote a *Life of Gallatin*, two novels, a nine-volume history of the Jefferson and Madison administrations, critical essays, and the fascinating introduction to the Middle Ages, *Mont-Saint-Michel and Chartres*. But his most successful literary creation is himself in *The Education of Henry Adams*. Seventy years are covered in the *Education*—years that spanned three wars, the advance of modern science, the rise of industrial nations, and the shift of power to the hands of the entrepreneur in business and politics.

Adams' bachelor life was outwardly uneventful. As he said in his third-person mannerism, "He never got to the point of playing the game at all; he lost himself in the study of it, watching the errors of the players." Apart from a stint as secretary to his father in London and seven years as a professor of medieval history at Harvard College (for four dollars a day) combined with the editorship of the *North American Review*, Adams had no regular employment. He confessed he ached to serve his country. Yet few historical periods have been observed by a better prepared or more perceptive critic. Imbued with the new scientific spirit, Adams tried patiently to reduce history to some sort of system. But he is remembered for his lifelong effort to educate himself, in the sense of learning from experience and finding a satisfactory pattern for his existence.

Adams' sardonic summing up of his experience as undergraduate and teacher at Harvard College has a core of meaning that may be suggestive to you. "The four years passed at college were, for his purposes, wasted," he says flatly. All of it, he maintains, "could have been easily put into the work of any four months in after life." Among the specific indictments, interestingly, are his failure to learn "to read mathematics, like any other universal language" or to hear the name of Karl Marx. Still, a course of lectures by Louis Agassiz on the glacial period and paleontology "had more influence on his curiosity than the rest of the college instruction altogether." He enjoyed the not slight privilege of a personal tutorial with James Russell Lowell. He discovered a bent for writing, and by reading papers in literary societies and acting in the Hasty Pudding Club, he achieved ease in speaking in public. Indeed, he was elected by his classmates Orator of the Class of 1858 and "in a heat that might have melted bronze" gave an address that a relative remarked was "singularly wanting in enthusiasm." Adams was not sure that this quality was a defect or a merit—"in either case, it was all that Harvard taught."

Adams labels the chapter on his seven years as professor and editor "Failure." President Eliot thought otherwise. Without a teacher's certificate, without even a Ph.D., Adams believed that the only excuse for a teacher is to help students to learn. The twelfth-century lecture system—"to teach the boys a few elementary facts and relations"—that Adams condemned is still what passes for teaching in most university classes. If the professor interrupts his monologues by an occasional question, he calls it discussion. Adams told his students that they could get their facts where they liked, and use him only to ask questions. "The only privilege a student had that was worth his claiming, was that of talking to the professor, and the professor was bound to encourage it." He acted on the rule that a teacher should join his students in trying to find the best way to learn his subject.

While Adams said he failed, he also said: "The students read what they pleased and compared their results. . . . The boys worked like rabbits, and dug holes all over the field of archaic society; no difficulty stopped them; unknown languages yielded before their attack. . . . They learned, after a fashion, to chase an idea like a hare through as dense a thicket of obscure facts as they were likely to meet." You can do much worse than to learn to chase ideas through your own reading and experience in the self-reliant way that Henry Adams' students did, and as he did himself. And you can draw many worthwhile suggestions for evaluating your own education from *The Education of Henry Adams*.

MICHEL EYQUEM DE MONTAIGNE, FIRST OF ESSAYISTS

Essays are autobiography in disguise. It is not much in fashion any more either to write or to read personal essays. Yet in few other places will you find such fresh and palatable advice about your development. You cannot possibly find better tutors than Montaigne, Bacon, Lamb, Hazlitt, Emerson, and Thoreau. A personal essay is brief, it is conversational in tone, and it is concerned with the author's judgments about matters that deeply affect you. The freshness of the six essayists mentioned comes to a considerable extent from their habitual championing of the opposite of the conventional position about many subjects.

The admired master of these independent spirits—and your

lifetime friend, I hope—is the French nobleman, Michel Eyquem de Montaigne (1533–1592). His dates make him a contemporary of Queen Elizabeth I. His *Essays* are really an intellectual auto-biography. He withdrew from the hubbub of a life of action in strife-torn France in order to analyze and record his reactions to existence in personal terms. To do so, he invented the essay form—the word modestly suggests a trial, an effort to express a thought. Sometimes you may think society is on trial. Montaigne is stubbornly insistent on judging matters without romantic hanky-panky, with the blend of objectivity and tolerance that we associate with the most enlightened modern point of view. He ranged over all experience, from the ignoble trivia of daily life to the largest issues of human destiny, and he used all the writings of the past as foils for his own thoughts, as a billiard player banks his cue ball off all the cushions of a billiard table.

In spite of the urbanity that suffuses Montaigne's essays, his ideas often have the force of a woodman's ax. "The cannibals and savage people do not so much offend me with roasting and eating of dead bodies, as those which torment and persecute the living." "Our follies do not make me laugh, but our wisdoms do." "Crosses and afflictions make me do nothing but curse them. . . . The course of my reason is the nimbler in prosperity." "I am so besotted unto liberty that should any man forbid me the access into any one corner of the Indies, I should in some sort live much discontented."

Of late we have had much writing about semantics and the ways in which our use of language conditions our behavior. Consider how clearly Montaigne states one of the main lessons of the semanticists, the tyranny of absolutism in language:

Many abuses are engendered into the world, or to speak more boldly, all the abuses of the world are engendered upon this—that we are taught to fear to make profession of ignorance and are bound to accept and allow all that we cannot refute. We speak of all things by precepts and resolution. The Stile of Rome did bear that even the same that witness deposed, because he had seen it with his own eyes, and that which a judge ordained of his most assured knowledge, was conceived in this form of speech: *It seemeth so unto me.* I am drawn to hate likely things, when men go about to set them down as in-fallible. I love these words or phrases, which mollify and moderate temerity of our propositions: *It may be; peradventure; in some sort; some; it is said; I think;* and such like. And had I been to instruct children, I would so often have put this manner of answering in their mouth, enquiring and not resolving: *What means it? I understand it not; It may well be; Is it true?* that they should rather have kept the form of learners until three score years of age than present themselves doctors at ten. Yea but there is some kind of ignorance strong and generous that for honor and courage is nothing beholding to knowl-edge—and ignorance, which to conceive rightly, there is required no less learning than to conceive true learning.

THE CONCORD SPRING

Once when I was an editor in a publishing house, I received the manuscript of a book on Ralph Waldo Emerson from a dis-tinguished Indian scholar, Madhava Rama, the Chidambaram Swami of Francis Yeats-Brown's *Lives of a Bengal Lancer.* In the accompanying letter he said, "For fifty years I have drunk daily from the pure spring of Concord." The circle was joined. A century earlier Emerson, Thoreau, and other "Transcendentalists" in the village of Concord, Massachusetts, were drawing inspira-tion from the Bhagavad-Gita and other Eastern philosophic works. The dissolution of the British rule in India had its seed in Concord. Thoreau's essay "Civil Disobedience" was a source of Gandhi's doctrine of passive resistance that led Britain peace-ably to turn over the government to the leaders it had trained.

The journals of the Concord friends, Ralph Waldo Emerson and Henry Thoreau, are high on my list of indispensable writings, the ones I would take with me to Antarctica, Devil's Island, or Cleveland over a weekend. Their ideas are as fresh as new-turned earth, and their style as aromatic as a bruised walnut hull. Con-sider some of Emerson's pithy sentences: "I like a man who likes to see a barn as well as a good tragedy." "Excite the soul, and the weather and the town and your condition in the world all disappear." "Culture is one thing and varnish another." "All the thoughts of a turtle are turtle." Whatever justification you may need for the effort you are making to cultivate your mind, you will find in Emerson's entry in his *Journal* for April 13, 1834, when he was thirty: "We are always getting ready to live, but never living. We have many years of technical education; then many years of earning a livelihood, and we get sick, and take journeys for our health, and compass land and sea for improvement by travelling, but the work of self-improvement—always under our nose—nearer than the nearest, is seldom engaged in. A few, few hours in the longest life."

Each of Emerson's essays is a great oak, a monumental natural growth filled with many sculptured bits like acorns. *The American Scholar, Self-Reliance, The Over-Soul, Experience,* and many another essay in his several volumes blend idealism and common sense in a manner as Yankee as a Massachusetts meetinghouse. Today, as individuality flattens beneath mass pressures, you are likely to find *Self-Reliance* offers you a credo for the preservation of your integrity.

Society everywhere is in conspiracy against the manhood of every one of its members. Society is a joint-stock company, in which the members agree, for the better securing of his bread to each shareholder, to surrender the liberty and culture of the eater. The virtue in most request is conformity. Self-reliance is its aversion. It loves not realities and creators, but names and customs. Whoso would be a man, must be a nonconformist.

You will not find a better answer to this problem than Emerson's own eloquent one in the same essay:

What I must do is all that concerns me, not what the people think. This rule, equally arduous in actual and in intellectual life, may serve for the whole distinction between greatness and meanness. It is the harder, because you will always find those who think they know what is your duty better than you know it. It is easy in the world to live after the world's opinion; it is easy in solitude to live after our own; but the great man is he who in the midst of the crowd keeps with perfect sweetness the independence of solitude.

Henry Thoreau, like his friend Emerson, also believed in the "unquestionable ability of man to elevate his life by a conscious endeavor." In this faith you might set your target beside his: "To affect the quality of the day, that is the highest of arts." How you might change the quality of your days, Thoreau spells out with eloquence and tart Yankee humor. By worldly standards and those of his Concord neighbors, Thoreau was close to shiftless. Even Emerson said that instead of being the chief of American engineers, Thoreau was but a "captain of a huckleberry party." He made almost no effort to better himself. Or so it seemed to the neighbors who equated accumulation of material things with betterment, as we do today. But Thoreau worked much harder at self-betterment than the most industrious Yankee farmer in his stony fields. From 1845 to 1847 he lived in a hut on the edge of Walden Pond, a mile and a half from Concord village. In a memorable sentence he explained: "I went to the woods because I wished to live deliberately, to front only the essential facts of life, and see what it had to teach, and not, when I came to die, discover that I had not lived." Henry Thoreau's method for "fronting life" was to simplify it in order to have time, for "Time," he said, "is but the stream I go a-fishing in."

Thoreau is a prime example of how foolish it is to imagine that among the millwrights of history the man of ideas is any less potent than the man of deeds. Would the foolhardy deeds of John Brown at Harper's Ferry have roused the conscience of the North had not his death been framed in song? Or if on October 3, 1859, while Brown was in jail, Henry Thoreau had not called together the citizens of Concord and addressed them with his blazing *"Plea for Captain Brown"*?

On one occasion the idle villager united deeds and word to help make the name of Concord revered around the world. The deed was small. Thoreau refused to pay his Massachusetts poll tax and spent a night in jail in consequence. The result was his essay *Civil Disobedience*, printed in 1849. It ranks with Milton's *Areopagitica* as a major statement in behalf of individual liberty. The refusal to pay the tax was a symbolic gesture, a protest a dozen years before the Civil War against the North for its tolerance of slavery and the iniquitous Mexican War. As mentioned, it helped mold the pattern of passive resistance adopted by Gandhi. More far-reaching, *Civil Disobedience* is a defiant assertion of the moral obligation of the individual to oppose by deed what he considers wrong. Thoreau says: "If one honest man in this State of Massachusetts, ceasing to hold slaves, were actually to withdraw from this copartnership and be locked up in the county jail therefor, it would be the abolition of slavery in America. For it matters not how small the beginning may seem to be: What is once well done is done forever."

Not the downtrodden alone but irresolute men of good will in many lands have had their destiny pointed out to them by this captain of a berry patch.

He can combat injustice who has experienced a little in his own person. Cast your whole vote, not a strip of paper merely, but your whole influence. A minority is powerless while it conforms to the majority; it is not even a minority then; but it is irresistible when it clogs by its whole weight. If the alternative is to keep all just men in prison, or give up war and slavery, the State will not hesitate which to choose. If a thousand men were not to pay their tax-bills this year, that would not be a violent and bloody measure, as it would be to pay them, and enable the State to commit violence and shed innocent blood. This is, in fact, the definition of a peaceable revolution.

What have these two citizens of Concord to say to you and me? More than anything else they believe passionately in the independence and integrity of the individual and in his responsibility to follow the voice of his conscience. They also remind us of the mysterious undercurrents of existence that cannot be apprehended except by drawing on that power we call insight. At a time when we are all trying to do the sensible thing, which almost always coincides with what some group thinks we ought to do, we need to drink at the Concord spring, even though we swallow a little heresy.

PRIVATE EYES—THE DIARISTS

"It's an odd idea for someone like me to keep a diary. . . . Still, what does that matter? I want to write, but more than that, I want to bring out all kinds of things that lie buried deep in my heart." So the thirteen-year-old Anne Frank, hiding in a neighbor's house in Amsterdam, began her timeless account of adolescence and first love, three years before she died in the Nazi gas chambers of Bergen-Belsen. Her reason serves to explain the incomparable insights offered by diaries—the uncovering of all kinds of things that lie buried in the privacy of the heart.

Candor makes the diary the most intimate of art forms. The fact that diaries are often written clandestinely at the end of the day in the privacy of a bedroom may be part explanation of this candor. Mainly, however, the diarist is indulging in a midnight soliloquy, is indeed conversing with himself. Of course, many diaries either only pretend to be private or openly have an audience in mind, as do those kept by public figures as historical records. Yet the nakedness of the form, its immediacy of reaction to event, its hurried composition and the uncertainty of future publication many times lure the writers of open and semi-open journals into much more frankness than they intend.

We need not linger over the pages that reveal the writers in their indiscretions. Yet if Samuel Pepys and James Boswell, for instance, had concealed their peccadilloes, we should have lost two of the best lessons in self-honesty. Both were vain men and strove to cut a figure in the London they loved, but neither tried to stand taller before his mirror than he really was. We pay psychiatrists princely fees to help us see ourselves as we really are. In Pepy's *Diary* and Boswell's *London Journal* we have remarkable examples of self-portraiture without hypocrisy.

LETTERS

All too often, collections of letters are boring because they deal with the transient and the trivial. Such letters are monuments to vanity. Like rosebushes, the letters of the famous, the infamous, and the obscure benefit from pruning. Therefore, some of the writers of the world's most memorable letters are represented by a single letter.

With these reservations, it remains true that letters embody some of man's noblest, most moving, and most charming utterances. Love letters are perhaps the least inspired of all forms of composition. But even among them there are gems. The actress

Sarah Bernhardt, telling her absent lover, the playwright Sardou, how desolate Paris is without him, writes: "It is like the face of a clock, bereft of its hands." The swift artless candid movie of seventeenth-century French society by Mme. de Sévigné has with justice been thought the most charming letter-writing of all. You will also find the letters of John Keats masterpieces of playfulness and poetic imagery together with surprisingly sound criticism of life and literature. Another English author, D. H. Lawrence, put some of his sharpest descriptive writing in his letters.

Letters have been the carriers of some of the finest of human sentiments. Herbert Spencer, an invalid at forty, discouraged by adverse criticism and lack of support, announced that he was being forced to give up his life work, a series of books that would apply the new theory of Darwinian evolution to social and political history. John Stuart Mill sent Spencer an offer to guarantee publication of his next work, not as a personal favor, but as "a simple proposal of cooperation for an important public purpose, for which you give your labour and have given your health." Mill's support led to American aid also and the prolonging of Spencer's career for many years. The splendid generosity of Mill's letter lay in the fact that he and Spencer held differing philosophies. By assuring the continued publication of Spencer's works, Mill brought on the eclipse of his own.

The most famous letter by an American is President Lincoln's to "Mrs. Bixby, Boston, Mass." The letter begins with simplicity— "I have been shown in the files of the War Department a statement of the Adjutant General of Massachusetts that you are the mother of five sons who have died gloriously on the field of battle." It closes with high eloquence—"I pray that our Heavenly Father may assuage the anguish of your bereavement, and leave you only the cherished memory of the loved and lost, and the solemn pride that must be yours to have laid so costly a sacrifice upon the altar of freedom." Lincoln was misinformed: Two of the Bixby boys died in battle, one was captured, and two deserted. Yet his four-sentence letter is a masterpiece of English prose and an enduring statement of human compassion for all mothers of sons who have died in battle.

A number of letters are still molten with anger over injustices that should never be forgotten. The best known is Dr. Samuel Johnson's letter to Lord Chesterfield. Poor and ill, Johnson had labored for seven years on his *Dictionary of the English Language* without receiving the financial aid that he had sought from Chesterfield. When at the end of the task Chesterfield praised the work publicly, Johnson wrote in polite fury recalling the indignities he had suffered. He asked bitterly, "Is not a patron, my Lord, one who looks with unconcern on a man struggling in the water, and, when he has reached ground, encumbers him with help?" and he declared his unwillingness "that the Publick should consider me as owing that to a Patron which Providence has enabled me to do for myself." The Earl, otherwise remembered for his own polished letters of worldly counsel to his natural son and to his godson, blandly expressed his admiration for Johnson's style.

5

THE SANITY OF THE ARTS

Fiction, drama, poetry, painting, and music have so much in common that, to avoid repetition, we need first to consider them as an entity, as the arts.

You live in about the only society in which the arts are not an important part of everyone's life. Singing, dancing, playing musical instruments, telling tales, and making things of beauty have been natural activities among all peoples since the most ancient times. Indeed, the magnificent colored drawings of animals on the walls of the Lascaux Caves of Dordogne (c. 50,000 B.C.), the ancient stories embedded like fossils in the *Odyssey* and all other early epics, the lovingly decorated weapons and utensils in prehistoric excavations, all tell the same profound truth: Man felt a need to dance and sing songs, paint pictures, mold images, and tell stories and became wonderfully adept at these art forms long before he bothered to master the useful crafts that we, like Robinson Crusoe, would give absolute priority. Children, who in some ways recapitulate man's history, never put the practical first, either. What is especially significant about primitive man's use of art forms is that they invariably make up a symbolic language through which he speaks his most serious interpretations of the mysterious world about him.

Art is fundamental in all human experience. In a literal sense art is everything that is not nature, everything that man does to his environment. We differentiate between the brushes, paint,

and canvas an artist works with and the painting that he produces. Yet the craftsmanship that turns out a fine sable brush,
the chemical research that leads to paint that will last, the
weaving of the grade of canvas used for portraits—these are arts,
and the quality of the activity involved may be superior to that
of the painting. We talk about the fine arts, and in this book we
are examining what are generally agreed to be great works of
art. But those things and events that make up your daily round—
clothes, food, house, work, love, friendship, recreation—have
their creative aspects. They can take on something of the orderliness and comeliness that captivate us in, let us say, Chinese
ceramics, paintings, poetry, and philosophy. This is perhaps the
basic contribution of any art—this imposing of order and grace
on the raw materials of experience. In addition, prolonged exposure to works by great creative spirits arouses a preference for
the ingenious and pleasing way of doing things, a pervasive
creative attitude toward life.

Finally, of course, art has meaning. It is a commentary on
human existence. Directly or indirectly, consciously or unconsciously, all works of art have something to tell us about life.
How can we possibly get a better inside view of French society
of fifty years ago than through the novels of Marcel Proust? How
better can we grasp the poignancy of various psychological states
than through the revelations of his characters? The problems
from which plays, novels, and even poems draw their energy are
human problems and have clear applicability beyond yourself.
But whatever meaning a symphony, a ballet, or an etching may
have for you is an entirely internal affair; yet the influence on
you may be profound. Owning a water color by John Marin may
be the beginning of liberation from mean material preoccupations by raising questions about their relative importance in your
scale of values. Listening to a season of symphony concerts may
beget a wholly new realization of the essential dignity, nobility,
and defenselessness of man, a feeling that may elevate your day
to day relations with your fellows. Though the influence of the
great teachers of the liberal arts cannot be measured and proved
any more than that of teachers in schools and colleges, it can be
a powerful force to contribute to your creative growth.

ART AS PLAY

Art starts as play. At the age of two years a child arranges blocks in a pattern, hums or improvises free verse to a melody of sorts, sways rhythmically to music or to his own sing-song. In the next two or three pre-school years, before matter-of-factness sets in, a child may make up stories, paint pictures, sing, and dance—all without inhibition and often with surprising ability.

To a degree little appreciated by the layman, the adult artist is also playing. In this sense the word has the expanded meaning of *not work*. Without audience, without pay, still the singer sings, the dancer dances, the playwright writes plays. But even in a simpler sense an artist is often playful. For instance, in his reminiscent "A Child's Christmas in Wales" Dylan Thomas turns a boy's lower-middle class Christmas Day in a dreary Welsh seaside town into a fantasy of marvels and poetic foolery. Among other mock-heroic events, he remembers two bundled-up citizens puffing on their pipes as they walk silently down to the water's edge—and perhaps on into the sea, their pipe smoke still streaming after them.

You can almost hear the great Johann Sebastian Bach laughing as he playfully develops a jig or other theme he has picked up from peasant sources. Papa Haydn even wrote musical jokes, as in the *Surprise Symphony*. The thirteenth-century creators of the gargoyles on Chartres Cathedral must have had fun with their impious monsters. Playfulness is the characteristic that unites a number of modern painters as different as Ensor, Chagall, Dufy, Klee, Miro, Picasso, Tanguy, and Dali. Marc Chagall is perhaps the clearest example you will find of pure playfulness combined with seriousness of artistic purpose in the graphic arts.

MYTH AND SYMBOL

Myth begins at the earliest stages of man's climb, when he is inferior to the animals, which are the embodiment—and thus in his art, the symbol—of the invisible powers that rule the universe. (We townfolk have no trouble understanding this point of view on those rare occasions when we spend a night in a forest.) Against the rage of winter, hunger, disease, and death only fertility seems potent. Therefore genitalia, the sun, and grain are among the earliest symbols everywhere. To play it safe, primitive man made symbols of the evil forces that bullied him and fetishes to appease them.

Ignazio Silone, the Italian novelist, in *Bread and Wine* sheds light on the way symbolism works. Four boys are playing a card game in which the king of diamonds is high card. Theirs is so worn that it is easily identified. One boy proposes substituting a low card. Another objects: The king of diamonds is always the king of diamonds, just as the Pope is always the Pope. A priest brings him to see that the card is only a piece of paper, that it has different values in other card games, and that it has no intrinsic value, only the value assigned it by the persons playing the game. So with real kings. Ultimately all art is symbolic, a system for reference to those intangible and ineffable realities that have the deepest meaning for us.

THE SENSE OF FORM

Art of any kind has form. Art gives order to experience. Order is an escape from chaos and tension. Experience is formless, except in bits and by accident. The events of the day rarely have any of the dramatic sequence of a short story or play. The objects in a landscape rarely arrange themselves as neatly as the artist arranges them in a painting. True, the studious eye or the microscope reveals nature as amazingly, often mathematically, structured. True, too, the sense of form that has actuated the artist since a cave was his studio has nature as its ultimate inspiration. But once experience becomes a song, a statue, or other kind of art, it is a new reality. Serious experiences can seem funny, and unpleasant ones can seem pleasant. For instance, children chant "Three blind mice" with happy voices, with never a shudder at the sadistic business that follows. The fairy tales of the Brothers Grimm are grim indeed when you take them out of their tinsel wrappings.

Form does not mean absolute regularity of structure, of course. Neither the shape nor the rhythm of breakers crashing on a beach repeats itself exactly. No two apple trees are ever the same; yet every apple tree is a beautiful instance of irregular symmetry. Complete symmetry tends to be as boring as a child beating on a drum. So the artist, sculptor, or architect rarely makes two sides of anything the same. Nature seldom does either, as you may see by looking in the mirror or at a leaf.

A sense of form is one of the basic driving forces that direct every artistic act, from the "And then the Little Bear cried . . ." of a nursery tale to the subtle gestures of a Balinese dancer's hands. Rhythm, pattern, design, balance, contrast—these are all aspects of form. Whether he is writing a symphony note by note, building a cathedral stone by stone, or writing a play word by word, the artist works within a simple plan of major divisions, such as three movements of a symphony or three acts of a play. Yet he has at all times an overriding sense of the relation of each isolated detail to the organic whole. This requires a sharp realization of what sections ahead will be like before they exist except as a buzzing in the artist's head or as sketchy notes.

In the time arts—music, dance, and literature—there is always a sense of progression, of bringing new forces into play, of moving toward a conclusion. This involves problems of length of passages, of tempo, and of tone. As the novel nears its end, description and exposition drop out, and the narrative moves faster. How the novelist handles a scene, therefore, varies with the point in the story. Thus, to experience a piece of literature, a musical composition, or a dance, you have to become aware of the parts within it that the creator strove to bring into harmonious relationship.

In the space arts—sculpture, painting and the other graphic arts, architecture, and decoration—the problems of relationships are more clearly apparent. If you look, you can fit most traditional paintings and prints within a basic compositional design of a triangle or a circle. At all times the artist keeps alert as to how the direction of a line or the intensity of a color or lighted area is related to the center of interest, which in hundreds of religious paintings, for instance, is the face of Christ.

I prize a water color of a sailboat by a young artist. He had spent the summer at the seashore and knew well what sailboats look like. Yet what did he paint? With brushes loaded with color, he boldly whacked in a gigantic triangle, a dainty hull, and one band of blue for the sea and another for the sky. Most fascinating, the sail is roughly divided into three areas of pink, green, and yellow. The young man had never seen a colored sail, let alone one so exotically patched. He had abstracted from his memories the essential form of the most interesting object—the sail—although the only shape he had seen was a gaff-rigged trapezoid. To assert the gaiety of all those sails gliding through his memory, the artist simplified and subordinated everything else to his sail and then intensified its interest by those three bright fields of color. Thus the artist takes his observations and memories of shapes and colors and forces them into formal arrangements that exist only in his imagination. This is the way every artist shapes his material in any medium. The artist in this instance, by the way, was three years old.

Form is present in the most extreme avant-garde poetry, music, sculpture, or painting. In the dripped-on paintings of Jackson Pollock, for example, you will see a canny distribution of the colors that create an over-all pattern. In the slashing brush strokes of the more violent contemporaries, the hand is obeying some inner control. For one thing it keeps the design from seeming like any previous type of painting, yet immediately identifiable as of the contemporary school. For another, the apparently formless design is inevitably painted with clear awareness of the size and shape of the space around it. It is never formless in the sense that a child's first crayon scrawls are. So with music and the other arts. The reason that they often strike us as formless is that they do not abide by a system that we are used to. In their time Keats, Cézanne, and any number of creative geniuses were derided by eminent critics for the same reason.

THE INEVITABILITY OF INNOVATION

Since World War II a revolution has occurred in industry. Before then a company went along for years with little change in its products. A family used the same sort of soap and breakfast food through generations. Today industry cannot hold its markets unless it constantly improves its products or introduces new ones. To achieve innovation American industry spends several billion dollars annually on research and development. In the arts innovation goes on with the same inevitability, and always has. The history of art, like the history of science, is a chronicle of great changes brought about slowly by innovations, a small number of which in retrospect are crucial in effecting major developments.

Since a piece of music or a play has no utility, it cannot be made better in measurable efficiency. In architecture and design practical improvement is a factor. But taste is the only arbiter of excellence in most arts. The only certainty that the artist can count on is that he can never achieve anything but mediocrity by imitating the models of the past, no matter how skillfully he works. Change is a must. The ordeal of the great artist arises from this knowledge. Actually, most artists stay timidly within established forms. Others strive to break away, but succeed in being merely ridiculous. A few have the discipline and inspiration to be fresh and original. The work of any great artist is a record of early imitative efforts followed by work that increasingly bears the stamp of uniqueness. Shakespeare's earliest narrative poem, "Venus and Adonis," is much like Marlowe's verse. Yet among the hundreds of plays by the numerous other Elizabethan playwrights, none resembles such diverse masterpieces as *Midsummer Night's Dream, Henry IV, Macbeth, Hamlet, King Lear,* or *The Tempest.*

You can see what the dilemma of the artist is: He must start within an established formal system of some sort. As Mark Van Doren once said to me, "I never would have written poetry if I hadn't read it." A mysterious chemical reaction sets in when a young person first has the experiences that later lead him to be creative in a certain field. Necessarily it involves admiration of particular works, often inferior. For a while they dominate his imagination, and shape his first efforts. Soon he adds other admirations and models. He grows in mastery of his technique. Then if he is worthy of the title of artist, he starts to fight his way to independence. This is the crucial period in the life of an artist. It may last for years. As his competence increases, he is sorely tempted to let well enough alone and try to develop as fully as possible within the accepted forms.

In stagnant cultures art becomes ritualistic, not personal; the function of the artist is to enhance the prestige of the existing order. With a few conspicuous exceptions, artists who have been successful in a worldly way in our culture have not been innovators—and they have been forgotten. I have just been looking at two enormous volumes of reproductions of paintings and etchings exhibited at the Columbian Exposition in Chicago in 1893. Except for two or three names, such as Cassatt, Hassam, and Zorn, these celebrities, chosen as their countries' best, are as unremembered as their incredibly bad pictures. One might think this the low point in the history of painting. Yet at this time Cézanne, Monet, Renoir, Van Gogh, and other great Impressionists and Post-Impressionists were at work; they are not represented.

The painter or poet or composer who decides to seek enduring fame through innovation faces a tough fight. By definition, he must do what has not been done. But the catch is that what he does must have a rationale of its own. He cannot just do anything. He cannot hit piano notes at random. Like a research chemist, he must invent or adapt so that he works within an intelligible order of some sort. Out of such an imperative came the twelve-tone system of music, "action" painting, the conversational rhythms of poetry, and other developments of modern art. But along the way thousands of artists try to be different but fail. What they do is meaningless because it lacks a logical structure, or because the system that gives it meaning is too limited to allow fruitful expansion. Jackson Pollock almost instantaneously pushed the drip technique of painting to its ultimate possibilities. In *Finnegan's Wake*, James Joyce reached the ultimate in dreamlike stream-of-consciousness narrative and fresh-coined vocabulary based on associations. No important artist has bothered to accept either Pollock's or Joyce's technique for his own efforts. Most good artists do not get beyond echoing past forms and adjusting present ones. Some great artists like Bach and Milton do not innovate so much as they exploit traditional forms to the limit. But they also stimulate generations of other artists to develop fruitfully in countless ways.

ART AS PROBLEM SOLVING

Artists do not progress in set ways. But playfulness does progress to problem solving. An architect may say to himself, What fun it would be to build a house on top of a pole, like a bird house or a boy's tree house! He lets himself go and plays with the idea. But as he draws rough sketches of his whimsy, he reacts seriously to the problem he has set himself. In time he finds answers for the various sub-problems and his playful idea turns to reality. (At the airport in Washington there are two such structures for stranded travelers to rest in.) Or Chagall thinks: Wouldn't it be amusing to ignore gravity and reality and paint red, blue, green, and yellow cows, roosters, and human beings floating about in the air! Then he works out his composition and his color combinations.

The artist faces problems of two kinds—of subject and of treatment, of content and of form, of what and of how. Suppose you are a writer, and you hear an extraordinary story about two brothers who competed against each other in everything, even love. You have never read a story just like it. Yet the chances that you will wish to write this story are remote. Why? As an artist develops, more and more he exists in a world of his own preoccupations. Relatively few subjects are congruous with the subjects his mind has been grappling with. One reason is tradition. Shakespeare never wrote a domestic tragedy because he worked within a tradition that deemed only nobles, not ordinary citizens, fit subjects for tragedy. You may not wish to write about the rivalry of brothers because you are concerned with problems of social change, race relations, or wholesome suburban life.

Or the rivalry of brothers may not seem the sort of subject that would allow you scope for your special style. A society portrait painter with a polished technique is likely to consider a handsome woman more suitable to his talents than a steel mill. Your problem may be one of medium. If you are a novelist or a playwright, you may believe that the uniqueness of the problem of the brothers is concentrated in one episode and that therefore the proper medium is a short story. Or you may be a short story writer. You may think the interest lies in the background and in the fabric of the lives of a number of characters over the years. A novel or a play is indicated, not a short story. Artists of all sorts are inclined to maintain vehemently that subject and treatment, content and form, are one and the same thing. It seems to me more exact to say that they have meaning for the artist only in association and have to be considered together.

Perhaps this may be the clue to one chief way that you can relate arts and letters to your own development as a creative person. As we have said, the creative artist is a problem solver. His restless scrutiny of experience leaves the serious artist bored with what is settled and known. Just as the true scientist has no interest in performing routine tests, so the true poet refuses to write neat little lyrics with conventional sentiments, or the artist to paint slick portraits, or the writer to crank out boy-meets-girl short stories. Even at a high level of seriousness, even when they do face new and challenging problems, many artists give in to a compulsion to "solve the problem" with final solutions. Thus they miss true greatness. One of the characteristics of great art is its enigmatic quality. Are the wonderful sculptures of the Yoruba and Benin African tribes beautiful or ugly? Do they exorcise evil spirits or praise them? Are they expressions of religion or of lust? The study of Greek tragedies, of Bach's religious music, of El Greco's paintings leaves a residue of doubt about final answers.

It is as though the most serious artists, poring over the mysteries of existence and struggling to subdue them by wrapping them in the form of drama or music or sculpture, must at last confess that there are various levels of certainty and that the peace that is the reward for the pursuit of truth comes at the highest level with a realization of the unknowableness of life. With this realization comes, not resignation, not despair, but an acceptance of ambiguity as a fact. Ambiguity to a Breughel or a Chekhov is not an absolute. Accepted as an absolute, it leads to fatalism, dogma, or inertia. Accepted as a fact, it injects a dynamic, unfinished element into existence. Toleration of ambiguity is an important aspect of the creative personality. Engagement with great art, therefore, is one of the most profitable actions in the cultivation of your mind, because it will help release you from the tyranny of closed systems of thought.

THE SOCIAL STATUS OF THE ARTIST

Among the natives of the Marquesas Islands no dwelling is finished and livable until a carved and painted post adorns its entrance. When the rest of the structure is completed, the artist is ceremoniously invited—wooed apparently—to live in it while he works at his task. If he is not well fed and treated with what he considers due respect, he walks out, casting a grave social stigma on the householder. The Marquesas Islanders and other primitive peoples recognize that the creative forces commanded by the artist are somehow allied with those mysterious ones that govern the universe. Thus the artist is esteemed and well rewarded. Even among European gypsies, who might be supposed to be long since corrupted by close association with modern industrial society, the young who reveal musical talent are dedicated to a life of music, rigorously trained, and excused from other labor.

The position of the artist in American society oscillates between that of a bum and a Hollywood star. Indeed, a Hollywood star occasionally is an actor of sufficient ability to be called an artist, and occasionally a genuine artist messes up his life to the point of deserving the label of bum—statistically almost as often as the rest of us do. There are good reason why the best artists in any field do not live dissipated or disorganized lives any more than do the best surgeons or best business executives.

First, the successful practice of any art is a demanding, wearing, daily discipline making hard demands on physical and emotional fitness. It is a lonely affair—lonelier than being a surgeon or an executive—for in many arts, such as writing, painting, and composing, the entire process is carried on in solitude, and even in the performing arts the public appearance of the actor, musician, or dancer is preceded by endless practice and rehearsals of the greatest severity. Few of us have the cold courage needed to sit at a typewriter, stand before an easel, or practice scales day after day without a boss to tell us what to do and without colleagues to sustain, and shame, us into continued production. Many would-be artists cannot stand the discipline, and they fall apart. The public too often confuses these less heroic souls with the men and women who are made of the steel necessary to become a true artist. Of course, some great creative artists have lived unconventional lives. Some have destroyed themselves and their talents. But these tend to be the men of moderate achievement, such as Poe and Modigliani, not a Wordsworth or a Velásquez.

A second reason why the serious artist does not generally deserve the familiar libel of him is that he is doing what he wants to do, and what he wants to do is both creative and identified with him personally. This way lies sanity. Perhaps the prime reason for the emotional troubles of modern man is his frustration at doing work that is uncreative and in no way identified with him. In most of his work he shares responsibility with others. Objectives and standards of performance are set by others. More often than not, the artist decides what he is going to do, does it by himself, and judges his own achievement. Since he is guided in the act of creation by a vision of shining perfection, he is much more critical of his performance than most of us who are guided by nothing more exacting than a job description and a set of specifications.

In an American plant manufacturing huge turret lathes, a German machinist chisels his initials on every part that he produces—"O.H.," Otto Herrlich. There is something splendid and pathetic in the gesture. Each part is a marvel of precision, a monument to skill come by through years of prideful effort. The sad truth, however, is that with all his cunning artisanship, the machinist follows a blueprint, another's conceiving. And even if he did not, the product of his hands is destined to years of impersonal service, and no man will ever say, Ah, an original Otto Herrlich! as we say, Ah, a Holbein!

Two more reasons why in a mad world the artist is among the

sanest members of society. First, he has a profound conviction that he is in touch with reality. He must feel this, or he cannot function. The president of an industrial empire once confided to me that every day he asked himself, Why am I doing this? What is it all about? The sculptor and the poet think that they know. Second, the reality that the artist apprehends always is more orderly than the real world. Even when, like the playwright Strindberg, an artist finds something akin to chaos at the heart of reality, he must organize his vision into a form that has order for him—and for others, if it is to be granted an audience.

THE ECONOMIC STATUS OF THE ARTIST

This brings us to the economic relationship between the artist and his public. Until the last century the artist almost always knew intimately the persons on whom his success depended—tribal chieftains, citizens of Athens, prelates, princes, the courtiers and groundlings of the Globe Theater, merchants, and statesmen. He spoke to them daily. With the spread of wealth and education during the past century and a half, the artist has apparently gained a degree of freedom rarely enjoyed by his predecessors. But at the same time he is no longer sure who his audience is or who will pay for what he creates. Lacking a definite or adequate source of financial support and often working amid indifference and hostility, the artist today becomes alienated from his public. Not infrequently, he works with no concern for any opinion beyond his own and that of a few cronies and critics. Until a wider public grows more discriminating in the arts and until it buys contemporary art even more generously, the artist will continue in his alienation.

Our affluent, wasteful society supports relatively few artists. A friend of mine provides a typical instance of the economic status of the artist in rich United States. He plays a violin in one of our best symphony orchestras during the musical season. Summers he plays in a "pops" orchestra. The year round he gives lessons and tries to sell insurance. His less versatile fellow musicians think him lucky. Only the exceptional artist makes his living from his creative efforts alone. These exceptions are worth considering.

A successful novelist, playwright, painter, singer, dancer, or actor is often paid far beyond the going rate for the other 98 per cent of the practitioners in his field. An ordinary novelist may publish three novels in ten years. If he collects $10,000 in all—an optimistic assumption—he has not made enough to live on. But if one or two of his novels are taken by a book club and the movies, they may make him wealthy. The average painter who tries to live by his brush alone is as poor today on Fourteenth Street, New York, or Montmartre, Paris, as he was a hundred years ago in the same places. Yet paintings by artists as recent as the late Nicholas de Staël and Franz Kline may sell for $30,000. The stakes are high.

Another difference in the role of the artist in our society is that his destiny is controlled to a considerable extent by what in business are called middlemen. The marketing of creative efforts *is* business. A successful violinist, actor, or novelist today nine times out of ten has an agent who handles his business affairs. Beyond the agents, between the artist and his public are the organizations, such as publishing houses, theaters, and museums, that present his wares to the public. Many a reputation is based on adroit management and publicity—and I mean critical as well as mass-appeal success. As a natural consequence, some artists, like Salvador Dali, spend almost as much pains on shaping their public image as they do on their art. Yet critical success is not usually manufactured out of inferior talents. Salvador Dali is a technically proficient painter with a flair for novelty.

Along with these factors the artist faces the hazards of chance. Thousands of books and plays have failed in spite of all expectations of success, and some that were thought too "good" to appeal to a large public have prospered. Once an artist achieves success, he remains a celebrity, the recipient of an ironic personal homage by Americans whose respect for a person who makes a name for himself transcends their dubious regard for him as an artist.

REACTING TO A WORK OF ART

Your interaction with a poem, painting, or other work of art is more complex than at first it may seem. What goes on may be exemplified in the following way: Let us say that Fenimore Irving, a playwright, writes a play about George Washington. The immediate impetus to do so may be the experience of reading a biography or a visit to Yorktown. But Irving also is influenced by whatever else he has heard about Washington. All this is his experience. The same is true when you see or read his play. You react to what you see on the page or on the stage. But you too have memories and attitudes that act as a transparent colored film between you and the play. Both the playwright and you, the beholder, have important secondary reactions. In the back of Irving's mind is some concern about what you and the critics will think about his play. There is also his special concern about all the technical problems involved. You also are influenced by the playwright's reputation, or lack of one, and by what critics have or have not said about his play.

Frequently, the work of art that you contemplate comes to you through intermediate transmitters. The written text of a play about Washington is interpreted by producer, director, technicians, and actors. The theater and the circumstances in which you see it affect your reaction. *Twelfth Night* performed by students and a polonaise played by a neighbor's daughter are distorted replicas of the art that lies hidden, like fire in coal, in the words of Shakespeare and the notes of Chopin.

All of this is by way of reminding you again that your response to art is exceedingly complex. Therefore, when you say, "I like that" or "I don't like that" about any work of art, you are passing a judgment on yourself, perhaps on your limitations, rather than on the work. You might, for instance, like a painting of a Dutch windmill and dislike a painting of a butchered beef carcass hanging on a hook. You might consider windmills picturesque and beef carcasses repulsive, except as roasts. Yet Rembrandt painted both subjects, and his beef carcass is much admired by critics. You might respond warmly to William Butler Yeats' early poem "Innisfree" and be left cold by his later "Sailing to Byzantium." The first is rhetorical in style and sentimental in mood; the latter, colloquial and philosophic. Critics consider "Innisfree" relatively trivial, "Sailing to Byzantium" one of the finest of modern poems.

You might find Chopin's "Fantasia" delightful, and be bored by Bach's "Goldberg Variations." On repeated exposure, you might tire of the "Fantasia" and grow fascinated by the "Variations."

Here is the secret—better acquaintance. It is not much of a secret, yet apparently hidden from millions of people. Give yourself a chance! Here lies the whole marvelous world of music, poetry, drama, fiction, sculpture, painting, and the rest of the arts, all wide open to your enjoyment. To form hasty opinions, even favorable ones, may cut you off from years of enjoyment. When Dylan Thomas' poems first came out, most of us were puzzled by his seemingly wild and mystical style. In time, we came to understand what he was trying to say and to separate the successful poems from ones that do not "come off." Any opinion not based on long acquaintance with an art form, though not necessarily on technical understanding of it, is bound to be superficial and untrustworthy. Give yourself a chance by suspending judgment of specific works of art until you have (a) background for judgment and (b) adequate acquaintance with the specific works.

Your experience is enhanced by knowledge of the tradition in which an artist is working. Without qualifying as a musicologist, you can soon distinguish the baroque tradition in which Bach composed, the romanticism of Schumann, and the modernism of Bartók. Your appreciation of colonial architecture and of New York State gingerbread is keener if you relate both to the revival of interest in Greece that flowered in every possible form, including printing and horticulture, in the eighteenth century.

As your awareness of cultural developments gradually grows more certain, you are able to place an unfamiliar work of art against its appropriate background. For instance, two of John Keats' poems, "On First Looking into Chapman's Homer" and "Ode on a Grecian Urn," are interesting not just as poems but also as romantic reactions to things Greek. But remember that familiarity with social trends and technical influences is only an aid to understanding a work of art. Few persons are more tiresome than those who in any field "talk a good game." Be sure you do not substitute an accumulation of pedantic jargon *about* the arts for the living, immediate, visceral experience itself.

6

THE HUMAN PREDICAMENT
IN FICTION

"The human soul is a very complex thing." George Eliot, the Victorian novelist, put this inscription in *Adam Bede* as a warning to her readers, I suppose, that her characters would not follow the predictable patterns of the usual fictional heros and villains, but would exhibit some of the enigmas of actual human behavior. The cultivated mind can best be distinguished from the merely well-informed mind by its superior understanding of the subtleties of the human soul. Of course, the soul is a vague entity. You might prefer to talk about understanding human behavior. In this chapter we will try to uncover some of the ways in which reading fiction can increase your insight into what has been called "the human predicament."

The special business of the storyteller is to explore what this predicament is. From the earliest times a few members of the population have been more sensitive than their fellows in reacting to the drama of human existence—its struggles, its agonies, its triumphs, its defeats, its comedy, its beauty, its joys, and its bizarre extremes of degradation and nobility. From Homer to Hemingway, the storyteller has created on three planes. First, he tells tales of action and suspense that give delight. Next, in so doing he sets standards of behavior by creating heros. And

finally he pours his gaze into the darkness of the world's evil and
the murky grottoes of his own soul to re-enact for us those predicaments of existence that torment only the human animal.
These are the three different levels on which the storyteller
functions: as narrator-entertainer, as hero-maker, and as student
of good and evil. To turn to the storyteller as a peddler of the
candy bars of escape from reality is childish. It is to ask to be
cheated.

A SENSE OF LIFE

At whatever level he writes, whatever his intent, the fiction
writer must create a sense of life. The conviction of authenticity
that you have in reading about medieval times in Scott, or Russia
during the Napoleonic wars in Tolstoi, or early nineteenth-
century England in Jane Austen, or post-World War I Germany
in Franz Kafka—the sense of rightness of the atmosphere and
psychology—is based on knowledge of the total environment
of the characters and the action. This knowledge comes from
thoughtful firsthand observation or diligent research. Either way,
the result is a quality of immediacy in the writing. You might call
it "thereness." This sense of being "there" is evoked to a large
extent by sensory images.

One of the greatest works of art yet produced in America—
in my opinion the greatest—is Melville's novel, *Moby Dick*. But
the tremendous drama of Captain Ahab's mad hunt after the
white whale, the mystic insights into the depths of the human
heart, the fashioning of an American myth, and the fantastic
humor, all would not be were it not for the rich imagery that
flickers through every page like luminous protozoa in the summer seas. From the opening page where Ishmael, the sailor
narrator, says that he goes to sea "whenever it is a damp, drizzly
November in my soul," until the awesome final struggle between
Ahab and the whale, Melville evokes the sights and sounds and
mood of every scene by means of nouns and verbs and compari-
sons that sting the senses like a walk at low tide on the sands of
old Sag Harbor.

The values you derive from reading fiction rest on this Merlin ability of the storyteller to beguile you into accepting the credibility of his characters and their environment. Whether you lose yourself in the world of Victor Hugo's Jean Valjean, Samuel Butler's Ernest Pontifex, or Henry James's Lambert Strether, you look into the souls of extraordinary people through the eyes of the shrewdest of observers. Vicariously you undergo a thousand experiences and become intimately acquainted with a great range of personalities, social groups, occupations, places, and times. Above all, you come to understand what problems bedevil human beings behind the Venetian blinds of respectability, what emotional drives and pressures move them to aggression or regression, and how they bear themselves in triumph and defeat. You increase your knowledge of human nature just as surely as you do knowledge of law by reading legal cases. Indeed, you might say that novels and short stories are case histories with the emphasis on why people do things and how they feel about what they do and what others do to them.

THE HOMERIC HEROES

In all societies a main service of the storyteller is to prop up the ego of his fellows by creating heroes. He may start by enlarging the deeds of the local champion, but more often he sings the praises of the great of the past. By identification, the lowliest member of the tribe or of the state feels larger, more virile, more successful than he really is. It follows, therefore, that the heroes of a society are indicators of the deeply cherished values of that society.

Of all the storytellers Homer is the greatest, both as teller of tales and as creator of heroes. Scholars in general agree that one man named Homer wrote both the *Iliad* and the *Odyssey*. He did not live in Greece but was a member of a Greek colony in what is now the city of Izmir (Smyrna) on the coast of Turkey. He lived about 800 B.C. and wrote about events connected with the siege of Troy, which undoubtedly took place three or four centuries before his time. Thus Homer drew on material handed down by oral tradition and already blurred in details. Since written history did not exist, he must have looked on himself as historian as well as entertainer. He composed orally in verse for recitation. Not for several centuries were his works written down. It is staggering to think that the thousands of lines of our two greatest epics were composed, memorized, recited, listened to, and handed down without a script.

Though the *Iliad* and the *Odyssey* were originally in verse, they take their place at the head of all fiction. The *Odyssey* has been called the greatest of novels. The *Iliad* and the *Odyssey* record just about every aspect of life of the Bronze Age—details of dress and dwellings and seafaring, weather and seasons, waging of war, morals, friendship, family relations, leadership, love, loyalties, death, the role of the individual in society, and the role of the gods in the scheme of things. The only works of comparable magnitude and seriousness are Dante's *Divine Comedy* and Shakespeare's plays. Even so great a novel as Tolstoi's *War and Peace* has no such scope. In addition Homer seems always confronting a universal question: What should be the wise man's course of action in a world where fate makes a joke of reason and justice? What should a wise man's purpose be and how should he fare steadily toward it?

Both the *Iliad* and the *Odyssey* are stories of men with purposes. Both are episodes within a larger action that begins with the flight of Helen, wife of a Greek king, Menelaus, with Paris, son of King Priam of Troy, and ends with her return and that of the Greek survivors, Odysseus being the last. During the intervening twenty years the Greeks under the leadership of King Agamemnon, brother of Menelaus, besiege Troy (Ilium), a walled town near the Dardanelles. The *Iliad* takes place within several weeks during the tenth and last year of the siege but well before the fall. The *Odyssey* covers the last several weeks in the ten years after the fall of Troy that it takes Odysseus to return to his home, the island of Ithaca on the west coast of Greece.

Odysseus' purposes are clear—to survive the hazards of his journey and then to drive away the suitors who have been badgering his wife Penelope to give up hope of his return and to marry one of them.

ACHILLES, THE DIVIDED HERO

In the *Iliad* the grand purpose of recovering Helen is subordinated to what seem at first odd personal objectives. The central figure is Achilles. In the pattern of war fought primarily by individual leaders, Achilles is by reputation the best fighter on the Greek side. Homer's purpose is to demonstrate that Achilles is indeed superior to all other Greeks and that their escape from imminent defeat depends on him alone. In order to accomplish this end, Homer puts Achilles through some strange paces. First, he has to give up his concubine Briseis to Agamemnon. Because of this, he refuses to fight and even prays that the Greeks will lose, and he goes on sulking even after Briseis is returned to him. His closest friend, Patroclus, borrows his armor and is slain and mistreated by Hector, the Trojan champion. Not Menelaus, Diomedes, Odysseus, or any other Greek hero measures up to Hector. As the Trojans under Hector are about to overwhelm the Greeks in their ships by the shore, Achilles, in ungovernable grief and fury over the death of Patroclus, goes into action, slaughters "thousands" of Trojans, chases Hector three times around the walls of Troy, kills him when he stands to fight, and savagely drags his body about by the heels for days. The grief-stricken King Priam, the old father of Hector, goes to Achilles with ransom and receives his permission to take back Hector's body for a hero's funeral.

This hardly sounds like great literature. In a first reading you may find the behavior of the Homeric heroes fantastic, contradictory, and ludicrous, and the behavior of the gods even more so. But in time you will find the power of Homer as narrator irresistible. For instance, after the brutal treatment Achilles has given Hector, he receives Priam with courtesy, weeps with him in grief for his own father and the dead Patroclus, and grants the old king's petitions with magnanimity. Priam's pitiful, "I put my lips to the hands of the man who has killed my children," has a raw power beyond artifice. This is one of the most moving scenes in world literature.

ODYSSEUS, THE NEARLY COMPLETE HERO

The *Odyssey* lacks the tragic intensity of the *Iliad,* but it has a wider variety of characters and exciting events. By the Greek definition, it is a comedy because the hero triumphs in the end. The *Odyssey* is put together with superb skill, with flash backs, rehearsals, and other sophisticated devices to control proportions, hold attention, and sustain tempo. It could easily have been an "and-then" chronicle of Odysseus' wanderings and homecoming. Instead it falls into three major units.

In a brief opening scene between Athene, Odysseus' helpful goddess, and Zeus, the king of the gods, the situation of Odysseus is revealed, but the focus shifts to Telemachus, Odysseus' son, grown to young manhood in the seventeen years or so that Odysseus has been away from Ithaca. Immediately the situation there is clarified—faithful Penelope holding off the many unruly suitors, hoping her husband will return; Telemachus powerless to resist. Telemachus goes off in search of his father (a much used symbol in modern literature) and visits Nestor and Menelaus, safely returned from Troy, the latter with Helen restored as his queen. This meeting neatly enables Homer to tell about what happened to some of the chief actors after the end of the *Iliad.*

The longer second unit covers the return of Odysseus from Troy to Ithaca. The account is ingeniously managed. It begins at Calypso's island, the farthest point west that Odysseus has been driven by storms, that is, by the sea god Poseidon, whom he has offended. As a result of the begging of Athene in the opening of the *Odyssey,* Zeus orders the beautiful goddess Calypso to free her reluctant lover. So after seven years she sends Odysseus off on a raft. He is swept ashore, salt-caked and naked on a river bank on the shore of Phaeacia.

In the morning sun he reveals himself to the princess Nausicaa, playing ball on the sand with her handmaidens while the clothing they have just washed, including their own, dries. Homer treats the whole incident with such delicacy and naturalness that it is one of the most charming of literary vignettes.

Odysseus is handsomely entertained at the palace of King

Alcinous, Nausicaa's father. Cunningly, Homer has Odysseus tell in the first person his adventures as he and his shipmates tried to cross the Aegean Sea from Troy to Ithaca. These capsule stories are so famous that for centuries all school children, except our own, have known and marveled at them, and all Western literatures are filled with references to them. Odysseus visits the Lotus-Eaters. He blinds Cyclops, the son of the god Poseidon, and escapes from his cave with some of his men. His greedy men open the gift of Aeolus, a bag of wind. Giants destroy eleven of his twelve ships and their crews. Circe turns half of his remaining crew to swine, but he rescues them. He descends into Hades and talks with the spirits of the dead. The conversations with his mother, Agamemnon, and Achilles and the glimpses of other illustrious dead are touched with unexpected pathos, but they also give the earliest surviving outlines of other famous stories, particularly Agamemnon's account of his murder on his return to Mycenae. Odysseus tops off his account with the most famous of all sea adventure stories—the passing of the Sirens, Scylla, and Charybdis, and the loss of his ship and men. Odysseus' rehearsal then catches up to where the action opened—his seven years under the spell of the lovely Calypso.

About half of the *Odyssey* is given to the third section, Odysseus at Ithaca. Disguised as a beggar, Odysseus is reunited with his son Telemachus at the hut of a loyal swineherd. At his own house, overrun with Penelope's suitors, the rowdy wooers give the beggar a rough time, but Odysseus carefully plans their doom. He beats the suitors in stringing and shooting his own bow, a test that Penelope has arranged to choose a husband. With Telemachus by his side he kills all of the wooers, and in a tender final scene reveals himself to Penelope and to his old father Laertes. This half of the *Odyssey* is almost a novel in itself, but its poignancy and savor and climactic force depend on the memories of the many hazards of battle, sea, and enchantment that broad-shouldered Odysseus has overcome before he faces these final odds and becomes master again in his own house.

MEN AND GODS

At first the behavior of Homer's heroes and of the gods, who intervene in human affairs as capriciously as children playing with dolls, does seem bizarre. So does the behavior of the Japanese or any other people whose culture is alien to our own. The puzzle of Homer's men and gods becomes the puzzle of ourselves and human destiny. We begin to realize humbly how impertinent it is for us to believe that our presuppositions about life, like the axioms we trusted in high school geometry, are necessarily true.

Our enlightenment begins when we understand that in the Homeric society and for some centuries after, the individual played his role on a small stage. Troy, Athens, Ithaca, and the other mighty-sounding places were small indeed. Odysseus' long-sought Ithaca is called a city; yet his establishment seems to consist of a largish farmhouse, some servants, and one or two swineherds and goatherds. Even in the city state of Athens at its height citizens were so few that everyone spoke for himself in the assembly as in a New England town meeting.

In this atomistic society two premises are accepted. They may shock us. One is that personal glory is the highest goal in life. The other is that, while the gods help and hinder the individual, they do so in unpredictable ways. The gods are not necessarily on the side of the just. Thus if the individual is to win glory, he must placate the gods as best he can, but he is strictly on his own, and he may lose, no matter how brave or virtuous.

Now the great adventure of reading the *Iliad* and the *Odyssey* should lead us beyond the rousing action and the wonder at the behavior of the characters to see ourselves in the light they kindle. Odysseus, fighting stormy seas and malevolent spirits, has the god Poseidon against him and the goddess Athene for him. He overcomes all dangers not because of supernatural aid, but because of his courage, intelligence, and unswerving sense of objective. In short he was master of himself, a nearly complete man, and thus, as far as it is possible in this world, the Greeks believed, he was master of his destiny. Achilles is a tragic figure because he is divided. He is mastered by his own emotions, and he elects to seek glory by spear and sword alone, knowing well that his time is short. He is to die at the hand of the unheroic Paris, though not in the *Iliad*. We will not meet again a storyteller who equals Homer as a recounter of the deeds of heroes who are at once so heroic and so human and also such quintessential symbols of their age.

DON QUIXOTE AND SANCHO PANZA

I have said that the storyteller plays three roles. The first two are as entertainer and as setter of standards. You can see both of these functions at their best in *Don Quixote* by Miguel de Cervantes Saavedra, who died in 1616, the same year as Shakespeare.

Much reading of old romantic tales of chivalry has befuddled the wits of Don Quixote, a Spanish gentleman whose estate seems to consist mostly of books. He decides to seek adventures in the manner of the knights in the romances he has read. He enlists the services of a poor farmer, Sancho Panza, to act as squire. Mounted on his bony horse Rosinante, cased in makeshift armor, and trailed by fat Sancho Panza on a donkey, the gaunt knight sets forth. His mission, inevitably, is to right wrongs, particularly those involving defenseless women in distress, and to serve his lady, Dulcinea del Toboso, really an ignorant country wench. Don Quixote has many adventures, in which he is invariably discomfited. Beguiled by his master's enthusiasms and promises, Sancho serves loyally, though not bravely, in spite of mishaps and poor fare. Briefly Sancho realizes his ambition to be a governor of an island but finds governing a troublesome affair. In the end knight and squire return home, Don Quixote disillusioned with knight-errantry, Sancho still full of bounce.

Not much plot in this. But *Don Quixote* is one of the greatest inventions of the human mind. A battle-seasoned ex-soldier, government supply officer, jail occupant, provider for four females, Cervantes published Part I in 1605 as a desperate bid for income his plays and poems failed to bring him. He was then in his late fifties, an old man in those days. The instantaneous success of the novel and its pirating led him to write Part II, published in 1615.

Cervantes started *Don Quixote* as a satire of the high-flown romances common from medieval times to his own day. He succeeded: The gale of laughter that greeted the knight of the lugubrious countenance blew all his solemn prototypes off the stage of public esteem. Chivalry was not again taken seriously until the romantic revival of medievalism, as in Scott's novels. But Cervantes did much more. Since he wrote in separate episodes, and since he had time to essay public reaction after the publication of Part I before he began Part II, he was able gradually to change his burlesque to something deeper.

THE AMBIGUITIES OF CERVANTES

Ultimately the character of Don Quixote grows ambiguous. He is funny, but he is sad. He is a total failure in the eyes of the practical world; yet he has become a symbol of the romantic idealist. In World War I the British officers who led their men out of the Flanders trenches carrying only swagger sticks were quixotic. The young man who exchanges his desk in an advertising agency for one in a school classroom is quixotic. Of course, the castles and giants and magicians and lovely damsels are only humble inns, windmills, shepherds, innkeepers' daughters, all delusions. Yet, we think, is not Don Quixote pursuing a vision of reality infinitely nobler than the grubby actuality inhabited by the miserable oafs he has invested with extraordinary attributes? Does not Don Quixote exhibit a superior kind of wisdom, like an old gentleman turning off his hearing aid while a crony reminisces, in declining to recognize the sorry limits of the everyday world we call the real one? In short, is not *Don Quixote* after all a tract in defense of chivalry, in celebration of those who, as Stephen Spender says in a fine poem, never allowed "the traffic to smother,/With noise and fog, the flowering of the spirit," "Who wore at their hearts the fire's center" . . . "And left the vivid air signed with their honor"?

So we think, until we remember Sancho Panza. Sancho starts out as the buffoon to the sad clown Don Quixote. He is as cowardly and as earthy as his master is foolhardy and ascetic. Gradually as the fable gained in philosophical depth, Cervantes made Sancho more explicitly a foil to Don Quixote. Especially in Part II, where Cervantes makes the most of his material, Sancho grows in significance. For several chapters as Sancho governs his island, Cervantes separates him from Don Quixote and gives him a lead role. By being true to himself, Sancho emerges as the man of good sense. His gluttony, cowardice, and hard-headed peasant estimates of situations sum up the argument for accepting the world as it is, enjoying fully its good things and avoiding the unpleasant. He is with his blood brother Falstaff the enduring symbol of the unromantic, the anti-sentimental. Did Cervantes mean through Sancho to deny Don Quixote, to point to the futility of the idealism of which he is the symbol? I think not. I think the old soldier is telling us that the truth has many faces.

THE NOVEL OF SOCIAL PROBLEMS

In the hands of Richardson, Fielding, Smollett, Sterne, and Scott the modern novel emerged in England in the eighteenth and early nineteenth centuries as an uncomplicated account of a central character. As the novel grew more sophisticated, the natural development was to shift the emphasis from the adventures of the hero to the problems of society. The simple episodic narrative of course persists to this day, but in hundreds of other novels the author has taken on himself the burden of moralist.

The development of science in the seventeenth and eighteenth centuries had much to do with establishing in literature the habit of examining actuality with scrupulous attention to fact. The thinking underlying literature as well as science for centuries was a construction of assumptions. Certain things must be true, everyone agreed, and so a man's behavior could be measured against what was in the original patent, so to speak. Tragedy in the Aristotelian sense of the fall of a noble man is possible only in a society that believes it knows what a noble man is and what immutable code of conduct he violates to make his fall inevitable.

As soon as science upset the applecart and began its search for causes for natural phenomena, the literary man also shucked off absolutes about human behavior. Paradoxically he became more deeply involved in the baffling questions of right and wrong, individual responsibility, and purpose in the universe immediately he had no preordained values to check against. In this climate of uncertainty most of our greatest novels were written.

SIN AND CONSEQUENCES
IN PURITAN BOSTON

Fittingly enough, one of the classics of this probing of human conduct in a field of blurred guidelines is Nathaniel Hawthorne's *The Scarlet Letter*. Published in 1850, it was written by a descendant of Puritans, one who had made himself at home in the narrow spiritual world of his Boston ancestors. It is a novel, not so much of causes, as of effects. Though melodramatic, the action is not the main line of interest. Hester Prynne, married to an elderly man who is away in captivity among the Indians, has a child by another man. She refuses to name him. She is exhibited on the scaffold of the pillory with her baby and thereafter forced to wear the letter A for adultery embroidered in scarlet.

Hester's aged husband turns up, gets her promise not to expose their relationship, and under the name of Roger Chillingworth applies himself to discovering the man involved. Chillingworth soon correctly suspects the Reverend Arthur Dimmesdale. As the young minister's physician and companion, for seven years he skillfully tortures him, yet without gaining his end, a private admission of guilt. Finally Hester persuades Dimmesdale that he should go abroad with her and the child Pearl to begin life anew. But after delivering a brilliant public sermon, Dimmesdale confesses publicly from the scaffold, shows a scarlet letter on his own breast, and dies. Hester goes abroad but returns some years later and dons her scarlet letter again.

You can see great differences between the life-of-the-hero narrative and the novel typified by *The Scarlet Letter,* and you can see that impulses similar to those that move the scientists are at work. First, in two senses in this novel there is no hero or heroine of the familiar Scott, Dickens, and Hollywood type. There are three main characters, and none is "good" and none is "bad."

The community is a fourth actor or force of equal importance in the drama. The citizens of Boston embody the values that the three leading actors are violating. But these citizens are divided and symbolize different forces that keep even a seventeenth-century Puritan society from ever being the rounded, tightly-sewed thing, like a baseball, that sociology textbooks describe.

Nor are the characters unified or static. Tom Jones, Candide, Don Quixote, and Odysseus grow in wisdom in the course of their adventures, but they are essentially at one with themselves at the beginning and they are basically unchanged at the end. Hester Prynne, Arthur Dimmesdale, and Roger Chillingworth are divided *within themselves*, as Hamlet was, and they change as the action progresses. This action is not merely exterior events. Paralleling the "plot" is a pattern of psychological changes. They are responses to events, decisions, interactions with the other characters. Many are transitory, but gradually they shape the characters so that at the end each character has run a course of significant change.

In what for 1850 is an amazing show of nonconformity Hester has refused to concede that sin is anything but being untrue to one's self. Her punishment by society is ineffectual, as is her leaving America. She wins spiritual peace only when *of her own will* she returns to Boston and resumes her badge of shame. The sensitive, verbalizing Dimmesdale gets no benefit from his terrible private penance. Only through suffering the subtle persecution of the man he has wronged, making public confession on the scaffold, and open acknowledgment of Hester and his child Pearl does he find release even in death. Old Chillingworth, who has let his sense of injury twist him from a quiet learned man into a creature obsessed with evil, returns at least to the peace of impotency when his foe escapes him on the scaffold.

This imaginary world is a projection of the world of reality—not what we call the real world, but the secret world of truth, in which each of us has an overwhelming sense of personal identity but finds himself unable to define himself and grow except in concessive relations with others and within the fabric of the tribal values he happens to inherit. In such a world, as in science, normalcy exists in equilibrium, and rest, rather than happiness, becomes the end of struggle.

THE WORLD OF THE BOVARYS
AND KARAMAZOVS

Two other novels, *Madame Bovary* by Gustave Flaubert and *The Brothers Karamazov* by Fyodor Dostoyevsky, may stand as French and Russian representatives of the tendency of the novel to reflect the scientific spirit of inquiry about human problems.

Madame Bovary appeared in book form in 1857. It has the significant subtitle "Provincial Manners." Though Emma Bovary is the central character, rural bourgeois society is anatomized. Emma Bovary, a vain, sentimental, extravagant woman with superficial refinement, is the second wife of a plodding country doctor, Charles Bovary. Emma is stifled by her dull life in the dreary places where Charles practices. She takes two lovers, bankrupts Charles, and commits suicide. As in *The Scarlet Letter*, the outward events are subordinate to the inward drama—the revelation of the characters of Charles and Emma Bovary, Emma's lovers Rodolphe and Léon, the chemist Homais, and the other middle-class principals.

Flaubert said that he was Madame Bovary. He meant, I imagine, that she was a symbol of the predicament of nineteenth-century man: He had been nurtured on revolution; now he was reaping the reward in the mean materialism of the new democracy. He had fed on the honeydew of the romantic individualism celebrated by Rousseau, Byron, and their followers; now he was petulantly discontented because the reality of the modern industrial world was such a poor showcase for his swollen ego. Possibly Flaubert was mistaken in some of his views. But nowhere else a hundred years ago could a person get a more scientific view of his personal world than in this study of the world of the wife of a provincial doctor.

Fyodor Dostoyevsky published *The Brothers Karamazov* in 1880, a year before he died after a troubled life. Like Michelangelo's Sistine Chapel ceiling paintings, it is one of man's great single achievements. Its opulence and brilliance make ordinary novels seem anemic.

The four Karamazov brothers are Dmitri, Ivan, Aloysha, and the illegitimate servant Smerdyakov. Their father Fyodor Karamazov is an evil old man. He embarrasses, frustrates, and outwits his sons endlessly until they loathe him. Someone kills and robs him. The profligate, emotional Dmitri is tried for the crime. He was present at the time, mad with jealousy for fear his sweetheart Grushenka had accepted his father's offer of 3,000 rubles to come to him. Circumstantial evidence piles up against Dmitri. Only the saintly brother Alyosha is sure he is innocent. The crafty epileptic Smerdyakov confesses to the intellectual brother Ivan that he did the killing but says that Ivan is the real murderer, for Smerdyakov thought Ivan wanted him to do it. He gives Ivan the money he has stolen and hangs himself. At the trial Ivan, on the verge of a breakdown, produces the money, reports Smerdyakov's confession, and grants his responsibility —he did wish for his father's death. The court thinks him mad. The neurotic Katerina, who loves Ivan but is not loved by him, offers damaging testimony against Dmitri, who does love her. Dmitri is pronounced guilty and sentenced to Siberia.

The Brothers Karamazov may seem melodramatic. Much of its power comes from the energy and excitement of events, from the beginning, through the gathering tension, to the turbulence of the trial and attendant scenes. But Dostoyevsky is much more than a great storyteller. He is master of characterization, of creating individuals who are immediately and permanently unique and believable, no matter how extraordinary or how minor. He is also master of the speech, daily behavior, and background of all classes of Russians—monks, gamblers, schoolboys, servants, peasants, lawyers, innkeepers. He is, therefore, a social historian of greater range than Flaubert. (Prophetically he likened Russia to a troika galloping to destruction.)

But Dostoyevsky is above all philosophic. He goes far beyond Flaubert in his passionate effort to wrest from the dilemmas of his tormented characters answers to age-old, ever-fresh questions about the struggle between good and evil and the existence of God. What disturbed him especially was the presence of demons within all of us. The irony of the conviction of the innocent Dmitri and the confession of guilt of the equally innocent Ivan might suggest that Dostoyevsky was uncertain about the final triumph of good.

CHARLES DODGSON IN WONDERLAND

The novels and short stories of the nineteenth and twentieth centuries are so infused with the scientific spirit that they have documentary value. Balzac, Zola, Stendhal, Proust, Gide, Camus, Tolstoi, Turgenev, Mann, Kafka, Eliot, Thackeray, Meredith, Trollope, Hardy, Butler, Lawrence, James, Lewis, Hemingway, and a long line of other fiction writers are authentic recorders of our cultural history. But it is well to note here that some storytellers stretch our imaginations by going beyond realism. One of the predicaments of our time is that we are mired in the matter-of-factness of our jobs, family chores, and news bulletins. The dreary realism of many best sellers and the sawdusty stuff fed to our children are poor substitutes for the robust imaginings of the anonymous tellers of folk tales or the followers of Homer.

There was a day when every schoolboy read most of Charles Dickens (1812–1870) out of sheer enchantment; now he skips through *The Tale of Two Cities*, Dickens' least typical book, as an assignment, to get the "plot." Dickens' fame rests not on his reflection of reality, but on his heightening of it. He turns the London of his drab and bitter boyhood into a pageant as colorful as the medieval one of Geoffrey Chaucer or as brave as the Renaissance one of William Shakespeare. He clothes the improvident and ineffectual characters of his memories in the radiance of his comic invention, and Mr. Pickwick, the Wellers, the Micawbers, and a score of others live on, unique, gloriously above probability.

A mathematician is the author of two of the most imaginative, delightful, and intellectually stimulating books ever written. He is Charles Dodgson (1832–1898), a professor at Oxford, and the books are *Alice's Adventures in Wonderland* and *Through the*

Looking-Glass. Dodgson, a shy bachelor with a speech defect, invented the *Adventures* on a summer's day boating on the Thames with a friend and the three young daughters of a colleague, Dean Liddell. It was natural for Dodgson to like little girls; he had seven younger sisters. When the outing was over Alice Liddell begged to have the inventions of the day written down. So Dodgson sat up all night writing what he could remember in a neat little manuscript book. This was in 1862; sixty-six years later Alice Liddell sold the manuscript for $75,000. Encouraged to publish the story, Dodgson reworked the first draft and in 1865, *Alice's Adventures in Wonderland* by "Lewis Carroll" appeared to captivate young and old. In 1872, *Through the Looking-Glass* followed. We refer to both books when we say *Alice in Wonderland,* but since they are often printed separately, you should take care not to miss *Through the Looking-Glass.*

However casually Dodgson set out to entertain the three Liddell girls, he soon began to write on a second, philosophical plane. Keeping the events always within the grasp of bright young minds, he also began to play with ideas on an adult level. He was fully conscious of this double game in *Through the Looking-Glass,* and it is therefore intellectually a much more brilliant performance than its famous predecessor. As an early investigator of symbolic logic—formal logic expressed in symbols, now used by mathematicians for computer programming—Dodgson found it child's play to demonstrate how ambiguously we use symbols to keep an unsteady balance as we try to distinguish between appearances and reality.

This theme is dramatized by Alice's penetration of the apparent space in the mirror above the fireplace—a feat that birds try on picture windows, often with fatal results. Throughout her dreamlike sequence of puzzling adventures in this illusory space, she constantly finds that things are not as they seem. For instance, she finds her own reality in jeopardy when Tweedledee and Tweedledum assert that the sleeping Red King is dreaming about her and "If that there King was to wake, you'd go out—bang!—just like a candle!" The birds, animals, and chess pieces that live in this looking-glass land are a crusty bunch, forever straightening out her logic or use of language. Her difficulty with Humpty Dumpty illustrates our own in communicating with the Russians:

"I don't know what you mean by 'glory,'" Alice said.

Humpty Dumpty smiled contemptuously. "Of course you don't—till I tell you. I meant 'there's a nice knock-down argument for you.'"

"But 'glory' doesn't mean 'a nice knock-down argument,'" Alice objected.

"When I use a word," Humpty Dumpty said, in rather a scornful tone, "it means just what I choose it to mean—neither more nor less."

"The question is," said Alice, "whether you can make words mean so many different things."

"The question is," said Humpty Dumpty, "which is to be master —that's all."

What is real, and what is illusion? What is substance, and what is symbol? These are no academic questions. Name the commonest goals that most of us spend our lives trying to reach—success, security, happiness. Our trite definitions of these terms become as meaningless as Humpty Dumpty's definition of *glory,* and our efforts to reach them as bootless as the shifting of places at the Mad Hatter's tea. At least this is our predicament unless we examine our lives with some of the detachment, humor, precision, and wisdom that Charles Dodgson explored the wonderland in which Alice wandered.

I have been calling Dodgson by his "real" name; but was not the author *really* Lewis Carroll? Or, for that matter, how little did Dodgson-Carroll suspect that his split-level divertissement had still another story, a psychological revelation of himself. The *real* Dodgson was a wifeless don who had taken religious orders. His world was a curious one of Prufrockian fears of drafts and being caught without change, of mathematical symbols, and of amusing children, especially little girls. The circumstances of his make-believe and the hierarchical nature of the symbolic society of playing cards and chess pieces let him float his way through Alice's wonderland on a stream of free associations. Did Carroll—the author who is so aware of the viscera beneath the skin and whose laughter is as merciless as a

child's—did he ever notice that in his fantasy the males are
timid and ineffectual, the women ugly and hostile, and only the
seven-and-a-half-year-old heroine appealing?

Whatever reality may be, realistic fiction cannot capture it.
But do not let my didacticism turn you away from the fun of
reading and re-reading *Alice*. You cannot help learning from it
some basic lessons in logic, semantics, and philosophy, but that
should not interfere with your relish of the delicious absurdities
that Lewis Carroll thought up to entertain three little girls a
century ago.

EVERYMAN, BLOOM, AND MITTY

We often speak about identifying ourselves with a character in
a novel. We do not literally think of ourselves as that character.
Rather we see in his fate—his relative position in the universe—
much that is comparable to our own. Perhaps the enduring
symbol of this universal applicability is Everyman in the medieval English morality play by that name. When Death comes to
fetch him, Everyman wangles a little delay time to round up a
companion to go with him on his stern journey. His cronies all
protest their loyalty but beg off. Everyman is frantic. Only one
finally offers to go along—the steadfast Good Deeds. Apart from
the moral of this medieval play, you will observe that the main
character is deliberately universalized. So you will find universal
elements in the characters in most serious literature.

Probably the most written about novel of the past fifty years
—perhaps in all English literature—is James Joyce's *Ulysses*. It
has no story, in the usual sense. The primary events record
nineteen hours of June 16-17, 1904, in the life of a Dubliner,
Leopold Bloom. He gets up, walks about the city, meets people,
listens, talks, eats, and finally goes home. All the while the past
floats along on his "stream of consciousness," and he carries on
an "interior monologue" as he associates the present with pieces
of the past. Two subsidiary characters, Stephen Daedalus and
Bloom's wife Molly, carry on similar but less extensive reveries.

Leopold Bloom's one-day ramble about Dublin is patterned
after the long journey of Ulysses (Odysseus) about the Mediter-

ranean on his return from the Trojan War. Bloom and Ulysses are both adventurers, seekers. The journey of each traces the perimeter of his known world, and the record of his wanderings is an inventory of its leading figures and events. Externally, Joyce's *Ulysses* is a near-burlesque of Homer's *Odyssey*. Yet Bloom's unheroic mixture of innocence, vanity, indecency, inquisitiveness, indecision, and cowardice is more nearly the stuff of modern man than whatever went into the hard-nosed Greek.

Bloom is not tragic. At the most he is pathetic, when he is not being foolish. He is, in short, Everyman in modern dress. His immense concern about himself and his fatuous day-dreaming about his prowess cast him in the same mold as James Thurber's hero, Walter Mitty. Mitty, henpecked driver of the family car on a shopping trip, metamorphosing himself into fighter pilot and other dauntless roles, is a figure of fun. But he is nonetheless also the suburban Everyman.

THE CONTEMPORARY SCENE

We have been looking at some aspects of fiction that are related to the purposes of this book, without attempting even a sketchy account of leading writers in English. We must have a look at contemporary fiction, for it is the mirror of the present age. In the thousands on thousands of novels and short stories written in our generation, every possible theme has been dealt with. Yet there have been two overriding ones—the exploration of self and the analysis of society. Most contemporary writers owe an enormous debt to Freud, though in the main they have picked up his ideas secondhand. But they also share the new awareness of the dynamics of social forces, especially of class and economics, within which the individual is often caught. The self-sufficient hero has become an anachronism in serious literature. He persists only in a few works such as the novels of Thomas Wolfe, as a Byronic hero with a Whitmanesque love of the American land and an Elizabethan love of rhetoric.

Your reaction to the characters in much of the fiction being written today may be "I couldn't care less what happens to them." In this judgment I must concur. The chief characters in many of the novels and short stories most seriously regarded by critics are miserable specimens of humanity. They have much in common. They are mixed up, self-centered, immoral, and destructive. They are not unreal, for their subhuman counterparts fill the newspapers with incredible doings. The authors, men and women of undoubted talents, seem to be writing compulsively, out of a horrible fascination with the sick side of contemporary life. But the trouble is that while the reader may share this fascination temporarily, in the end he does not care what happens to someone for whom his main feeling is revulsion, contempt, or perhaps worse, indifference.

Perhaps, then, you have a simple test for picking your contemporary novels: You ought to care what happens to the main characters. The distinction does not, I think, lie in what the characters do so much as in how they are handled—in the depth of understanding of the writer and in his ability to project a set of admissible standards for measuring the behavior of the characters. In a sense the distinction is between negative defeatism and something positive.

WILLIAM FAULKNER OF YOKNAPATAWPHA COUNTY

To the rest of the world the most significant modern American writer is William Faulkner. The award of the Nobel Prize in literature is evidence of this judgment. Russians and even Western Europeans with no firsthand knowledge of the United States may imagine that the nightmarish events that occur in Faulkner's Yoknapatawpha County are typical of what goes on everywhere in America. You may find them unbelievable, perhaps sordid, a libel of the South. You may put his characters in the "couldn't care less" basket. You may consider Faulkner's style at times involuted to the point of self-parody.

Yet *Sartoris, The Sound and the Fury, As I Lay Dying,* and *Light in August* are novels of undeniable power. Through them and his other novels and short stories Faulkner threads an almost mythical representation of life on this planet rather than in

Mississippi. He uses characters and scenes that are as native as yellow clay, no matter how extreme they may be. But his interest clearly is in man everywhere. He is intensely absorbed in the characters he creates; yet he is always looking beyond them at their universal prototypes.

Light in August is filled with cornered, damaged people, with violence and cruelty and meanness, but chinks of tenderness and compassion light up the gloom here and there. Joe Christmas murders Miss Burden, a spinster whose paramour he has been, gives himself up, runs away, and is shot to death and emasculated. Around this bloody core—still, hardly more violent than that of *Oedipus Rex, King Lear,* or *Samson Agonistes*—Faulkner twists a tangle of dark ambiguities.

First, Joe Christmas is illegitimate, and he is a mulatto. Faulkner does not allow himself the ease of a clear-cut racial problem. Christmas believes that he has Negro blood, but he chooses to live among whites. From his earliest experiences as a nameless waif in an orphanage, through a bruising adolescence, to his final episode with Miss Burden, he has suffered ambivalent feelings toward women. Because he is an outcast, he resents Miss Burden's kindness toward him. When she prays over him, he cannot resist his compulsion to kill. Yet he gives himself up, his escape is not meant to be successful, and he makes no effort to defend himself when cornered.

In *Light in August,* Faulkner writes with unaccustomed directness but with the poetry that makes his best passages seem incandescent. Even at the first level of narrative, you will find yourself deeply concerned about Joe Christmas and the people about him without liking him or any of them. You do care. Then you wonder whether or not Faulkner intends a second level of meaning, a symbolic one. The divided soul of Joe Christmas, his mixed blood that takes turns, Faulkner says, in dominating his actions, may make him a symbol of the divided South. Or perhaps, as his name suggests, Faulkner means him to be, if not Christ, a symbol of modern man doomed to a sort of crucifixion by his own destructive impulses and his spiritual insufficiency to deal with them. In any case you will find much to ponder in William Faulkner, much to give you both the disturbing impact of a tragic work of art and a purview of man's destiny beyond the boundaries of Yoknapatawpha County, Mississippi.

THE O. HENRY TASTE

O. Henry has had an unfortunate influence on American taste in fiction. More than any other writer he fixed the vogue of the flashy style and the surprise ending. Poe and Maupassant and a host of other writers, and of course editors and publishers, share the responsibility. But O. Henry established the popular appetite for the meretricious story with the contrived ending—one that comes about through the manipulation of plot rather than through the logic of character and events.

In "The Furnished Room," for instance, a young man searches for his lost sweetheart. He rents a room in the theatrical district of New York. The room smells of his beloved's favorite perfume. But the landlady assures him the girl has not been there. While he is ending it all with gas, we learn that the girl has occupied the room just before him and has left by the same means.

Compare this meaningless irony with another search—with the Pardoner's Tale, Geoffrey Chaucer's rendering of a medieval story of the "Three Revelers." Three young toughs set out from a tavern to find and slay Death, the killer of one of their fellows. An old man directs them to a grove where they find a great amount of gold. Two guard the treasure, while one goes to town for wine. When he returns, the two kill him, in order to possess the gold for themselves alone. They drink the wine, which the other has poisoned, and thus all three cheat themselves out of the gold but find what they were looking for. While this is a sketchy medieval morality tale, the neat ironic ending grows out of the kind of characters involved, and it embodies the logic of poetic justice. The double suicide of O. Henry's lovers is merely deplorable and clumsily coincidental.

Chaucer's story survives after nearly six hundred years; O. Henry's is painful after the first reading. The millions that O. Henry wrote about—the new middle class bubbling up in the democratic melting pot—were also his readers. As in domestic architecture, furniture, and home decoration, their literary taste was undeveloped. But long after we have rid ourselves of cupolas and horse-hair rockers festooned with antimacassars, we still find the taste even of college graduates runs largely to fiction in which plot and trick endings dominate. This tendency is helped along by the practice in high schools of writing book reports that never get beyond a synopsis of what happens and a hurried "I like it because the characters are so true to life."

To say that a fictional character is "true to life" usually implies only that he is easily recognizable as a type. On occasion, as in such novels as Sinclair Lewis' *Main Street,* the author seems to make a fresh discovery of new types of people. These types result from the pressure of social change on human beings in certain environments such as the small town. Lewis' novels have value as social documents. At the time of their publication in the boom 1920s, they turned a spotlight on the kind of crudities and spiritual poverty that exist in the midst of material abundance. But the over-all quality seems thin because Lewis relies so heavily on photographic surface realism in his social satire.

Truth to life in the highest sense in fiction as in the graphic arts demands more than literal representation of surface appearances. Even Sinclair Lewis points up the thesis he develops in each of his novels by trying to create chief characters who are more remarkable than their average associates—Carol Kennicott, George F. Babbitt, Martin Arrowsmith, Elmer Gantry, Sam Dodsworth, Anne Vickers. Ease of recognition and of pigeonholing cannot be the measure of greatness of characters in fiction. The most typical of Shakespeare's characters—his nice heroines —are forgotten. Only the sinister Lady Macbeth has joined the gallery of immortal characters.

THE SHORT STORY

The short story as we know it parallels the rise of the novel as a device for studying human beings under pressure. A long line of distinguished writers have used it with all the skill and seriousness of specialists in internal medicine using X-rays. One of the earliest of modern practitioners was Robert Browning, even though he wrote poetry. His dramatic monologues, such as "My Last Duchess" and "Fra Lippo Lippi," do precisely what Maupassant, Chekhov, and the best of contemporary short story writers accomplish: Through a single episode they cast a bright light over the lives of the chief characters.

In "My Last Duchess" the speaker is showing a guest his art treasures. He pauses before the portrait of a woman—"My last duchess," he explains and coolly tells how she failed to please him, that he "gave orders," and that she died. Between the lines the reader sees that the duchess was only a child, loving laughter and sunlight and natural things and people. Obviously she was frozen by the stuffy name-proud aristocrat. Whether the orders so smothered her happy spirit that she died, or whether the orders were more sinister, is not clear. In the high Renaissance Italian society that Browning was presenting, disposing of close relatives was common. The double irony of this short story in blank verse is that the cruel and haughty duke is a genuine connoisseur of art and that he is about to haggle with the visitor about the dowry his next duchess should bring with her.

ANTON CHEKHOV, CREATOR OF THE MODERN SHORT STORY

The creator of the modern literary short story—to distinguish the type from the commercial magazine story—is the Russian fiction writer and playwright, Anton Chekhov (1860–1904). A typical Chekhov natural slice-of-life story is one called "An Unpleasantness." A doctor at a provincial hospital works in a constant state of exasperation because of the slovenliness of the place and the ineptness of his assistant. One day when the assistant is more befuddled than usual by a hangover, the doctor strikes him and tells him he is fired. Then remorseful but confused, he rejects the assistant's apology and insists that the fellow sue him. At the home of the judge, the chairman of the hospital board simply orders the assistant to apologize and sends him back to work. The chairman says to the doctor, "Everything has to be logical with you; you drag in principles and worry about fine points, and as a result you get things all balled up." The doctor cries: "This is absurd! This is comedy! It's vile." But he drinks some vodka with the judge and the chairman, and the next day he begins again the endless round of frustrating dealings with the miserable assistant. Nothing whatever is changed.

Now this is not entertainment in the sense that a shoot-'em-up Western or detective story is. Yet I remember this story, while I have forgotten completely the TV thriller I saw last night. But more than that, this apparently artless, anticlimactic tale brings in a rush of fresh air like the opening of an outer door on a stuffy room. There in an out-of-the-way spot the troubled figure of an insignificant doctor crystallizes our own unheroic posture in the face of the small exasperations that abrade our spirits. Yet we realize that in an unromantic sense the doctor has the stuff of heroes in him, at that. He is not permitted the luxury of burning for a cause like Joan of Arc at Rouen or even of gunning down the bad man in the dusty street of a Texas town. He simply must go on trying to heal the sick, trying to make use of his inept assistant, trying to curb his own frailties.

Is such a story uplifting? Not exactly. It offers neither solace nor hope. It does not offer the illicit promise that what is wrong today will somehow be righted tomorrow. It encourages no Cinderella daydreams about unmerited rewards. It does not even offer the distraction of catastrophe. The doctor has not the stature to win release through tragic downfall any more than he has through fairy-tale triumph. Yet with our realization that of course he must stay and live with his problems, we experience relief. This is reassuring reality, the same mixture of accomplishment and frustration that gives texture to our own days.

Numbers of writers have practiced the short story with variations on the Chekhov manner, and often with distinction. The form seems especially congenial to us today, perhaps because in our fragmented society we are relieved to confront only a small segment of experience at a time. In any case, modern writers have shown great virtuosity in evoking a considerable sense of life from the three to five thousand words of an average story.

A good short story lights up details selected for their revelation of character and background, much as on a dark night the headlights of a car for a moment show up a farmhouse in sharp relief. The novel moves forward by addition of events, impressions, and comment. The short story, like poetry, relies on subtraction, on the power of suggestion with the minimum of means.

FOCUS AND POINT OF VIEW

Two of the chief decisions a short-story writer must make in order to extract the full significance from his material are in relation to his *focus* and his *point of view*. These choices can make or break his story. Focus in effect is the answer to the question, Whose story is this? Another way to put this question is, Which character is most worth revealing? Point of view means literally, From what point is the action presumably seen? It may be seen from the objective point of view of the omniscient author, from the subjective point of view of one of the characters or of one side-line observer, or from a combination of the two. You can add a great deal to your ability to savor the nuances of a story by observing how a writer uses these two devices—for every fiction writer must make decisions about both.

Ring Lardner's "Haircut" exhibits what a superior writer can do in a short story and how he does it. A gabby small-town barber chatters along about local characters and events as he cuts a stranger's hair. Out of his monologue emerges this incident: Paul Dickson, a retarded boy, is the butt of the village humor, particularly that of a brutal fellow named Jim Kendall. Paul is treated kindly by a sensitive thirty-year old woman, Julie Gregg, and by a new young doctor, Ralph Stair. Julie falls in love with Dr. Stair. Smarting at being rebuffed by Julie, Kendall sends her a false message that the doctor wishes to see her at his office at night, and then he and his cronies hide nearby and jeer when the poor girl flees miserably from what she had thought was to be a sentimental meeting. Paul tells the doctor, who is indignant. Later, to amuse himself, Kendall takes Paul along on a duck-hunting trip, and Paul accidentally shoots him dead.

The focus in this story is unusual. It is not on any one character because it would destroy the values to elevate one character to a dominant position. The focus is on the group or, if you like, on the village. Now what about the point of view? The entire story, every word, is the monologue of the barber. Why? What Lardner is doing is writing a savage indictment of the crudeness and cruelty of a small town. The barber has no grasp of the significance of what he is telling. A symbol of the insensitive natives, he thinks that Jim Kendall "certainly was a card," the humiliation of Julie and the doctor exquisitely droll. He is too dull to realize that the half-witted boy Paul has more human feelings than he has and that the shooting was not an accident. Any shift of point of view to that of the author or any perceptive character would shatter the effect that the barber's insensitivity bestows.

Through the centuries the storytellers have created make-believe characters in tales as fantastic as those with which Shahrazad beguiled King Shahriyar and as realistic as those of twentieth-century United States by such authors as Garland, Norris, Dreiser, Cather, Sinclair, Anderson, Lewis, Dos Passos, and Farrell. Following the fortunes of these imaginary people seems certain to sharpen your insight into the lives of the human beings about you and to extend your compassion for them. It also seems as true that you will come to a more perceptive reading of the character you play in the novel of your days, one that may save you from the vanity of exaggerating the importance of your triumphs or your troubles and may also give you more sympathetic appreciation of the vulnerability you share with everyone else in the human predicament.

7

LIFE ON THE STAGE

Of all the arts, drama seeks most to be lifelike. In this obvious fact lies the fascination and the instructiveness of the theater. It is as though on the stage we had a chance to see the events of life—those leading to the death of Joan of Arc or a salesman, for instance—played over, more or less as they might have happened. Or we can see life restructured, nobler, funnier, more exciting, more significant.

The theater has been marvelously inventive in creating illusions of reality and unreality. The Greek players wore masks that depersonalized them. Shakespeare's Roman Caesar and Egyptian Cleopatra acted their parts in Elizabethan dress on an almost empty stage. Ibsen's mid-nineteenth-century problem plays were acted within three walls of the middle-class Norwegian living quarters that nurtured them. The combination of scene, sound, and action gives drama means of achieving effects beyond the command of any other art. Indeed, drama may also call on song, dance, instrumental music, and painting. Because of this richness of resources, a play exists only in the individual performance. The text is only a pretext for the play.

A play's approach to lifelikeness conceals the fact that it is the art form most dependent on artifice for its success. The restrictions of time and space make it imperative for the playwright to observe a number of conventions of the theater and to learn many more devices for making plausible what happens on the stage. A play has a much tighter structure than a novel. Every line must obey an inexorable logic. Whatever is set up in the original premises of the play must be sustained. All the developments in the course of the action must be consistent with those premises, if the end is to seem inevitable. They do not necessarily have to be "true to life"—they must be true to the basic logic of the specific play.

In *Pygmalion*, Shaw asks us to believe that an uneducated London flower girl can be taught the speech and manners of an upper class gentlewoman. The fact that such a metamorphosis is not uncommon is not important. What Shaw has to do is to convince the audience at the outset that Higgins is a fanatically determined linguistics teacher and that Liza Doolittle, the flower girl, is innately intelligent. Whatever happens in the play must grow out of the kind of characters involved. The conventions of what this may be vary with different types of plays—tragedies, comedies, fantasies, expressionistic plays, and so on. But consistency of character the playwright must observe.

In order to have the characters act plausibly, in order to get the action to move, a play like a short story must have a basic situation of sufficient emotional significance to the main characters to generate action. As in a short story or a novel, the action need not be external. In Chekhov's *Cherry Orchard,* as in his story about the hospital doctor mentioned in the chapter on fiction, the meaning lies largely in what does *not* happen. Members of an old Russian family might save their heavily mortgaged estate by selling their cherry orchard for a suburban development. The sentimental aristocrats cannot think of doing this—or anything else. They reminisce and float away. The son of a former serf of the family, who has urged them to sacrifice the orchard in order to save the rest of the property, buys the estate and starts cutting down the cherry trees. The behavior of the feckless, sensitive aristocrats and that of the practical new owner reflect their basic personalities. At the same time Chekhov reveals sharply, but not unsympathetically, Russian society at a crossroads.

BALANCED CONFLICT

Whether the action is overt or psychological, the basic situation usually has within it the seeds of a balanced conflict. When in *Pygmalion* the bachelor Higgins undertakes to educate an attractive young woman, his scientific coldness and her feminine warmness are equally enough matched to guarantee a collision. In the *Cherry Orchard* the representatives of the old order stand for certain civilized values that make their refusal to be sensible not unadmirable in contrast to the crude materialism of the new order.

The conflict may be within the leading character. In fact, Aristotle in his *Poetics*, the most influential work on drama, says that the hero of a tragedy has to be a noble person with a fatal flaw. In many Greek plays that flaw is *hubris* or pride. Mary, Queen of Scots makes an excellent dramatic figure. She was beautiful and intelligent, but her overweening desire to rule led her into shady transactions and finally to death. Had she not been a queenly person, she could not evoke the empathy the audience must feel for her situation.

Empathy is a feeling of emotional involvement in the action, a feeling of understanding the behavior of the characters. It usually leads to sympathy for one or more characters, but not necessarily so. Consider your feelings for Lady Macbeth, for instance. One of the contributions drama makes to individual development is a heightening of empathic reactions—a greater insight into the degree of emotional tension in a disagreement between friends, say, or the intent behind the words in business negotiations.

The classic example of balanced conflict is Sophocles' *Antigone*. Antigone, daughter of Oedipus, faces a dilemma. A conflict often takes this form—a choice of two courses, either of which will have disastrous consequences. It is her sacred duty to bury her brother Polyneices, killed by another brother in an attempt to gain his rightful turn as ruler of Thebes. It is also Antigone's duty to obey the new king, her uncle Creon. On penalty of death, Creon has ordered that Polyneices must lie unburied.

Antigone chooses to obey what she considers the higher law of her duty to her brother, with inevitably disastrous consequences.

Beyond this dilemma Antigone's inflexible belief in the rightness of her ideas is in conflict with the uncertainty as to what is right of her sister Ismene and with the realistic attitude of King Creon. Conflicts between loyalties and conflicts between idealism and realism are among the most common in drama. Conflicts grow out of as many personal and social problems as there are plays. Plays, therefore, have the extra value of offering in dialogue what often becomes sparkling debates on problems of current interest and enduring importance. And playgoing, the most sociable way of taking an interest in an art, also leads to good conversation, for the problems at stake can be discussed as well as the play and the production.

GREEK DRAMA

The Greek drama of fifth century B.C. was a part of the life of the people to a degree that we have a hard time imagining. Each spring in honor of Dionysus, god of fertility, the state held a contest. Three playwrights were chosen. Each was allowed a day to present three tragedies and a short satire. The one, two, or three actors were furnished by the state; the chorus of citizens by a patron. The seventeen thousand citizens sat in the open tiers of the Theater of Dionysus, and a panel of citizens judged the winner.

The gods and heroes of Greek myths were the subject of the plays. Thus the Athenians—and citizens of other Greek city-states, since this was a period of peace and Greek unity—attended cycles of plays based on material with which they were completely familiar. They brought considerable sophistication to judging the dramatic treatment, the poetry—the plays were chanted in verse—and the symbolism by which the events were related to human destiny and the welfare of the state.

As in so many other aspects of Western civilization, greatness in the drama begins with the Greeks. And greatness in drama means tragedies. The Jews had no tragedies, for a jealous Yahweh would not permit man to take himself that seriously.

The Buddhists had no tragedies, for happiness consisted in squelching the passions from which tragedy springs. The Christians produced no tragedies while earthly existence was only a prelude to the hereafter. Not until the Elizabethans blended Christian conscience with a Greek sense of the importance of man in this world did tragedy again reach the heights of the Athenian theater of the mighty three—Aeschylus, Sophocles, and Euripides.

Aeschylus (c.513–c.546 B.C.) is the oldest of the three great Greek tragic poets. He fought at Marathon and Salamis, and one of his seven extant plays, *The Persians*, celebrates the Greek victories. In 468 B.C. he lost the Dionysian contest to Sophocles. Ten years later, in 458 B.C., competing for the last time, Aeschylus won the prize with the *Oresteia* trilogy, of which *Agamemnon* is the first play. He is said to have written ninety plays. The seven extant plays of Sophocles (c.495–406 B.C.)—he may have written one hundred and twenty-five—reveal powerful characterization. The greatest, *Oedipus the King*, is the source of Freud's Oedipus complex. The youngest of the trio, Euripides (c.480–406 B.C.), is also said to have written ninety plays. In his eighteen surviving plays some, such as the *Suppliants*, *The Trojan Women*, *Electra*, and *Orestes*, overlap material handled by Sophocles and Aeschylus. His treatment is more modern and realistic. Plato was twenty-two in 406 B.C., the year that both Sophocles and Euripides died. Euripides was the butt of the satire in the *Frogs* and another of the eleven comedies by Aristophanes (c.448–c.380 B.C.), one of the greatest of all comic writers. His *Lysistrata*, adapted for Broadway in recent years, is a funny exposition, with serious overtones, of how women might take over government and stop war, if they had a mind to.

THE *AGAMEMNON* OF AESCHYLUS

For our purpose, the *Agamemnon* of Aeschylus serves to illustrate the nature of the problems in the tragedies the Greek dramatists wrought and the terrible events they used for lumber. They also wrote the noblest poetry ever written.

The scenario of *Agamemnon* is brutally stark—straight from

the ancient Greek myths and the mythic events of the Trojan War. King Agamemnon returns to Argos after leading the Greeks successfully in the Trojan War. He is welcomed ceremoniously by his wife, Queen Clytemnestra. After they go within the palace, Agamemnon's war prize, Cassandra, the daughter of the King of Troy, prophesies the murder of Agamemnon and of herself. Clytemnestra kills her husband and Cassandra and, with her paramour Aegisthus by her side, boasts that she has done so, primarily, she says, because Agamemnon had sacrificed their daughter Iphigenia for the sake of the Greek army, becalmed on the way to Troy. Aegisthus brags that his villainy has been part of a long-laid plan, part of the curse put by his father on the house of Atreus. The two defy the citizens to oust them from rule of Argos.

A tangled web of family history precedes and follows this, the first of Aeschylus' three plays, the *Oresteia*. Let's go back. Agamemnon is the son of Atreus. In vengeance for the seduction of his wife by his brother Thyestes, Atreus feeds Thyestes the flesh of two of his sons. Aegisthus, who escaped his brothers' fate, makes revenge his life mission. Meanwhile, during Agamemnon's absence at Troy, his boy Orestes is sent from Argos. Years later Orestes returns and avenges his father by killing his mother and Aegisthus. Against this horrible background the adultery and murders of *Agamemnon* forge a link in a chain of events related to a central theme.

This theme seems the problem of retribution, of crime and punishment. Crime is evil; yet what besides further evil comes from vengeance? Does the crime against his family give Aegisthus any right of revenge? Is Clytemnestra justified in considering the sacrifice of Iphigenia the same as murder? And may she be allowed the luxury of indignation at the arrival of Cassandra as Agamemnon's concubine? Feeling himself responsible for the becalming of the Greek host at Aulis on the way to Troy, was Agamemnon bound to sacrifice his child? Was the abduction of Helen by Paris provocation enough to launch the Trojan War that led to the death of the finest of Greek youth and the brutal destruction of Troy under the iron hand of Agamemnon?

"THE CATCHER IS CAUGHT"

Aeschylus brings out his tremendous issues by what at first seem odd techniques to a modern playgoer. But their strangeness helps make the symbolic power of the play deeply moving. A watchman on the roof of the palace opens the play. He grumbles about his lot, watching through the years for a signal that the war is ended and Agamemnon returning. When the signal comes, he is happy for the queen, though he suppresses a hint of evil within the palace. He is like any of us, getting to work on time, tending our gardens, and leaving world affairs to the "politicians." There is a chorus of old men. They mutter among themselves, telling over the past events, raising questions, suspicious but nerveless, men of words and not of action when Cassandra tells them what is about to happen and Clytemnestra throws the facts into their faces. They are the many-tongued public, you and I and people everywhere, who stand back while the decisions of a few men bring war or peace.

There is Agamemnon, the simple soldier, still tasting the triumph over the Trojans, but meekly submitting against his will to Clytemnestra's insistence that he walk into his house on purple tapestries. This unheroic treatment of Agamemnon, the incidental realism about his harsh management of the war, and his failure to ask for his children or to mention Iphigenia, all builds up a character of the insensitive man of action, who does the dirty work we want done and sleeps well—as we do.

Finally there is Clytemnestra, one of the great evil creations of literature. With steel-nerved effrontery she plays the part of the faithful wife who wept through the ten years of waiting her husband's uncertain return. Amazing, then, is her turnabout as she opens the palace doors on the bodies of Agamemnon and Cassandra and recounts in detail her bloody deeds and her reasons. Who can say that her grief for Iphigenia is feigned or no? Or that she is insincere in her fruitless hope that now the evil genius of the house of Atreus will leave this house and "rid these walls of the mad exchange of murder"? We can only agree with the Chorus: "Reproach answers reproach, it is hard to decide. The catcher is caught, the killer pays for his kill. But the law abides while Zeus abides enthroned. That the wrongdoer suffers. That is established."

Ultimately in the third play of the trilogy, the *Eumenides,* Aeschylus resolves his dilemma as best he can: Orestes, in *The Libation Bearers,* has killed Clytemnestra out of a disinterested sense of justice. The Eumenides, the Furies, pursue him, but Athena intervenes. He is tried, and he is acquitted. So Orestes' guilt is lifted. The avenging Furies become the peaceful guardians of Athens. Out of the horror-haunted folk fantasies from which like amanitas in a drear wood spring sinister myths, Aeschylus works his way into the sunlight of the rule of law.

THE ELIZABETHAN THEATER

Two thousand years lie between the two golden ages of the drama—that of Athens under Pericles and that of London under Elizabeth I and James I. These two millennia brought changes to the physical theater as well as to the structure of society. Both influenced the style of playwriting. Aeschylus, Sophocles, Euripides, and Aristophanes immobilized their two or three chief actors with elaborate costumes, platform shoes, and towering masks with megaphonic effects. They had to do this for the actors to be seen and heard by the thousands of outdoor spectators. Thus in Greek drama acting was negligible, the chanted line all important.

By the time of Marlowe, Jonson, and Shakespeare the stage had become an infinitely more intimate affair jutting out into an unroofed courtyard, or "pit," about the size of a tennis court. Around three sides rose two or three tiers of balconies. The gentry paid half a crown and sat in "rooms," or boxes, in the balconies. The "groundlings" paid a penny and stood in the pit. The back of the stage had alcoves and balconies that served for changes of scene. Few props were used. This stage created plays like movies. The scenes unfolded virtually without pause, since there were no curtains to bring down and up while sets were being shifted.

The most significant difference, then, is that Elizabethan drama is one of action. The stage permitted a great deal of movement. Eloquent as is Elizabethan blank verse, the common medium of the playwrights, its function is to supplement and heighten the acting. Along with this change came another. The Greeks had to concentrate the play, as in *Agamemnon* and *Antigone*, on the final events. With straightforward rehearsal of preceding events, the Elizabethan play can roam at will over time and space and start the action earlier, including the causal events that bring about the final catastrophe or delay the happy ending.

THE MATERIAL OF ELIZABETHAN DRAMA

By 1600, social, intellectual, and spiritual changes profoundly affected the material of drama. England had exchanged the simple Christian piety of the Middle Ages for a troubled conscience. The austere Judeo-Christian view of the universe was incongruously married to the radiant spirit of the Renaissance with all its gusto for this life, its love of fine show, and its humanistic belief in man's unconquerable mind.

From this alliance arose a great innovation in drama as in religion and society—the individual. To the medieval writer, as to the medieval theologian, the uniqueness of every individual had no existence. In the Renaissance the single soul began to take on value, the particularities that differentiate one personality from all others began to be recorded by portrait painters and playwrights. Instead of the one, two, or three heroic actors of the Greek civic-religious plays, the Elizabethans filled the stage with sharply individualized characters of high and low degree.

The Elizabethan playwrights did abide by the convention that the chief figure in a tragedy had to be noble. Not for a long time will the beggar, the merchant, or thief be fit for anything but comedy. But as the colorful life of the streets flowed into the Blackfriars, Globe, Rose, Curtain, Fortune, and other London theaters, the merging side by side of comedy and tragedy in drama as in life brought another liberation from classic restrictions. Elizabethan drama is gamy in characters, action, and language straight from the hedgerows and taverns, but its spirit is not naturalistic but romantic. Characters are nobler, wickeder, funnier than anyone the audience knew, the action more violent, more delightful than life, the language more elevated, saltier, more poetic. Elizabeth and her loyal men were shaping a brave new world, and the bravery spilled onto the stage.

But the playgoers in Shakespeare's day were not citizens of Athens come to take part in a solemn civic occasion. Nor were they Broadway critics and first-nighters out to render sophisticated judgments. They were much more like the crowd at a baseball game or a carnival, out for an afternoon's fun, courtiers and men-about-town in the tiers of balconies and even seated at tables on the stage, servants, sailors, apprentices, and other fun-loving fellows standing on the ground about the stage. Women were rarely present, and then usually masked, nor were any sober citizens of a puritanical cast in the audience. In a city that tolerated prostitution, the theater was deemed too disreputable for actresses. Boys played women's roles, and there were companies of boys only. Like any Cape Cod summer stock group, an Elizabethan company, though licensed under the protection of a noble, had to please the customers. Its foremost responsibility was to provide fast-moving, hard-hitting action.

WILL SHAKESPEARE OF STRATFORD

Your confrontation with greatness necessarily includes the bravest of the Elizabethan poet-playwrights, William Shakespeare (1564–1616), and his most famous play, *Hamlet*. Who is this Shakespeare? The son of a well-to-do village tradesman, after a grammar school education he marries Anne Hathaway at eighteen. Leaving Anne in Stratford, he goes to London and becomes an actor in minor roles. Later he is a regular member of the Lord Chamberlain's company of players, but he acts little. He begins writing about 1591. The country boy soon associates himself with nobility, for two long poems in 1593 and 1594 are dedicated to Henry Wriothesley, Earl of Southampton. At this time Shakespeare also writes his famous sonnets. In ornate language the poet promises immortality to his dear friend through the power of his verse. The object of his affection, a young man, possibly Southampton, is stolen from him by his mistress, a dark lady. It is not improbable that this is autobiographical, but proper in Elizabethan times because of the social distance that separated the poet from his noble nineteen-year old patron, Southampton.

Meanwhile Shakespeare settles to his trade. His job is to turn out plays for his company, and until 1610 he does this in the same journeyman way that Bach composed his masterpieces. Shakespeare also is part owner of the Globe Theater. The company holds together loyally and prospers. Shakespeare becomes well-to-do, buys the biggest house in Stratford and one in London, retires, and spends his last half-dozen years as a country gentleman. His playscripts are the property of his company; he never bothers to edit any for publication. Apparently an ordinary sort of fellow, Will Shakespeare.

SHAKESPEARE'S *HAMLET*

In Christopher Marlowe's *Doctor Faustus* the hero sells himself to the devil in exchange for twenty-four years of knowledge and power. At one point he cries, in what might be the motto of the Renaissance, "Resolve me of all ambiguities!" In *Hamlet*, William Shakespeare makes one of the supreme efforts to grapple with the ambiguities of the nature of man and his relation to the universe. The play is based on a blood-and-thunder story that was lying around. It belonged to a long line of revenge plays that, as we have seen, go back to Aeschylus. The problem facing Hamlet is almost precisely that facing Orestes. The significant difference lies in the degree of certainty about the facts. In *Agamemnon*, Clytemnestra's guilt is explicit: She has committed adultery and murder. Orestes must still consider the value of vengeance. But Hamlet starts the decision-making process much farther back. His royal father is dead, and his uncle has taken over both his mother and the throne. But can he believe ghostly testimony that his uncle murdered his father and that it is Hamlet's responsibility to secure revenge?

What did Shakespeare give the raffish, boisterous customers

on that day—night performances came later—in 1601 when *Hamlet* opened at the Globe Theater? First, Shakespeare gave them a whopping good thriller. Superficially, as playwriting, *Hamlet* is an elaborate piece of stalling whereby Shakespeare with great inventiveness thinks up reasons why Hamlet should stay his hand while tension builds up to the slaughterous final scene. The genius of *Hamlet's* Shakespeare shows in how he pieced out that two-hour interval.

In the early stages of the play, Hamlet is understandably depressed. Shortly after his father's death, his mother had married his father's brother, an incestuous relation in Elizabethan times. Furthermore, instead of Prince Hamlet, the despised uncle Claudius had been elected to the throne. Hamlet is in love with Ophelia. She bows to the orders of her sanctimonious, prurient father Polonius to have no more to do with Hamlet. The ghost of his father tells Hamlet how he was poisoned by Claudius and demands revenge. Hamlet has problems.

Hamlet feigns madness as a screen while he finds opportunity to carry out his assignment. His act convinces Polonius that he is mad for love of Ophelia. But astute King Claudius fears Hamlet and sets two spies on him to ferret out the truth. Hamlet berates himself for not killing Claudius but wonders whether the ghost might not be a devil tricking him. He hits on the stratagem of a lie-dectector test by inserting the poisoning of his father in a play performed before the king and queen. The king reacts guiltily. He tries to pray but cannot. Hamlet, now for the first time certain of Claudius' guilt, finds him on his knees but refrains from killing him because to do so when he is praying will send him to heaven. He will catch him when he can send him to hell. Meanwhile he gives his mother the third degree, kills Polonius eavesdropping behind a curtain, forces his mother to admit her guilt, and destroys her loyalty to Claudius.

The king ships Hamlet to England with instructions that he be killed on arrival. At this point Ophelia goes mad just as her brother Laertes storms at the head of a mob into the castle seeking vengeance for the death of his father, Polonius. Ophelia falls into a brook and lets herself drown. Hamlet, returned to

Denmark by pirates, struggles with Laertes at Ophelia's grave to prove his love for her.

The king arranges a doubly-rigged fencing match between Hamlet and Laertes as a safe way to get rid of Hamlet. The queen drinks from Hamlet's cup of poisoned wine. Hamlet is mortally wounded by Laertes' poisoned rapier, but in a scuffle exchanges rapiers and stabs Laertes with the poisoned one. The queen dies, the dying Laertes confesses the plot against Hamlet, and Hamlet at last kills the king before he himself dies. So Shakespeare keeps conflict between the two clever opponents agitated to the maximum intensity until the pins all go down in the final catastrophe.

SHAKESPEARE'S POETRY

Yet while Shakespeare was filling the stage with intrigue and violence and building up suspense to the cracking point, he was filling the air with poetry of enchanting loveliness and breath-stopping eloquence. It seems hard to believe that the rough and tumble Elizabethan audience relished their melodrama decked out in verse. But they had grown used to Marlowe's mighty line before Shakespeare had achieved his mastery of blank verse. Only once in history has it seemed congruous that soldiers should say: "But, look, the morn in russet mantle clad,/Walks o'er the dew of yon high eastward hill." Or that a ghost should say: "And duller shouldst thou be than the fat weed/That roots itself in ease on Lethe wharf." No single character in literature has ever matched the ease and variety of Hamlet's lines. At the one extreme is the pure Anglo-Saxon prose he speaks when he pretends madness or when he speaks on a level of low intensity, as to Rosenkrantz and Guildenstern, the players, and the grave-diggers. This prose itself varies from such spare simplicity as, "How long will a man lie 'i th' earth ere he rot?" to such racy idiom as Hamlet's dismissal of Polonius' complaint that a player's speech is too long: "It shall to the barber's, with your beard. Prithee, say on; he's for a jig or a tale of bawdry, or he sleeps: say on; come to Hecuba."

Hamlet's blank verse is one of the supreme achievements in art. It can be appreciated only as heard spoken by a professional Shakespearean actor and after it becomes familiar line by line. Yet there is virtue, too, in an unassuming trial of your own. Take the familiar soliloquy in Scene 1, Act III, that begins "To be or not to be." Imagine that you are Hamlet and read aloud without exaggeration, just with such changes in your expression as reflect your feelings as the thoughts on suicide flow through your mind. Read the entire soliloquy several times. After a hundred readings it grows more magical. Shakespeare develops the thought in a great arc that begins in feverish questioning in broken ascending rhythms, slows down at the thought of what the dreams of a suicide might be, and then beginning with "For who would bear the whips and scorns of time" descends in three slow sentences to the admission that, just as men go on living for dread of something after death, so too much thinking leads to irresolution and the defeat of important actions. Throughout the soliloquy images toss in the surge of the thought like whitecaps in the sea. What image of death has ever been more ominous or more beautiful than "The undiscovered country from whose bourn/No traveller returns"?

THE PROBLEMS OF A RENAISSANCE PRINCE

Behind the melodrama, behind the poetry, what sort of problems does Shakespeare come to grips with? Are we not unwary to think the theme is indecision, the problem that of the man of thought in a world of action, of the neurotic who cannot make up his mind? As we have seen, Shakespeare's key problem as a playwright was to hold Hamlet back until the big final scene. Then, too, is not Hamlet decisive in feigning madness, arranging the play to trap the king, coming to an understanding with his mother, killing Polonius, sending Rosenkrantz and Guildenstern to their deaths, grappling with Laertes at the grave of Ophelia, apologizing to him, accepting the fencing bout, killing the king, and with his dying breath bestowing his vote for the throne on young Fortinbras? Hamlet seems no more truly indecisive than he seems to deserve the title "Melancholy Dane."

Rather Hamlet is a Renaissance prince "be-netted round with

villainies." He is intelligent, witty, sensitive, brave, and magnanimous—a fictional version of Castiglione's courtier and Sir
Philip Sidney. True, like Shakespeare himself, he was susceptible
to periods of depression. Who but an oaf could contemplate the
evil that envelops Hamlet and not be depressed? Hamlet meeting
Rosenkrantz and Guildenstern on their arrival at Elsinore and
Hamlet in his two preliminary scenes with the players is a cultivated witty person, and in his make-believe mad scenes he is
funny. Hamlet's conduct toward Laertes is always correct and
generous. Though knowing that he is in mortal danger from his
murderer stepfather, Hamlet is fearless in his dealings with him.
Claudius, an intelligent man, never for a moment underrates
his nephew. Hamlet is exhilarated at the prospect of outwitting
Rosenkrantz and Guildenstern. His toughness in sending them to
be killed evokes Horatio's admiring, "Why, what a king is this!"

The fall of princes was the chief tragic theme of the Middle
Ages and Renaissance. Shakespeare could use no other, and
never did. Hamlet is therefore no common hero with whom we
can identify ourselves in his triumph over unequal odds. Nor
is he an average man, flawed with the ignobilities of the rest
of us. If he is a symbol, is he not universalized from a particular
prince surrounded by evil in particular forms to man with all his
essential goodness and intelligence still barred by the imper-
fections of his nature from inheriting the ideal society that is
rightfully his?

COMEDY AS SOCIAL CRITICISM

The discrepancy between reality and man's ideal potentiality
is at the heart of tragedy. The discrepancy between men's pre-
tensions and reality is the root of comedy. In tragedy the hero,
like Agamemnon and Hamlet, is at odds with the society about
him. In comedy he is, too—only the author and the audience are
on the side of society. The comic spirit is social, conservative, and
critical. It may include criticism of a particular society itself for
not living up to its own standards, but more often it condemns an
individual's deviation from norms of group behavior. If one
country bumpkin meets ten city slickers, he finds nothing to laugh

about. But if he and nine of his cronies meet one city slicker, he is much amused. Comedy is a majority matter.

In Shakespeare's *Twelfth Night* the vain and humorless Malvolio is held up to ridicule for being foolish enough to imagine that the lovely Olivia is in love with him. But what puts a cutting edge on the laughter is the fact that Olivia is a rich countess and Malvolio only her steward. Shakespeare's comedies are mostly romantic with the interest divided between romance and farcical mistaken-identity mix-ups that come down from the Roman playwrights Plautus and Terence. Shakespeare used comedy both as comic relief in his tragedies (and to keep the clowns of his company busy), as in the gravediggers' scene in *Hamlet,* and as delicious fantasy, as in the rehearsal of the play in *Midsummer Night's Dream.*

Plautus and Terence were the inspiration for the comedies of Ben Jonson. *Every Man in His Humour* (1598) was played at the Curtain Theater by Shakespeare's company with Shakespeare in the cast. The "humour," or eccentricity, of the main character is jealousy. He is an early member of a long line of city merchants with pretty wives who are "gulled" by young gallants. Bobadill, a cowardly braggart, and Brainworm, a mischief-making servant, have many successors. Jonson's most famous play is *Volpone,* or *The Fox.* The rich and childless Volpone pretends that he is dying. Mosca, (the fly), his confederate, extracts gifts for Volpone from the greedy would-be heirs—Voltore (the vulture), Corbaccio (the crow), and Corvino (the raven). In the end the cheats and double-crossers are all exposed. Mordant as the satire is in *Volpone* and a host of other Elizabethan comedies of humours, the characters tend by definition to be gross exaggerations and in time to become stereotypes.

Jean Baptiste Poquelin (1622–1673), actor, playwright, producer, and director, used the name Molière. It is the greatest name in the theater after Shakespeare's day. Using the picture-frame stage with which we are familiar, Molière developed the comedy of social criticism that lives on today, notably in the work of George Bernard Shaw. He broadened the target to ridicule the French society of his day. This is amusing, for the satirist of the false sophistication and insincerities of the society of Louis IV worked for Louis. Such titles as *The Miser, The Bourgeois Gentleman, The Learned Women, The Imaginary Invalid* name some of Molière's targets. *Tartuffe,* a satire of religious sham, and *The Misanthrope* are his best-known plays.

In *The Misanthrope* the central figure Alceste finds the insincerities of society unbearable and insists on expressing his opinion on all occasions. These occasions range from telling a poetaster that his sonnet is execrable to criticizing the coquetry of Célimène, the young widow he loves. Molière finds plenty of foolishness and hypocrisy to exasperate Alceste, but Alceste's excessive righteousness makes him ridiculous, too. Today we would call him a neurotic perfectionist. Molière is saying that, while society is an irrational affair, the man of good sense must develop a defensive tolerance if he is to live sanely within society.

THE COMEDY OF MANNERS

In England, with the reopening of the theaters following the Restoration of Charles II in 1660, the reaction against the overthrown Puritan rule led to the development of the comedy of manners. The world is constricted to that of fashionable society. The underlying moral purpose of Aristophanes, Jonson, and Molière is absent. The Restoration playwrights are concerned in exhibiting on the stage the virtues of their unvirtuous society. These were manners, gaiety, sophistication, and above all verbal wit.

The Way of the World (1700) by William Congreve (1670–1729) is the English masterpiece of the comedy of manners. The hero and heroine, Mirabell and Millamant, might be described as a pair of Shakespearean lovers who have made all the adjustments necessary to be comfortable in a Molièrean society. The way of the world is a good-humored cynical one. Mirabell and Millamant do not wish it different. The end of the complex action is that Mirabell wins Millamant and her fortune by frustrating the plot of his friend Fainall to gain control of Fainall's wife's fortune and that of her mother. The upside-down Restoration values are revealed in the fact that Fainall's wife is Mirabell's former mistress and that she aids Mirabell in his own comic but cruel plot against her mother, the foolish Lady Wishfort.

But *The Way of the World* lives by its dialogue. The subtle individualizing quality bestowed on their speech gives Shakespearean solidity to Congreve's roster of fantastic characters, all in their varying levels and modes of deviation from good taste— the vulgar Lady Wishfort, the would-be wit Witwoud, the fake roaring-boy Petulant, the Scotch countryman Sir Wilfull Witwoud, and the low-comedy servants. Congreve's own wit lies in giving all of his characters good lines. They may make us laugh at the character uttering them, but they are always colorful. Instead of being filled with mechanical malapropisms, Lady Wishfort's speech varies from the highfalutin, "But as I am a person, Sir Rowland, you must not attribute my yielding to any sinister appetite or indigestion of widowhood" to her tongue-lashing of her maid Foible: "Away, out, go set up for yourself again!—do, drive a trade, do, with your three-penny-worth of small ware, flaunting upon a pack-thread, under a brandy-seller's bulk, or against a dead wall by a ballad-monger. Go, hang out an old Frisoneer gorget with a yard of yellow colberteen again! do! an old gnawed mask, two rows of pins and a child's fiddle; a glass necklace with the beads broken, and a quilted nightcap with one ear." Witwoud is not witless. His epigrammatic "A wit should no more be sincere than a woman constant; one argues decay of parts, as t'other of beauty" is a line Congreve might have assigned to his good friend Anne Bracegirdle, who played Millamant. In a hundred other parts Anne Bracegirdle taught Restoration belles how to be ladies.

Congreve faces his greatest challenge when his hero and heroine, Mirabell and Millamant, are alone and natural and must exemplify the kind of society Congreve would have the audience believe admirable. How well he succeeds is shown in this speech of Millamant's in a famous scene in which they bargain about the conditions of their marriage:

Trifles—as liberty to pay and receive visits to and from whom I please; to write and receive letters, without interrogatories or wry faces on your part; to wear what I please; and choose conversation with regard only to my own taste; to have no obligation upon me to converse with wits that I don't like, because they are your acquaintances; or to be intimate with fools because they may be your relations. Come to dinner when I please, dine in my dressing-room when I'm out of humour, without giving a reason. To closet inviolate; to be sole empress of my tea-table, which you must never presume to approach without first asking leave. And lastly, wherever I am, you shall always knock at the door before you come in. These articles subscribed, if I continue to endure you a little longer, I may by degrees dwindle into a wife.

THE PROBLEM PLAYS OF IBSEN AND SHAW

Under fiction we have noted that the tandem forces of democracy and industrialization left the nineteenth-century writer preoccupied with the problems of the new society. Hendrik Ibsen (1828–1906), a Norwegian who wrote plays about Norway from voluntary exile, is the father of modern drama and the creator of the problem play. The problem play differs from others in dealing with specific current social problems. Of course, behind these are universal ones. In *Ghosts*, for instance, Ibsen attacks the hypocrisy of middle-class society for failing to face the serious question of hereditary venereal disease. In *The Doll's House* he deals with a modern woman's struggle to keep marriage from blocking her efforts to achieve an identity of her own. *An Enemy of the People* is a sardonic comedy, in which the blunt hero is condemned by his townsmen when he tries to serve them. In these and his other problem plays Ibsen turns his ironic vision on the difficulties of the individual in maintaining his integrity against the hypocrisy and stupidity of the crowd.

In *The Wild Duck*, Ibsen moves away from realism toward the symbolism and expressionism that have played so interesting a role in the modern theater. It is a strange mixture of satire and tragedy. Old Werle, typical of the pillars of society that Ibsen liked to pull down, has ruined his business associate, old Ekdal. His son, Gregers Werle, a militant idealist, persuades Ekdal's son, the befogged Hialmar Ekdal, to take several actions contrary to his sentimental, self-indulgent nature. When young Ekdal learns that the elder Werle is the father of his fourteen-year-old daughter Hedvig, he makes a gesture of abandoning his family. Hedvig is egged on by the righteous Gregers Werle to prove her love to Hialmar by sacrificing the thing she loves most, her pet wild duck. Instead, the child emulates the supposed habit of an injured wild duck and kills herself.

Ibsen has a strain of ironic humor that sometimes, as in *An Enemy of the People* and *The Wild Duck*, seems to be turned against himself. In the earlier plays the hope behind the lugubrious events is that society may be redeemed by leadership of high integrity. Yet Dr. Stockman, the hero in *An Enemy of the People*, and young Werle in *The Wild Duck* are rendered ineffectual by an overdose of integrity. Against Greger Werle's advocacy of the "claim of the ideal," Ibsen seems to recommend through the drunken Dr. Relling the "life-lie," the illusions that permit inadequate human beings to be happy in an imperfect world. Ibsen is not being inconsistent. He is correcting the record to make clear that muddleheaded "nice guys" such as young Ekdal and inflexible idealists like young Werle can cause as much trouble as wicked characters such as old Werle and dull-witted citizens at large.

Ibsen's plays roused all Europe to furious debate of the issues he raised. But they have had the dramatic power to hold the stage to this day and to influence generations of playwrights. Chekhov, Strindberg, Hauptmann, Shaw, Galsworthy, and O'Neill all stand in his debt.

George Bernard Shaw (1856–1950) carried on the problem play but added wit and greater intellectual range. Shaw also had a love of controversy and a flair for publicity, and he published his plays in book form with elaborate prefaces and epilogues. His ideas never lacked exposure. Shaw had his first play staged by Ibsen's producer in 1892, and was working on a play at the time of his death at ninety-four, an awesome record exceeded by the three great Greeks, Lope de Vega, and whom else? Long after the public ceased to be shocked by his subjects, such as prostitution in *Mrs. Warren's Profession* (1902), and his attacks on everything orthodox, about a dozen of his fifty or so plays continue as fixtures of the stage on their merits as good theater.

Shaw's gifts in profusion are demonstrated in such plays as *Arms and the Man* (1894), *Candida* (1895), *The Devil's Disciple* (1897), *Caesar and Cleopatra* (1899), *Man and Superman* (1903), *Major Barbara* (1905), *The Doctor's Dilemma* (1906), *Androcles and the Lion* (1912), *Pygmalion* (1913), *Back to Methuselah* (1922), and *Saint Joan* (1923). In this long and distinguished career Shaw accomplished the remarkable tour-de-force of managing his stagecraft skilfully, writing dialogue that almost matches the sparkle of Congreve's, and of editorializing through his characters on every major issue touching the public welfare. In using a play to offer his personal opinions on everything from war and womanhood to phonetic spelling, Shaw defied the canons of playwriting. But he demonstrated that one man with fresh ideas and command of an art form to express them can make the world listen to him, even when what he says undermines everything they believe.

EUGENE O'NEILL'S TRAGIC CENTURY

In the twentieth century artists have reacted with far more intense moral feeling to the tragic conflicts of our time than have members of any other segment of society. The horror expressed by press, pulpit, and public at man's inhumanity to man during the past sixty years seems soon eased by words. But the work of graphic artists such a Käthe Kollwitz, Georg Grosz, Picasso, and Georges Rouault and of writers such as Franz Kafka and Boris Pasternak are voices of the conscience of mankind that will never be stilled.

The modern tragedy, of which even war is a symptom, is man's loss of a unifying purpose in the universe. As he has gained more and more knowledge of the physical world and has wrung from it increasing material comfort, he has lost the sense of a personal identity and of belonging to a society in which work, art, and religion are shared as a common experience—a state that, in spite of all the miseries of the past, he has often enjoyed. A Mexican peasant works in the fields, worships in the one village church, and dances in the village square with members of families he has known all his life. He has a sense of personal and communal wholeness, no matter how poor his lot.

An American or European lives in an apartment or a suburban box, surrounded by strangers. He spends his days away from his family among other strangers making and selling things and services that give him no pleasure. He is transferred to Milan or São Paulo or Wheeling, West Virginia. His children leave home, marry strangers, and become strangers. His ability to gather messages from all over the world brings him no solace— only the conviction that civilization is doomed. No matter how much better off than the poor Mexican he may seem, he is filled with a sense of anonymity, of loneliness, of meaninglessness, of despair. His greatest need is to be somebody, somehow.

In "Dover Beach" the Victorian poet Matthew Arnold neatly described modern man's position as being between two worlds, one dead—the world of past faith—and one "powerless to be born"—the world of the future, to be realized perhaps through science. Modern man's lack, he pinpoints, is certitude. The century since "Dover Beach" has brought more rather than less uncertainty about human destiny. To a significant degree man has lost confidence in his own importance and his sense of relatedness to other men. We see this feeling of isolation and anonymity reflected in all of the arts.

No artist has sought more persistently, variously, or honorably to deal with the destiny of man in this tragic century than has the playwright Eugene O'Neill (1888–1953). The moral seriousness that moved him at all times, his bold technical innovation, and the weight of his success in the theater make him the foremost figure in the history of American drama and our greatest American creative artist since Mark Twain.

O'Neill's plays fall into three groups: The early expressionistic ones include *The Emperor Jones, The Hairy Ape, Anna Christie, All God's Chillun Got Wings,* and *Desire Under the Elms.* They appeared on Broadway in the 1920s and are now classics of the American stage. The second group is characterized by greater technical and psychological complexity. Its most important representatives are *The Great God Brown, Strange Interlude,* and *Mourning Becomes Electra.* The autobiographical pieces come last: *Ah, Wilderness, The Iceman Cometh,* and *Long Day's Journey into Night.* These eleven works give O'Neill stature because the originality of what he has to say is fused with the originality of his technique. This balance is rare, especially among American playwrights. Broadway box-office pressure has given good theater precedence over philosophical content. O'Neill wrote a number of plays such as his first success *Beyond the Horizon, Marco Millions,* and *Lazarus Laughed* that fall short of his best work, but even his failures are major creative efforts.

The central theme running through O'Neill's plays is the eternal struggle of man to justify his existence in a scheme of things that includes not only hostile external forces but also the destructive elements within him. Today we have an international school of playwrights who accept this state of affairs with casual nihilism. What ties O'Neill to Shakespeare and the Greek tragic poets is precisely his refusal to accept. His plays are full of damaged souls overwhelmed by evil. Defeat is their inescapable end. Yet O'Neill shares the true tragic sense that this is not man's proper state. He declares his modernity, however, by stating his characters' problems in the social and psychological conditions of their times. He never found any satisfactory answers, but neither did he give up the effort nor turn by default to the answers of the past. Painful confrontation with truth is as close as his characters get to answers.

THE HOUSE OF O'NEILL

Never repeating himself, O'Neill carried on his arduous search for man's lost dignity through the three groups of his plays. In the first group *Emperor Jones* is an exciting introduction to the modern theater. Brutus Jones, an ex-Pullman porter, takes on the title, trappings, and power of ruler of a West Indies island. The natives, led by a witch doctor, rise against him. In his flight through the jungle in a night of terror, Jones casts off one by one parts of his gaudy uniform and with them the values of the Western white man in which he is also masquerading. He is true to himself only when he finds his way back to his African origins, though he has to die to do so.

In *The Hairy Ape,* Yank, a ship's fireman, tries to validate the proposition that only people like him really "belong" in the modern world of machines because they make them run. He fails to make his point and comes to his death in the arms of a gorilla in the zoo. In *Desire Under the Elms* the hardness of life on a rocky New England farm and the hardness of the Puritan faith of his fathers have made Ephraim Cabot a hard man, hated by his son Eben. Marriage to his young third wife, Abbie, softens him. He promises to cut Eben out of his mother's share of the farm, if Abbie will give him a baby. With Eben's help she does. But then Abbie can prove her love for Eben only by killing the baby. Ephraim returns to his natural granitic condition. And again O'Neill seems to say that the evils that poison our social system cannot be cast out by denial alone but only by first recognizing the monstrous nature of the system itself.

Mourning Becomes Electra is O'Neill's chief work. It consists of three connected plays based on the house of Atreus myth in the Aeschylus trilogy mentioned in the beginning of this chapter. But since he was retelling the grim story in Freudian terms, O'Neill introduced material from the Oedipus myth. In place of Agamemnon returning to his palace in Argos after the Trojan War, General Ezra Mannon returns to his white-pillared Greek Revival house, in a New England seaport at the end of the Civil War. The other members of the Mannon family re-enact the parts of Clytemnestra, Aegisthus, Orestes, and Electra, with Orin (Orestes) given an Oedipus attraction toward his mother Christine (Clytemnestra) and an incestuous attraction toward his sister Lavinia (Electra). O'Neill also makes Lavinia the main character, rather than her brother. All die violently except Lavinia, whose punishment is to live on among the ghosts in the House of Mannon.

O'Neill is not merely doing over Aeschylus in Civil War costumes, nor is he translating the terrible deeds of the house of Atreus into a psychoanalytical case history. During the twenties the popularization of Freud's theories coincided with the postwar condemnation of the joylessness of the narrower side of the Puritan tradition in American life. Yet *Mourning Becomes Electra* is not basically any more an indictment of Puritanism than *Desire Under the Elms* is. O'Neill uses the New England characters and their environment because he knows them. But more immediately he is enacting through them the tragic fission that man's animality introduces into life in a society that keeps its equilibrium by imposing on the individual a harsh system of sanctions and repressions. Beyond this conflict at the sexual level is the larger drama of man's dream of a world of love and peace and beauty destroyed by the dark promptings of man's baser passions.

Towards the end of his career, the thrust of O'Neill's creative powers carried him back, surprisingly, to plays of orthodox construction and personally experienced matter. The first, *Ah, Wilderness!* (1933) is usually described as a nostalgic comedy derived from O'Neill's memories of his adolescence. The title from the *Rubaiyat* is a symbol of the intoxication young Richard Miller extracts from first love and the verse of the fleshly school of late nineteenth-century poets. The trials of the family of a romantic boy and the small-town pleasures of a simpler day show O'Neill in the unsuspected role of master of domestic comedy. But Richard's skirmish with a harlot and drunkenness and his alcoholic uncle's messed-up life are too painful to be comic.

In *The Iceman Cometh,* O'Neill moved from his boyhood memories of New London, Connecticut, to memories of his young manhood as he lost himself in drink and the fellowship of down-and-outers. A motley group hanging around a waterfront bar console themselves with what they are going to do as soon as circumstances permit their return to their former existences. When the chance comes, not one gets away; they all are happier as failures cherishing their illusions. Coming after the elevated striving of the middle plays, the ambivalent handling of defeat in *The Iceman Cometh* is disconcerting. For once, O'Neill seems to endorse defeat as a state of being.

The posthumous publication and performance of *Long Day's Journey into Night* made clear that O'Neill's plays were to a considerable extent transcripts of the tragedy of the House of O'Neill. In this last unendurably sad play, Eugene O'Neill tried, like Orestes, to come to an accommodation with the Furies pursuing him by putting his family and himself on the stage without concealment. So he confronts his father, who won cheap success as the star of the melodrama, *The Count of Monte Cristo,* and who turned stinginess to sin. He contemplates his older brother, a useless alcoholic. He faces again toward the horror of his mother's addiction to narcotics. And he forces himself to live over the bitter experiences of a hypersensitive boy burdened by the knowledge of evil. *Long Day's Journey into Night* does much to show how an artist may recombine the raw materials of his life into a work of art and how his private agonies may drive him to play God and fashion imperfect microcosms of his own. O'Neill won the Nobel Prize, but he did not escape the doom on his house by writing plays. He was himself a sorry father. His two sons became alcoholics, one of them ending by suicide his promising career as a student of Greek drama.

Eugene O'Neill lacked only one gift, eloquence. His dialogue never reaches a level to match the high seriousness of his themes and the originality of the rest of his dramatic inventions. He stands, however, as a major figure in world drama and the playwright who has made the most profound effort to deal in universal terms with the spiritual problems of our tragic century.

8

THE POET'S TRADE

The Irish physician-poet Oliver St. John Gogarty says:

> What should we know,
> For better or worse,
> Of the Long Ago,
> Were it not for Verse?

The question is serious. Much of what we call history has its first draft in oral recitation, not writing. Much of what we know about early English history goes back a thousand years to the Anglo-Saxon poets, who were called *scops*, or "makers," and to their predecessors. Since it is easier to memorize verse than prose, the making, memorizing, and reciting of verse have been a natural act in all human societies. Chaucer, one of the subtlest of poets, wrote clumsy prose. In Albania and in our own mountains today there are men and women who cannot read or write but who can recite historical verse narratives and ballads by the hour. Poetry has played an active role in human affairs for many centuries. Perhaps you have missed the value it may have for you.

Of course, the forms and functions of poetry have been extended beyond those of early narratives. If you are not accustomed to reading verse, you will have to be patient with yourself until you gain the understanding that will lead you to the rewards ahead.

WHAT IS A POET?

First of all, what is a poet? If you have in your mind an image of an effeminate fellow who is of no use in everyday affairs, you have merely been taken in by a late nineteenth-century caricature. Most good poets have been serious and intelligent men of the world. (Curiously, only two poets of first-line importance have been women—Sappho and Emily Dickinson.) Some poets have carried heavy practical responsibilities. Before he wrote his greatest poems, John Milton had spent years as a propagandist for the Puritan cause. Goethe gave as much of his life to science as to literature. Two leading poets of our time have been businessmen—T. S. Eliot, partner in a publishing house, and Wallace Stevens, vice president of an insurance company—and two, William Carlos Williams and Oliver St. John Gogarty, have been practicing physicians. Today most American and English poets work at full-time jobs in universities.

Even among poets who have not seemed to be gainfully employed, the ones who have achieved anything like greatness have worked hard at their trade. Take Lord Byron. In looks and behavior he created the image of the romantic poetic personality —elegant, amorous, undisciplined, morbidly introspective, antisocial. True, he engaged in various sensational love affairs and did not shun publicity. Yet in his short life he published as much verse as most poets who have lived twice as long, and he was paid handsomely for it, possibly as much as any poet who ever lived. And he gave his wealth, his prestige, and his life to the cause of Greek freedom.

What is a poet? He is first of all an observer of scientific persistence and precision. He is acutely aware. He sees more than the rest of us, whether he is a Byron looking at society, a Wordsworth looking at a flower, or a Keats looking at himself. He is a sensitive reactor. A poet feels what he sees with what may seem abnormal intensity. He is delighted, angered, or depressed to a greater degree than most of us are. A characteristic habit of mind of the poet—he associates. He remembers what he has experienced; he puts together not merely A and B but A and Q. Finally, he records. This last act is the special one that separates the poet from the poetic person—the musician, the child, or perhaps the florist or hardware store owner. He not only writes verse; he has to write it. This is a sort of compulsion, a reflex involving the mystery of creativeness. The record of experience, therefore, is never a literal account of an event or thoughts about an event—nor is meant to be. The record is not even what the poet thinks an event *means*. It is a poem. No matter what the event was, no matter what the reaction to the event was, *the poem is the experience,* for the poet and for you, the reader.

CREATING A POEM

Robert Herrick, the seventeenth-century Devon curate, wrote one of the most perceptive accounts of the way in which poetry is written.

NOT EVERY DAY FIT FOR VERSE

'Tis not ev'ry day that I
Fitted am to prophesy.
No, but when the spirit fills
The fantastic pannicles
Full of fire, then I write
As the godhead doth indite.
Thus enraged, my lines are hurled
Like the Sibyl's through the world.
Look how next the holy fire
Either slakes or doth retire;
So the fancy cools, till when
That brave spirit comes again.

As in science, the act of creating a poem involves an element of what for a better explanation we lamely call inspiration. But the mind must be prepared; to put it to use when it comes, the craft must be already mastered. In a statement matching Herrick's, Archibald MacLeish has expressed the way that a poem takes hold of a poet with irresistible urgency.

WORDS IN TIME

Bewildered with the broken tongue
Of wakened angels in our sleep—
Then, lost the music that was sung
And lost the light time cannot keep!

There is a moment when we lie
Bewildered, wakened out of sleep,
When light and sound and all reply:
That moment time must tame and keep.

That moment, like a flight of birds
Flung from the branches where they sleep,
The poet with a beat of words
Flings into time for time to keep.

MacLeish's poem serves to illustrate what a poet is doing and
how he does it. He says that the arrival of the final concept of a
poem—the time of writing—is like waking from a dream. For a
moment everything is vividly immediate. That is the moment
the poet must seize to put his vision into words.

IMAGES, ASSOCIATION, AND METAPHORS

MacLeish thinks of the act of writing his thoughts into a poem
as an "act of flinging." As he imagines words being flung, he is
reminded of birds being startled from a branch where they have
been sleeping. And since, once written, words take on a certain
permanence, they are flung "into time," into the future.

This one problem illustrates perfectly the poet's approach. It is
impossible to fling words. MacLeish knows it as well as you do.
But *it seems as if* he flings them. You might take "it seems as if"
as a basic clue to poetry. A poem is a statement that cannot be
made equally well in prose. A poet has some thoughts, he writes
them as words on a piece of paper; the words are printed in
books and magazines; they are read, often centuries after they
are written. Such a prose statement does not include what the
poet considers most significant—what he *feels* he is doing. He
feels—well, as if he were flinging his words into the future. You
probably have noticed that Herrick used the same image; he

felt as if his words were "hurled through the world." And Shelley in his famous "Ode to the West Wind" felt as if his words were driven over the universe and scattered among mankind.

Each of these three poets finds his statement of what he feels he is doing is inadequate. Each adds something—how this "as if" *seems*. Herrick says his lines are "hurled *like the Sibyl's* through the world." Shelley says:

> Drive my dead thoughts over the universe
> *Like withered leaves* to quicken a new birth! . . .
>
> Scatter, *as from an unextinguished hearth*
> *Ashes and sparks*, my words among mankind!

And MacLeish finds the perfect image in "Like the flight of birds flung from the branches where they sleep." So you go one step farther in your understanding of a poet's trade. In his effort to say what his feeling about an experience seems, he reaches out to find something that it is like—a comparison, a metaphor. The poet tries to make the reader feel what he feels. If you will close your eyes and think about an experience that involves *feeling*— say, about someone you love—you will discover that it is impossible for you to feel in abstract terms. You can say, "She is a lovely person of great charm." But that is not really what you feel. Nor does it communicate to me the least bit of what you feel. But if you were to say—had not Robert Burns said it first— "O, my love is like a red, red rose," I would catch something of the fervor of your feeling, as well as the loveliness and charm of your beloved. A rose is tangible. It evokes an *image*, sensory impressions—in this case of smell, sight, and even touch. Much of the content of poems, you will find, is concrete imagery. And much of it is metaphoric—various sorts of figures of speech that try to arouse in you, by *association*, the feeling the poet has about his unique experience.

Metaphors are at the heart of the difficulty most persons have in understanding poetry. The average adult lives in a world of matter-of-fact problems. He has patiently disciplined himself to identify a spade not merely as a spade but as a long-handled instrument for digging, or something of the sort. That is, the practical affairs of life inevitably force us to think factually and to use words in literal ways. But small children are not so conditioned. They say things like, "Look, Mommy, the sky's full of whipped cream." And the poet Richard Wilbur can say, "Outside the open window the morning air is all awash with angels."

INTENSITY, COMPRESSION, AND SUGGESTION

Any work of art to be first rate must continue to generate in the experienced observer intensity of feeling. This is brought about to a considerable extent by tensions in the work itself. After a few readings many of the poems by such poets as Tennyson, Elizabeth Barrett Browning, Meredith, Swinburne, Longfellow, Whittier, and Poe seem intolerably limp. The lack of tension usually is not in the themes, which are emotional enough. It comes from a certain slackness in the entire poetic process. The two leading causes seem to me to be (a) over-explicitness and (b) colorlessness of statement. Read through this poem by Matthew Arnold:

REQUIESCAT

Strew on her roses, roses,
　　And never a spray of yew!
In quiet she reposes;
　　Ah would that I did too!

Her mirth the world required;
　　She bathed it in smiles of glee.
But her heart was tired, tired,
　　And now they let her be.

Her life was turning, turning,
　　In mazes of heat and sound.
But for peace her soul was yearning,
　　And now peace laps her round.

Her cabined, ample spirit,
　　It fluttered and failed for breath.
Tonight it doth inherit
　　The vasty hall of death.

The first three lines have an admirable simplicity and hit a fresh note—let the lovely rose, not the dismal yew, be the symbol of the death of this woman. But the last line of the first stanza is distressingly explicit. It is embarrassing. From the prosaic first line on, the second stanza is colorless, and its second line is pure bathos. The first two lines of the third stanza are striking, though puzzling. The third and fourth lines are commonplace. Then in Herrick's words, the godhead must have filled Arnold's "fantastic pannicles" full of fire, for the fourth stanza is one of the great ones in English. The adjectives "cabined" and "ample" are unusual in combination with spirit. The image of the spirit fluttering and failing for breath is gripping. Then the last two lines, lifted by the brilliantly chosen words "inherit" and "vasty" rise to a wholly new level of intensity. Arnold compressed into one stanza a universal statement about death, one that faces the inevitability of death forthrightly, yet rises above personal grief and affirms the essential nobility of the individual human spirit.

You might almost define intensity in a poem as the result of the amount of suggestion evoked by the greatest economy of means. Folk ballads are often masterpieces of evocation by a minimum of words. You will find in the wonderful Scottish ballad of "Sir Patrick Spence" how much tension can be generated in a few lines. Like all true folk ballads it is anonymous. It probably goes back to a fifteenth-century version. I have anglicized the dialect for easier reading.

SIR PATRICK SPENCE

The king sits in Dumferling town,
    Drinking his blood-red wine;
"Oh where will I get a good sailor
    To sail this ship of mine?"

Up and spake an eldern knight,
    Sat at the king's right knee:
"Sir Patrick Spence is the best sailor
    That sails upon the sea."

The king has written a broad letter,
    And signed it wi' his hand,

And sent it to Sir Patrick Spence,
  Was walking on the sand.

The first line that Sir Patrick read,
  A loud laugh laughed he;
The next line that Sir Patrick read,
  The tear blinded his ee.

"Oh who is this has done this deed,
  This ill deed done to me,
To send me out this time o' the year,
  To sail upon the sea!

"Make haste, make haste, my merry men all,
  Our good ship sails the morn!"
"Oh say not so, my master dear,
  For I fear a deadly storm.

"Late, late yestreen I saw the new moon
  Wi' the old moon in her arm,
And I fear, I fear, my dear master,
  That we will come to harm."

Oh our Scots nobles were right loath
  To wet their cork-heeled shoon;
But long ere a' the play were played,
  Their hats they swam aboon.

Oh long, long may their ladies sit
  Wi' their fans into their hand,
Or e'er they see Sir Patrick Spence
  Come sailing to the land.

Oh long, long may the ladies stand
  Wi' their gold combs in their hair,
Waiting for their own dear lords,
  For they'll see them na mair.

Half o'er, half o'er to Aberdour
  It's fifty fathom deep,
And there lies good Sir Patrick Spence
  Wi' the Scots lords at his feet.

The most apparent act of compression in this ballad is the omission of the sailing of the ship and of its sinking. Instead with great artfulness the poet slides from the omen of a storm to the grim humor of the nobles who were loath to get their cork-heeled shoes wet but nevertheless ended with their hats floating above them. He then shifts to wives waiting with their fans in their hands and gold combs in their hair. The final stanza matter-of-factly gives the depth of the water and then the stunning image of the drowned Sir Patrick with his lords ranged at his feet. If you are able to see why this is one of the great poems in the English language, you are able to understand almost any poetry. If only you see how absolutely vital to good art it is to get effects by suggestion, not by explicit statement, you are well on your way.

To understand poetry, you have first to grant the premise that the experiences that count in your own life are not matter-of-fact but emotional. What is left of a man's job once his two main emotional satisfactions—pride in craft and knowledge that loved ones are cared for—are removed? Many of our emotional experiences—our reactions to mountains seen from an airplane at sunset, for example, or to one of Beethoven's Rasoumovsky quartets, or to a seaport in a foreign country—are indefinable. We all spend a large portion of our lives in reverie. In this twilit state between conscious thought and dreaming, as well as in the buried river of the subconscious, we act out the disconcerting secret realities of our lives, as we have noted in our mention of James Joyce's *Ulysses* and James Thurber's "Secret Life of Walter Mitty." Some of the tensions and anxieties that trouble us are reflections of terrors, desires, and anguishes as vivid as they are unreal. If you grant these premises, you will see why the poet, like all other artists, can be your valuable guide. He can make you more perceptive of emotional reality, and thus help you to achieve more insight into your own personality and that of others.

VERSIFICATION

You will be just as well off if you postpone much attention to technical questions of versification until you have read enough poetry to feel tuned in, so to speak, on all kinds. A good deal of the failure of adults to enjoy poetry goes back to misguided efforts to teach youngsters what is to them the tiresome business of the mechanics of verse. Only three points need be discussed here: pattern and variation, the rhythms of contemporary verse, and the language of poetry.

PATTERN AND VARIATION

Technically, a poem is a complex interrelation of rhythms, stresses, pauses, consonant and vowel sounds, rimes and deliberate not-quite rimes, repetitions and echoes, and a number of other devices, all aimed at unified sense and effect. All artists are mechanics. No one ever wrote a sonnet or a rime royal stanza by accident. Yet it is also true that, like a good chemist, diemaker, or shipwright, a poet in time so masters his technique that he is hardly conscious of its mechanical aspects and arrives at his happiest effects by feel.

But a poet is never unaware of what he is doing. W. H. Auden ends one poem with the lines "Round the rampant rugged rocks/ Rude and ragged rascals run," and another poem with the couplet "Calmly till the morning break/Let them lie, then gently wake." The first poem, "Jumbled in the Common Box," is a savage indictment of our mismanagement of human affairs. The ugly gutturals and hammering stress forced by the repetition of initial sounds are as expressive of disgust as the meaning of the words. The second poem, "Now Through Night's Caressing Grip," is a compassionate invocation that night bring peace to the sore beset. Whereas the stopped consonants—d, p, t, g, ck, sc —in "Jumbled in the Common Box" make you bite off the words, the liquid *l*'s and the soft *m, n, a* and *ee* sounds in the second poem are as gentle as Auden's intent. Yet though a poet is aware of what effects he wants and how to get them, he does not calculate his effects by any mechanical system, as some English teachers seem to believe.

The versification of first-rate poets is never completely regular. This is a point of great importance. The commonest line in English verse, iambic pentameter, has five beats, or feet, each one having two syllables with the accent on the second, as i-AM. You will not find a poet of distinction who does not take liberties with this basic accenting. Take the opening of one of Shake-speare's sonnets: "When, in disgrace with fortune and men's eyes,/I all alone beweep my outcast state." Clearly the first accent is on the first syllable, *when*, and the second is on the fourth syllable, *-grace*. The accent in the first foot of the second line hovers over both *I* and *all*. This is not mechanical regularity. If you study these two lines for a few minutes, you will see how subtly the master maintains his five beats while he varies their fall. The vogue of the heroic couplet—lines riming aa, bb, cc, etc.—in the eighteenth century led to a vast amount of dreary, wooden sing-song versifying. This lodged like a pest in hymnals and school readers and became the verse that the new middle class took as the hallmark of elegance. Yet the eighteenth-century master, Alexander Pope, managed his couplets with delicate variety, as did Geoffrey Chaucer, who introduced them into England. Our first point, then, is that variety is as much a neces-sity in verse as in music or any other art.

THE RHYTHMS OF CONTEMPORARY VERSE

The second point: Contemporary verse often uses no regular beat at all. Instead it uses what might be described as the tightened-up rhythms of ordinary speech. For instance, you can-not identify any traditional pattern in Wallace Steven's "Dry Loaf," which ends:

> It was soldiers went marching over the rocks
> And still the birds came, came in watery flocks,
> Because it was spring and the birds had to come.
> No doubt that soldiers had to be marching
> And that drums had to be rolling, rolling, rolling.

Yet if you will read this stanza aloud, you will find that you fall into a natural stressed rhythm, engineered mainly by echoing words and sounds. Robert Frost's poem to an apple orchard, "Good-bye and Keep Cold," begins: "This saying good-bye on the edge of the dark/And the cold to an orchard so young in the bark." George Whicher tells how Frost had a professor of po-mology at the state agricultural college at Amherst, Massachusetts, check the poem. The professor reported it factually correct but said the meter needed tidying up.

The irregular rhythms of conversation have released poets from one bond of traditional verse. The use of echoing words and syllables and off-rimes, both within lines and at the end, have released them from another, the necessity for perfect rimes at the end of lines. This double freedom assures the reader of modern verse of great variety and subtle adjustments of form to subject. Of course, many poets also use traditional forms when it serves their purpose, or they blend regular and irregular as Frost blends end rime and conversational rhythm in the example given.

THE LANGUAGE OF POETRY

The third technical matter to note is the language of poetry. Again, because of the poor fare offered to children and the inadequacy of many teachers to deal with poetry, most adults have mistaken notions about the language of poets. They think of the fancy "poetic diction" of the past—"Ere Heaven's orb ascend o'er yon verdant copse, Inspire thou me, O Muse." Only a third-rate poet would use such archaic, personified, Latinized language today; the second-raters know better. But just as the rhythms of verse often take their accent from ordinary speech, so contemporary verse draws its vocabulary from the same source. In both cases, of course, an adroit heightening and adjustment to purpose takes place.

T. S. Eliot, leader in establishing the modern idiom, opens "The Love Song of J. Alfred Prufrock" in these words: "Let us go then, you and I,/When the evening is spread out against the sky / Like a patient etherized upon a table." The first line is the idiom of casual conversation. The second line is so inelegant it is refreshing. The third line is so inconceivable, by Victorian standards of poetic propriety, that it is shocking. All of this is not mere striving to be different. This language is precisely fitted to record the indecisions of modern man in the person of Prufrock.

Of course, the poet's choice of the kind of words and their arrangement still leaves the mystery of *which* words. Why did the anonymous composer of "Sir Patrick Spence" ever think of referring to the Scots lords' cork-heeled shoes, of all the details he might have picked? They were the height of fashion and thus suggested by contrast how unappealing the trip in the storm must have been. The principle of *selection of the significant,* common to all arts, in poetry depends on the power of suggestion in the words selected. In the opening of Eliot's "Prufrock," the mention of a patient under ether on an operating table suggests immediately a condition of sickness. This gives a clue to the serious theme behind the trivial problems of Prufrock, another Everyman-Bloom-Mitty. Suggestion operates by association. The cork-heeled shoes of the Scots lords and the fans and gold combs of their ladies by association evoke the whole world of the nobles. A traction engine in Auden's poem "Now Through Night's Caressing Grip" evokes the harsh problems of industrialism that beset us.

Another way of saying much the same thing is that the poet uses words as symbols. At no place does Eliot have to say explicitly that modern society is sick. He surrounds the indecisive Prufrock, worrying about petty matters such as how he should part his hair or wear his trouser cuffs, with disturbing items: a patient in an operating room, cheap hotels, yellow fog, lonely men in shirt sleeves leaning out of windows, a pair of ragged claws scuttling across the floors of silent seas, and so on. These are all symbols, as Prufrock himself is a symbol. You do not necessarily make definite associations as you read symbolizing words, but you feel their significance, perhaps subliminally, as the psychologists say, that is, below the threshold of consciousness. Creating such effects by the management of images and symbols throughout a poem is at the heart of the business of being a poet. Unfortunately, some modern poets, including T. S. Eliot at times, have chosen to employ symbols that have referents only for the poet and a limited number of readers.

At all times, no matter how ornate the style that might be fashionable, the best poets have always drawn on contemporary speech. John Webster, the Elizabethan playwright, in a mannered poem on the mortality of man, decries the ambition of kings who seek "To leave a living name behind, / And weave but nets to catch the wind." This is eloquent and metaphoric, but it is colloquial. Yet the reverse is also true. At all times good poets have felt no constraint about using something besides plain speech. William Wordsworth made a dogma of using the language of plain people in poetry. Yet one of his finest sonnets, "To Toussaint L'Ouverture," ends "Thy friends are exultations, agonies, / And love, and man's unconquerable mind." The polysyllables "exultations" and "unconquerable" are necessary for the organ roll he wishes. You will find that good poets use every resource our rich many-rooted language bestows on them. What they avoid with unerring taste is the artificial, pretentious, and hackneyed. Just as unerringly, the uninspired versifier makes these his stock in trade.

READING ALOUD

You will find your shortest route to lasting enjoyment of poetry is to read it aloud. All poetry, with the possible exception of some modern examples, is written to be read aloud. A poet writes with almost as much awareness of sound as a composer of music does. When William Butler Yeats finishes his beautiful "Song of Wandering Aengus" with the lines "And pluck till time and times are done, / The silver apples of the moon, / The golden apples of the sun," he is almost literally writing music. You get only a small fraction of the contribution of the lines to the whole effect of the poem if you do not hear them.

Some of the most exquisite experiences in poems are found in passages that delight the ear all by themselves. Shakespeare is the supreme master of noble lines and single phrases, in which the absolute rightness of the words to express the idea is matched by their sound. His sequence of 152 sonnets, which trace the dissolution of a friendship, may not be the passionate autobiographical account they purport to be, but merely an exercise to show how much better he could do what was then a literary fad. Yet much as Beethoven took a theme offered by a publisher, Anton Diabelli, and elaborated it brilliantly, Shakespeare clothes a series of familiar ideas in splendor by the eloquence of such lines as: "When to the sessions of sweet silent thought / I summon up remembrance of things past"; "Not marble, nor the gilded monuments / Of princes, shall outlive this powerful rime." Here is Sonnet 65, one of his most tremendous efforts, though the final couplet sags:

> Since brass, nor stone, nor earth, nor boundless sea,
> But sad mortality o'er-sways their power,
> How with this rage shall beauty hold a plea,
> Whose action is no stronger than a flower?
> Oh how shall summer's honey breath hold out
> Against the wrackful siege of batt'ring days,
> When rocks impregnable are not so stout,
> Nor gates of steel so strong, but Time decays?
> Oh fearful meditation! Where, alack,
> Shall Time's best jewel from Time's chest lie hid?
> Or what strong hand can hold his swift foot back?
> Or who his spoil of beauty can forbid?
>   Oh none!—unless this miracle have might,
>   That in black ink my love may still shine bright.

You will be surprised at the demands reading verse aloud will make on you. Try Sonnet 65. First, you cannot read well at all unless you understand what Shakespeare is literally saying and also what effect he is trying to get. This requires thought and more than one reading—fine training in analysis. Further, reading aloud is excellent for improving your speech. You cannot read such lines as "Against the wrackful siege of batt'ring days" as though you were telling the dry cleaner to call at your house. You must bring out the eloquence the poet puts into his lines. A poet savors words as a gourmet does sauces. "The wrackful siege of batt'ring days"—Will Shakespeare must have been pleased with that. To do justice to such phrasing, you have to use your lips and put resonance into your voice. And notice: Although this is a sonnet in form, actually it is a dramatic soliloquy. To follow the emotional line, as the poet-speaker terrifies himself with questions on the transient nature of love and life, you have to vary the volume and tension and pace of your reading. Now read "Sir

Patrick Spence" aloud. The tragic understatement of this ballad makes totally different demands on your voice. Poems vary so widely in their effects that you are forced to develop the power and flexibility of your voice—a wonderful change from our customary flat, lipless speech.

Read the following fine poem by Sidney Keyes, an English poet who died during World War II at the age of twenty-two. Read it aloud several times, and note how the beats fall. See how adroitly the devices we have been discussing enrich the effects.

PLOWMAN

Time was I was a plowman driving
Hard furrows, never resting, under the moon
Or in the frostbound bright-eyed morning
Laboring still; my team sleek-hided
As mulberry leaves, my team my best delight
After the sidelong blade my hero.
My iron-shod horses, my heroic walkers.
Now all that's finished. Rain's fallen now
Smudging my furrows, the comfortable
Elms are windpicked and harbor now no singer
Or southward homing bird; my horses grazing
Impossible mountainsides, long-frogged and lonely.
And I'm gone on the roads, a peevish man
Contending with the landscape, arguing
With shrike and shrewmouse and my face in puddles;
A tiresome man not listened to nor housed
By the wise housewife, not kissed nor handled
By any but wild weeds and summer winds.
Time was I was a fine strong fellow
Followed by girls. Now I keep company
Only with seasons and the cold crazy moon.

GEOFFREY CHAUCER, THE POET AS MAN OF THE WORLD

In his book *Two Cheers for Democracy*, E. M. Forster, the novelist and critic, has an essay about the role of the author's personal life in the effect of literature. He wonders what difference it makes that we know *The Rime of the Ancient Mariner* was written by Samuel Taylor Coleridge. "Coleridge signed other poems and knew other poets; he ran away from Cambridge; he enlisted as a Dragoon under the name of Trooper Comberback, but fell so constantly from his horse that it had to be withdrawn from beneath him permanently; he was employed instead upon matters relating to sanitation; he married Southey's sister and gave lectures; he became stout, pious, and dishonest, took opium, and died." But, he concludes, when we read the *Ancient Mariner*, we forget all about Coleridge; it is anonymous, like *Sir Patrick Spence* and the other folk ballads. And he concludes that "literature tends toward a condition of anonymity"—"It wants not to be signed." Writing in which the writer attracts attention to himself is not of the first order of literature.

Yet knowing about a poet and the circumstances in which he worked may quicken your interest in his poetry and your understanding of it. One of the greatest of poets is Geoffrey Chaucer. You may not be acquainted with his works because he wrote in Middle English, a language midway betwen Anglo-Saxon and our own English. But you can enjoy his poems in Modern English versions by Coghill, Krapp, Lumiansky, and others. Besides the freshness this experience may have for you, it may also correct the impression that poetry is mostly made up of short lyrics. When many persons speak about poetry, they really have in mind only a few familiar lyric poems taught in superficial surveys of literature.

If you have wondered who might be a prototype of the cultivated mind, one answer is Geoffrey Chaucer. This busy man wrote the *Canterbury Tales, Troilus and Criseyde,* and a considerable body of other works out of sheer bubbling creative force. He did not do it for money or for what we would consider fame. The *Canterbury Tales* was one of the earliest books published by William Caxton, the first English printer, but that was a century later. Chaucer had one inspiration modern poets do not have—he read his poems aloud at court. He thought about fame a good deal, but mainly about its passing. What made him steal untold hours from sleep and from the pleasures of social life to suffer eyestrain and chills in drafty, ill-lit rooms while he scratched out his poems? The same drive that led Edison to work in his laboratory in forgetfulness of food and sleep—the compulsion to make something new from a fresh idea or two—the need to create.

Geoffrey Chaucer was born about 1343 and died in 1400, a long span for his times. As a boy he was a page in the service of Elizabeth Countess of Ulster and her husband, Prince Lionel. Thus he saw much of court life early, and he spent his life close to it. He soldiered in two campaigns on the Continent and had to be ransomed after being captured in the first. He did not attend Oxford or Cambridge but may have studied law in the Inner Temple. His poetry will seem to you extraordinarily personal and chatty; yet it says virtually nothing about Chaucer's life or times. Wars and plagues and other events that he was close to, he passes over in silence. He does not mention his wife Philippa, who was a lady in waiting to the Queen, nor his son Thomas, but he did write a treatise on astronomy for "Little Lewis my son." Strangely, too, the official records—those prosaic gossips that tell us most of what we know about many great men, such as Shakespeare—of the reigns of Edward III and Richard II fail even to mention Chaucer as a poet. Instead he appears as a busy, competent man of affairs, far too burdened, it would seem, to write several hundred pages of enduring verse.

He held three posts, from which he took leave to go on a number of diplomatic missions. From June 2, 1374, to 1386 he was Controller of Customs for the Port of London. In 1389 he became Clerk of the King's Works, in charge of the Tower of London, Westminster Palace, and eight other royal residences. In 1390 he repaired St. George's Chapel, Windsor, and constructed scaffolds for jousting tournaments. He was a member of a commission responsible for bridges and sewers. Perhaps because he was robbed and beaten as he rode about on the king's business, he gave up this post and in 1391 became the King's Forester in Somerset. For one year he sat as a member of Parliament from Kent. In the course of this varied life Chaucer must have known the great and the humble, the trades and the professions, city and country, as few men have ever known intimately the face of their times. To add to the insights provided by his duties, he lived rent free during his years as Controller of Customs in a house built above Aldgate, an unparalleled spot from which to look down on the medieval pageant passing in and out of London, then still a walled city.

His contemporaries must have looked on Geoffrey Chaucer as an eminently practical, industrious, discreet, well-off, conservative government official. He was just that. That he read books in his roost above Aldgate until all hours and that he wrote verse violates our image of the executive type. But though his readers and listeners were a poorly educated lot by our standards, especially the women, they apparently delighted in Chaucer's poems, for nearly ninety manuscripts of the *Canterbury Tales* are extant. He wrote his first poems under the French influence dominant at the court. Then he has a period when his works reflect his discovery of the richer literature of Italy during two or three missions there. But the remarkable fact is that from the first he writes in English. And the more he writes, the freer is his treatment of the stories he borrows and the more natural his language, until the last dozen or more years he is thoroughly "English."

Chaucer's two masterpieces are his *Canterbury Tales* and *Troilus and Criseyde*.

CANTERBURY TALES

The *Canterbury Tales* is a series of stories in verse tied together by the original device of being told by thirty pilgrims as they ride together from London to the shrine of St. Thomas à Becket in Canterbury and back. Each one is to tell four stories, two each way. Several of the thirty do not have even one turn, for the band never reaches Canterbury. Chaucer left his monumental task unfinished. But the twenty-three tales, one or two still incomplete, with the general Prologue and the connecting links of the talk of the pilgrims as they ride along, make up the most vivid cross-section of a people and their culture in existence.

In the first place, a pilgrimage places the action at the center of medieval man's world, his religion. Yet though the occasion makes revelation of religious attitudes natural, it also has a holiday atmosphere that makes the telling of jolly tales as appropriate as the telling of pious ones. On a pilgrimage, most important, representatives of all classes of society except nobility might theoretically come together. In the Prologue, Chaucer introduces his pilgrims at the Tabard Inn at Southwark across the Thames from London, and an immortal band it is: a knight with his son and yeoman; a doctor, a lawyer, and a merchant; a university scholar; a monk, a friar, and a parson; a miller, a plowman, a shipman, and a cook; three women—a prioress, a nun, and a Wife of Bath; a dozen or so more, including the Host of the Tabard, who goes along to act as master of ceremonies, and not least Chaucer himself. This cross-section of medieval society offers great contrasts of personality, interests, and tastes, and the linking passages between the tales sparkle with the play of these differences. Yet separated into classes as the pilgrims are, they have strong cultural unity and ride along in a sort of turbulent harmony that can be duplicated today only by a baseball crowd.

The tales that Chaucer's pilgrims tell make up an anthology of medieval literature and lore and sum up the interests and tastes of the time. They include romances such as the Knight's earnest tale of friendship and love, the Wife of Bath's Arthurian tale of magic, and the Squire's flowery fragment of the Tartar princess Canace and her falcon. There are moral tales such as the Clerk's of the patient Griselda and the Physician's of the virtuous Virginia. There are pious tales such as the Prioress' of the Christian boy killed by the Jews and the Second Nun's Life of St. Cecilia. There are several fabliaux that Chaucer raises far above the stag-dinner level by his creation of characters who have the disreputable charm and credibility of Falstaff and his cronies. The Shipman's tale is typical. A monk borrows money from a merchant, gives it to his friend's wife in return for her favors, and tells the man he has repaid the wife. She then brazens her way out of her dilemma. Three of the most fascinating tales are neither pious nor ribald. The Pardoner's grim tale of the Three Revelers has been mentioned under fiction. The Canon's Yeoman's tale of a canon who swindles a priest by teaching him the secret of making silver from copper gives a brilliant account of alchemy. The Nun's Priest's tale of the rooster Chanticleer, Pertelote his wife, and the Fox is a wonderful mock-heroic rendering of the familiar fable with a witty satire of married life added.

Chaucer's mastery of verse is an extraordinary accomplishment. He wrote almost all of his *Canterbury Tales* in five-beat couplets, that is, with each pair of lines riming. The story flows through these lines with ease, vigor, and variety, never hobbled by the successive rimes as in the eighteenth- and nineteenth-century couplets we are familiar with. With reasonable diligence you can learn to enjoy Chaucer's verse. Apart from his vocabulary, his language sounds different from ours mainly because the vowels still have about the same quality as in European languages today—for instance, *e*, not *a*, gives an ay sound; *i*, not *e*, gives ee. Then, too, the soft final *e* is always pronounced at the end of a line and often elsewhere.

Perhaps you can get a taste of Chaucer's gusto and sly humor, though not of his melody and exquisite effects, from this slightly altered sample from the Prologue:

A Monk there was, a fair for the maistrie [*surpassing all others*],
An outrider, that loved venerie [*hunting*],
A manly man, to be an abbot able.
Full many a dainty horse had he in stable,
And when he rode, men might his bridle hear
Jingling in a whistling wind as clear
And eke as loud as doth the chapel bell.
There as this lord was keeper of the cell,
The rule of St. Maur or of St. Beneit,
Because that it was old and somewhat straight
This same Monk let old things pace [*pass*],
And held after the new world the space.
He gave not of that text a pulléd hen,
That saith that hunters are not holy men,
Nor that a monk, when he is reckless
Is likened to a fish that is waterless—
This is to say, a monk out of his cloister
That same text held him not worth an oyster . . .

TROILUS AND CRISEYDE

Chaucer's fame rests chiefly on the *Canterbury Tales*. Yet *Troilus and Criseyde* is the supreme long narrative poem in the English language. Chaucer borrowed the story from Boccaccio, but he expanded it, humanized it, and made it into a great work of art. *Trolius and Criseyde* has been called the first psychological novel, and it might, like the *Iliad* and the *Odyssey*, have been discussed as fiction.

The Trojan War is the background for *Troilus and Criseyde*. Troilus, the son of Priam, King of Troy, a debonair young man about town, falls in love at sight with a young widow, Criseyde—Cressida, in Modern English. In accordance with medieval courtly love conventions, Troilus suffers in an exaggerated fashion. By good luck, his friend Pandarus is Criseyde's uncle. After high-comedy negotiations, Pandarus persuades Criseyde to grant Troilus an interview, before he perishes of love. The two become impassioned lovers. Their happiness is shattered by the decision of the Trojan leaders to send Criseyde to her father, the seer Calchas, who has deserted to the Greeks, in exchange for a captured Trojan warrior. Criseyde finally goes, promising to return, but her letters to the distraught Troilus grow indefinite: she has accepted Diomedes of the Greeks as her benefactor. Troilus dies recklessly in battle.

The extraordinary aspect of *Troilus and Criseyde* is its sophistication. The interest is psychological. Whereas Boccaccio and later Shakespeare treat Criseyde as unvirtuous, Chaucer traces her development with surprising subtlety and insight. At first she is a knowing and witty player in the stylized game of love. She grows into a happy mature woman. Then hard realities push her reluctantly through ambiguous compromises, in which she tries not to make disloyalty to Troilus and loss of her own integrity the price of self-preservation. But she is defenseless and comes to terms with reality because she must.

On the other hand, Troilus is a romantic who finds no argument more compelling than his passions. That passion deepens under adversity, but Troilus does not grow up. He has no substantial solution for the problem he and Criseyde face. The intensity of his devotion and his self-destroying recklessness embody a principle that Chaucer treats with respect, but he is fascinated by Criseyde's relentless undoing. Clearly in this opposition of the idealistic and the realistic, Chaucer's sympathies are with the latter. His spirit is humanistic and, in the highest sense, comic, not tragic. His handling of Pandarus offers parallel testimony. In the first half of the poem within the context of comedy, Pandarus is the likeable affable fixer, easily verbalizing away the scruples of normal behavior. When trouble comes, he has nothing better to offer than the bankrupt suggestion that Troilus find another love. Useless, he moves backstage into the shadows. This tale of subtle shifting values, so natural in its language, so sophisticated in its humor, and so poignant in its reckonings with realities, was written about 1385.

THE REWARDS OF POETRY

Thomas Mann has a disillusioned character in one of his stories say:

Ah, how I have learned to hate them, those poets who chalked up their large words on all the walls of life. . . . Poets have said that speech is poor. "Ah, how poor are words," so they sing. But no, sir. Speech, it seems to me, is rich, is extravagantly rich compared with the poverty and limitations of life.

In this exaggeration there is some truth. One of the rewards of reading poetry is to realize how man can transcend his limitations. The poet with his gift of words can so deal with death, for instance, that this dread subject becomes interesting, even attractive. Of all the ways of stating a reaction to death, poetry is the most versatile and apparently satisfactory. Death is the theme of more poems than any other subject.

Consider how Shakespeare handles death in the following:

FEAR NO MORE THE HEAT O' THE SUN

Fear no more the heat o' the sun,
Nor the furious winter's rages;

Thou thy worldly task has done,
   Home art gone, and ta'en thy wages.
Golden lads and girls all must,
As chimney-sweepers, come to dust.

Fear no more the frown o' the great;
   Thou art past the tyrant's stroke.
Care no more to clothe and eat;
   To thee the reed is as the oak.
The sceptre, learning, physic, must
All follow this, and come to dust.

Fear no more the lightning-flash,
   Nor the all-dreaded thunder-stone;
Fear not slander, censure rash;
   Thou hast finished joy and moan.
All lovers young, all lovers must
Consign to thee, and come to dust.

No exorciser harm thee!
   Nor no witchcraft charm thee!
Ghost unlaid forbear thee!
   Nothing ill come near thee!
Quiet consummation have;
And renownéd be thy grave!

This is an elegy sung as a duet by two young men in *Cymbeline* on the supposed death of the heroine Imogen, who is disguised as a boy and is really their sister—as artificial a situation as you can imagine. But the song without its music has achieved an immortal separate existence as one of the most nearly perfect of English lyrics. It seems not an expression of personal grief. Yet with what other accent, one wonders, would the enigmatic Shakespeare have written about that shadowy boy with the odd name Hamnet, his son who died? Here in a handful of words addressed to the dead Imogen in the conventional manner of the elegy is stoic consolation. The refrain of the passing of the young and beautiful and the high and mighty is a medieval commonplace, but Shakespeare freshens it with the invention of what the dead boy need no longer fear and the plain statements of what he need no longer do. But the miracle lies in the way that the homely Anglo-Saxon words, adroitly set off by three Latinized ones in the last stanza, the skillful marshaling of vowels and consonants, and the subtle melody of the lines suffuse the grief with beauty. The raw fact of the death of a boy takes on dignity in the universalizing poetic statement. At the same time the music and splendor of the English language afford some of the most exquisite pleasure art in any form can offer. This two-level appeal to the mind and to the senses makes the reading of poetry one of the most rewarding of the experiences of a cultivated mind.

9

PAINTING, MIRROR OF THE AGE

One of the most popular books of the Middle Ages bore the inclusive title *Mirror of the World*. Every artist is engaged in mirroring his world. No matter how unconscious he is of such a purpose or how private the world may seem, his work is in some degree a reflection of the spirit of his age. Prehistoric rock paintings reflect the drama of survival in a grim world of man, beast, and weather. At the other extreme the portraits of Reynolds, Raeburn, and Gainsborough bespeak the landed aristocracy of eighteenth-century England. At the same time in the same London, William Hogarth catches in the mirror of his engravings the seamy tale of the poor and the profligate.

In France in the next century, Honoré Daumier, another mordant satirist with more pity in him than Hogarth had, writes in his lithographs the history of the petit bourgeois world of Paris. The bloody French Revolution and the silent industrial revolution have substituted middle-class tedium for the vices of the rich and the poor. With incomparable realism Daumier immortalizes on his stones the rich array of new types crowding the streets, shops, and courtrooms of Paris. The Pre-Raphaelites— Morris, Rossetti, Hunt, Millais, Burne-Jones—mobilized painting, wood-engraving, printing, and even furniture and wallpaper in a revolt against the dullness, ugliness, and materialism of English industrialism in the reign of Queen Victoria. They succeeded only in being Victorian.

Paintings, prints, photographs, sculpture, architecture, and related visual forms—all these are plastic arts. Plastic is used in the primary sense of being modeled and also in the secondary sense of giving form to impressions. In this chapter we limit ourselves to painting, but you may discover special delight in ceramics, in stained-glass windows, or, as I have, in drawings and wood-engravings. The plastic arts mirror the real world more directly than any other form except the drama. When you look at a marble figure by Praxiteles, a Ming vase, or a moonlight seascape by Ryder, you have definite pleasurable reactions. But the immediacy of the visual arts and the emotional response you may have toward the subject tend to hurry you into judgments irrelevant to works of art. The commonest confusion arises from judging a work of art according to notions of what is supposed to be beautiful in nature. How irrelevant to the purposes of the artist this may be is revealed by a remark of Goya's: "I see in nature only advancing and receding planes."

THE ARTIST'S JOY

Your approach to the plastic arts needs to start with some realization of the artist's joy in the physical act of applying paint, or chiseling stone, or drawing lines. Plato said long ago that the sculptor learns as much from the stone as he brings to it. The artist, that is, delights in his medium and at the same time submits to its limitations. For instance, much of the pleasure I have in the tedious business of wood-engraving comes from my struggle with the intractable wood on which I engrave. Lingeringly I handle the polished blond blocks, pieces of boxwood with the finest grain known. And I look with pride on my engraving tools, burins and scorpers and spitstichers, all patiently whetted at just the right angle on Arkansas oilstone until they are so sharp that, balanced loosely on a finger, they will not slide on the polished block. Graving a clean line through the crisply resistant wood with a triangular burin or oval spitsticher is as sensuous an act as biting into a ripe Bartlett pear.

All painters love to squeeze a tube of cadmium red or burnt sienna or cobalt blue and then pick up the creamy paint on brush or palette knife and spread it on canvas, masonite, or other surfaces. Some painters today are using lacquers and other fast-drying media that permit them to repaint areas and finish a painting at one sitting. Some are incorporating sand and other materials in their paint to get rough textures. Just as you may like the feel of calfskin or beech bark, so an artist likes the texture of paint and often, like Rembrandt and Van Gogh, applies it with a palette knife in a thick layer, or impasto. When you look at a lithograph, to enter vicariously into the artist's experience, you must share his pleasure in the luminous grainy blacks and grays that bloom from the union of greasy crayon, Bavarian limestone, or other specially prepared surface, ink, and paper. As the musician is delighted by the rich growl of a cello or the snarl of a brass, so the artist takes joy in the physical effects of his medium.

THE SUBJECT IS INCIDENTAL

Most artists are dismayed by laymen's talk about their works because it leaves out what activates them. To a degree unsuspected by the layman, an artist preserves, or recaptures, a child's ability to react directly and intensely to visual impressions. A champion athlete has faster reflexes than the rest of us, and an artist has more acute color perceptions and sensitivity to texture, line, form, and design. At the same time, though, he sees pictures. This is simple; yet it is apparently what many of us miss.

The artist is excited by a face, say, but he immediately has a vision of what it will look like when he translates it into paint. He really is interested in paintings, not faces. Eugene Speicher and Henry Mattson, the one a famous painter of people, the other of the sea, once told me that their subjects were wholly incidental. Speicher said he might just as easily paint seascapes; Mattson, portraits. The layman looks at a picture and goes back to what the artist has long since finished with—the subject. If the subject were more important than the artist's treatment of it, then looking at a colored photograph, or better yet the object itself, would be the thing to do.

Often a painter bases his final painting on preliminary sketches, not on direct observation. And in his preoccupation with problems inherent in creating a painting that will be in the mood and style he strives to establish, the artist gradually loses a sharp image of the original subject and any great interest in it. The French painter Georges Rouault puts it this way: "In truth, I have painted by opening my eyes day and night on the perceptible world, and also by closing them from time to time that I might better see the vision blossom and submit itself to orderly arrangement." Actually, creative workers of all kinds have a kinship with carpenters, machine-tool operators, and other mechanics. All great artists in every field have been great technicians. They have to be. And the difference betwen a popular work of art and one by an artist of stature—say, between a Broadway song and one by Brahms, or a magazine cover and a Leonardo canvas—lies to a considerable extent in the much greater range of technical complexity of the work of the master.

In traditional painting the technical problems include drawing of likenesses of objects, arranging them in a composition, and applying color. This oversimplification gives no clue to the extent and subtlety of the technical problems the artist grapples with. You might consider just one—the contrast of warm and cool colors, the reds, browns, and yellows on the one hand, and the blues and greens on the other. No matter what his style or what his medium, a painter has only warm, cool, black, white, and neutral colors to work with. He works with these in complex harmonies and distributes them in various intensities and amounts to emphasize significant parts of his subject. Yet at the same time, he is playing a separate chess game with his warm and cool colors, usually by placing them in contrasting juxtaposition. Study the paintings in a gallery or in a book of colored reproductions of masterpieces. You will be surprised at the universality of this game within a game through all the periods of art and changing styles. True, occasionally someone like Matisse paints a picture with all warm or cool colors to get a special effect. But you will find painters all the way from Mantegna to the latest abstract expressionist, or painters of the same period but different styles, such as Rembrandt and Velásquez, or a painter of many styles such as Picasso, all clearly using this counterpoint of cool and warm colors. And this is only one of the technical aspects that engrosses the artist's attention as he paints a picture.

From the moment an artist spreads paint on a canvas or uses any other medium to turn his vision into visible symbols, he commits himself to what for a better term we shall call a philosophy. Consciously or unconsciously, he must do so. He may say: "Oh, no, I have no philosophy. I just paint what I see." That is a philosophy, a basic commitment to try to represent objects faithfully, as Vermeer and Chardin did. Furthermore, they chose for their subjects only objects and settings from the calm everyday life they loved. If an artist says, "I am not interested in the subject but in the light it's bathed in," then he follows the impressionists such as Monet and Pissarro. If he says, "I am deeply interested in my subject, but I paint it as it makes me feel," he is subscribing to the same philosophy as Van Gogh and other expressionists. If he says, "I am mainly concerned with the essential form of things, with questions of volume and space around objects," he is working in the tradition of Cézanne and the abstractionists and Cubists.

He may say, "I like to paint things literally, but they may be imaginary things occupying an imaginary environment." In that case he is guided by fantasies, dreams, and the subconscious in the manner of Bosch or modern surrealists such as Tamayo, Tanguy, and Dali. Should he say, "I am not interested in representing anything at all in any state; I want to divide the space at my disposal into pure patterns of color," then he is nonobjective like Mondrian. If he lets himself go and spreads or drips his paint automatically in obedience to some inner command, then he is of the contemporary school of abstract expressionists such as Winter, De Stäel, Pollock, and Afro. Whatever style an artist uses, it represents some sort of philosophical belief. Beginners who try to do a vase of flowers with botanical accuracy, color-camera faithfulness, but little skill to sustain them rarely suspect how many other philosophies besides literalism there are.

MUSEUM VISITING

Some persons limit their exposure to art to an amble through a museum every six months or six years. They remember little except their fatigue. If you are able to visit a museum frequently, you can be highly selective. On one visit concentrate on one wing, one gallery, one artist, one form of art, or even one painting or piece of sculpture. For instance, when I am in Washington, I usually manage to visit the Phillips Museum. It is so small and selective that each room can be enjoyed at leisure. After repeated visits, I find that many of the paintings have become precious old friends. The glorious big Renoir boating scene, the superb Matisse interior, and the brilliant Vieira da Silva, one of the finest contemporary paintings, are alone worth an hour of your time.

No trip to Washington is complete unless you go to the National Gallery. It is so large and so rich in priceless treasures that limiting a single visit in time and scope is a necessity. The free distribution of information sheets about the works in individual galleries is a wonderful aid. In each visit to the National Gallery, I always manage to renew my acquaintance with three of the most charming persons I have ever met. First, I stop—to chat, I almost said—before Ranuccio Farnese, a boy about ten painted by Titian. Ranuccio is as alive and beguiling as a New York shoe-shine boy, though his rich dress, sword, and Maltese crown show that he was born to the burdens of one of the great houses of Italy. Here, I think, is life, breathing and natural, timelessly arrested. Grandson of a worldly pope, son of an evil father who was murdered, Ranuccio was gifted and lovable and grew up to become a cardinal.

Around the corner in the next gallery is the "Portrait of a Young Man in Red" by Giovanni Bellini, Titian's teacher. The youth wears a red gown and a black head-covering. His head is silhouetted against a blue background. For sheer elegance, for breath-taking richness of color to state the new pagan affirmation of the goodness of life in this world, this portrait is a symbol of one of the most engaging aspects of the Renaissance spirit. On the wall next to the unknown "Young Man in Red" is Titian's "Andrea dei Franceschi," one of the greatest of portraits. The "Young Man in Red" and the "Ranuccio Farnese" are springtime pieces; the "Andrea" is mellow fall. Andrea's red gown and the brown background are autumnal. The long narrow face, delicate-lidded eyes, chiseled nose and cheekbones, straight banged hair and sparse mustache and beard—all contribute to make Andrea the epitome of the Renaissance humanist, aristocratic, learned, wise, and tolerant. He was Grand Chancellor of Venice, 1529–1552.

You cannot look on these three sensitive faces without coming under the spell of Renaissance man's delight in being alive, his sense of the importance of being civilized, and his deep faith in the dignity of the individual human being.

REMBRANDT, THE KING OF SHADOWS

Greatness is rare and enigmatic. What shapes the genius of a Rembrandt is ultimately a mystery within the mystery of art itself. The greatness of Rembrandt's art cannot be accounted for by biographical, social, or technical means. Yet more than almost any other great creative artist, he is explicable, as far as that is possible, as he stands caught at the intersection of these three forces.

The parallels and contrasts between Rembrandt Harmenzoon van Rijn (1607–1669) and his great senior contemporary, Peter Paul Rubens (1577–1640) are extraordinary. Rembrandt, a Dutchman, breathed the heady air of freedom because Holland had just wrested its independence from Spain. Rubens, a Fleming, besides painting, labored loyally as a diplomat to further better relations in Europe for Spain. Rubens, a Catholic, went to mass every morning. Rembrandt, deeply religious, had uncertain Protestant connections. Rubens traveled to Italy, Spain, France, and England. Rembrandt moved only from Leyden to Amsterdam. Though he spent years in diplomatic missions, in his lifetime Rubens was enormously productive, rich, and famous. After early popularity and high living, Rembrandt did his greatest work in the last quarter-century of his life in poverty and eclipse, though not entirely without recognition.

The duplicate pattern of their private lives is fascinating. Rubens married the well-to-do Isabella Brant in 1609. They were happy together until her death in 1626, leaving two handsome sons, Albert and Nicolas. Four years later the middle-aged Rubens risked ridicule by marrying sixteen-year-old Hélène

Fourment. Rubens was the most successful painter who ever lived. During his lifetime, his paintings were sought after by the mighty of Europe. His carefully itemized contracts were executed with the help of a number of assistants, among them for a while his greatest pupil, Anton van Dyck. Making a teen-ager the mistress of his palatial home, where he conducted his social life, his painting, and his business, made even the self-possessed Peter Paul think up elaborate explanations. Hélène was the mother of five more of Rubens' children. Rubens liked to paint her, as he did her sister Suzanne. They lived happily in the Castle of Steen outside Antwerp until Rubens' death in 1640.

SASKIA, HENDRICKJE, AND THE BOY TITUS

Rembrandt married well-born Saskia van Uylenburgh in 1634. She died in 1642. Her death coincided with serious money troubles for Rembrandt. To care for him and his little boy Titus, about 1645 he brought into his house the girl Hendrickje Stoffels (or Jagers). Rembrandt outraged the Calvinist burghers by having a child by this servant girl. Though he was a profoundly moral man, he never married her. The reason, probably, is that he would then have had to account for Saskia's fortune. This he could not do because he had spent it. As devoted as any church-wed wife, Hendrickje followed Rembrandt into the shadows of the Jewish quarter and shared his lean fortune until her death in 1662.

The eight years that Saskia and Rembrandt were together were years of happiness, of worldliness, and of growing artistic powers. The seventeen years with Hendrickje were years of poverty, of withdrawal from the world, but of realization of the ultimate in artistic achievement. What a role for a servant girl—to share the years of destiny, of outer defeat and inner triumph, with genius. She cooked and washed and sewed for him, she mothered his motherless boy, she slept in his bed, she bore him a daughter, and she was an ever-available model for his pictures. What did she think, this snub-nosed, brown-eyed Hendrickje Stoffels, or Jagers —even her name seems uncertain—as she dried her hands on her apron, put on one of the rich red "prop" gowns or the favorite long rippling-sleeved white blouse that may have been Saskia's, and obediently took the position Rembrandt gruffly indicated? What did she think of this furrow-faced man staring at her with bemused concentration? Did she have the faintest inkling that he was immortalizing her? Did he talk to her, brag to her, tell her his dreams as Browning's Andrea del Sarto did his Lucrezia? I think not.

Through the long hours doubtless she tried hard not to move, not to doze, and contented herself with looking her love and planning how she would scrape together a nourishing supper for her little band. Except, that is, when he had her pose nude, as he did for "Bathsheba," and she turned blue in the drafty studio while he stared at her flesh exactly as he did at such subjects as the flayed ox that he painted the next year. Sometimes, of course, it must have seemed play. There was the morning he saw her in her chemise and had her hike it up and pretend she was wading while he sketched her. Later he developed the sketch into a painting, one of his few rapid ones. For "Potiphar's Wife" she had to sit for days with her legs crossed and one hand thrust out. For the "Flora" he dressed her in a fantastic get-up of a great boat-shaped hat with a branch of blossoms stuck on it—also a relic of the bountiful days with Saskia, no doubt—the favorite white ruffled blouse, and a heavy yellow-lined tablecloth that he tied around her waist inside out and filled with little roses.

Titus, of course, took his turn as model, either in a robe or as himself. Doubtless as a baby he served as the Infant Jesus. Among the winsome portraits of children, from Holbein's and Velásquez' superb royal offspring and Rubens' handsome Albert and Nicolas to Renoir's enchanting red-haired son Jean, none has the wistful spirituality of the six- or seven-year-old Titus as the boy Samuel kneeling at the knee of a stern Hannah, his hands in prayer, but his eyes peering up from beneath his red curls. In the painting of "Daniel's Vision," Titus, now about ten, kneels while a golden-haired, golden-winged girl angel, who might logically be his half-sister Cornelia, touches his shoulder. The wistful Samuel has become a thin-faced Daniel. What was his life like, this sad-looking boy, growing up with genius and poor Jews as his compan-

ions? Did he draw? We imagine so, for lacking other diversions in
the dedicated household, he must needs have amused himself
with drawing materials as a carpenter's son with wood-working
tools. And Rembrandt was a good teacher, as the brilliant work
of his student Fabritius testifies.

Six years or so after the Daniel, about 1657, Rembrandt did
a portrait of Titus reading, and we can imagine that books were
the lonely boy's companion. His plain brown coat of coarse material contrasts sharply with the elegant silks of the Rubens boys,
as does his withdrawn look with their aplomb and sense of being
at home in their mansion. Titus' red curls are still abundant, but
his cheeks are ominously hollow. What did Titus do as he grew
old enough to begin his own career? We do not know. We know
only that he moved away and that he married about 1668. The
sunken-cheeked groom of the gold, green, and red masterpiece,
"The Married Couple," looks like Titus as he would be at this
time. If so, it is a magnificent memorial. Titus died in this year
1668 and his bride shortly after him. He left a baby and his own
changing image in prints and paintings that measure the gray
years of his father's greatness.

THE AUTOBIOGRAPHY OF THE
MILLER HARMEN'S SON

In the forty-two years of his career Rembrandt wrote one of
the world's greatest autobiographies. He wrote it in sixty-two
drawings, etchings, and paintings of himself that record the
passage of the years over his face and soul with an intimacy,
ruthlessness, and compassion never equaled in any medium by
any artist except Beethoven.

About 1626, just out of his teens, Rembrandt begins telling
what manner of man this miller Harmen's son is. A droll stubby
figure rigged out in a long blue gown with sash, a white ruffed
collar, and a floppy velvet hat stands back from a crude easel
in a bare room full of strong light and deep shadows. He holds a
brush and palette. This is "The Artist in His Studio" (Museum of
Fine Arts, Boston). From the same earliest days is the first oil
of the head alone, that of a curly-headed youth whose unlighted

eyes are stones in a muddy pool, while the neck, jaw, and ear-lobe glow melon-gold. It is, one would swear, the face of a village bumpkin, an apprentice miller, perhaps, never an artist. Like any other young artist, Rembrandt is imitating the current vogue, in this case Caravaggio's tricky chiaroscuro as practiced by Ter-brugghen and others. So from the start Rembrandt dealt with shadows, and though these shadows are optical only, his first statements of himself have a pitiless objectivity for a youth of twenty or a little more. From the beginning Rembrandt makes the painting of a portrait a search for truth. He will not flatter even himself.

Drawings, etchings, paintings—the self-history goes on year by year. A 1636 etching shows him in the plenitude of his early success as a portrait painter in Amsterdam. Richly dressed, his features refined, he stares serenely outward, while Saskia, close at hand, symbolizes the happiness that shone on him in these years of light. These are the years that Rembrandt, like Rubens, surrounded himself with the works of other artists, including one of the best collections of prints ever assembled, with books, and with costly objects that came to Amsterdam on ships that furled their sails at the docks close to his door. The face in the self-portraits of this period show worldly pride and sensuous delight in the turbans, plumes, gloves, gold chains, and other richly textured things the miller's son now owns.

But the weather turned around. Saskia died. Rembrandt's growing unorthodoxy of treatment lost him his only market in Protestant Holland, the portraits of well-to-do merchants and professional men. By 1652 the change in his fortunes is mirrored in the seriousness of his look, the deepened cleft between his eyes, and the soberness of his dress. The shadows are gathering within him. Wars, civil troubles, a new taste for smooth techniques, and the compulsion to create according to his own vision without compromise, all conspired to drive Rembrandt deep into debt. In 1656 he was bankrupt. In 1658, stripped of everything but his Bible, Hendrickje, Titus, his child Cornelia by Hendrickje, and his tools, he went into the depths.

THE YEARS OF ADVERSITY AND GREATNESS

The last dozen years of adversity are the years of Rembrandt's greatness as a painter. Just as his life is drained bare, so his paintings, once filled with figures and movement, grow quieter. The areas of golden highlight contract, but the shadows are suffused with warmth. Apart from the self-portraits and the prints, this is the time of such supreme achievements as "The Polish Rider" (The Frick Collection, New York), "Flora," "The Auctioneer," "Lady with a Pink," "Aristotle Before a Bust of Homer" (all four, Metropolitan Museum, New York), and "The Mill," (National Gallery, Washington). Throughout his career Rembrandt had relied on warm colors—brown predominantly with red, gold, and cream. Now he orchestrated them in richer harmonies. Now he spread them broadly in patches not brushed neatly together. He had no time for trivia, for distracting detail or for virtuosity. Taking his place beside Homer and Shakespeare and Bach and Beethoven, Rembrandt van Rijn fused into one essence his subject, his emotional reactions, and his use of his medium.

In your confrontations with human greatness you will find few experiences more moving than your study of Rembrandt's portraits of himself in his last years. Four are among the greatest of portraits. The full-face head in Vienna, probably painted in 1656 because the thick hair is still brown, goes as far as paint can go to realize the tragic condition of being human. It is clear by now that Rembrandt is no longer using himself for a convenient model but as a means of studying humanity, in the same way that a medical scientist tries a new drug on himself. He has become Everyman. Suffering has crumpled the brow, and defeat has kneaded the plebeian face. The eyes are anxious, yet they are indomitable. The old black velvet hat and the red jerkin with the wisp of white linen at the neck are the only muted diversions, the only escape from pity for the world's wrongs held in those tragic eyes.

The 1659 three-quarter face in the National Gallery, Washington, shows an aging man, though Rembrandt has reached only fifty-three, the age at which Rubens remarried. The face over the upturned coat collar seems shrunken. The lines of care are bitten deep. The curly hair is gray. Everything is dark, insignificant, except the golden mask of the sad face, from which the eyes still scrutinize the world in aware appraisal.

Four years later in the handsome Kenwood House half-length portrait Rembrandt seems to have weathered the storm. He stands four-square to the world, his palette, brushes, and maulstick in one hand. The shadows have fled from the background; it is only dark enough to set off his white hair and to permit his soft white beret to be a dramatic episode. The face is full and serene, the eyes as intelligent as ever. It is a great affirmation of the supremacy of art, for Rembrandt here has lived beyond the defeats of his personal fortunes and has won the peace that has been his only goal since at twenty he began to explore the shadows—the peace of complete mastery of his profession. Here, in what in his day was old age, he is able to match vision with craft, to evoke with ultimate simplicity a monumental figure that is at once Rembrandt the king, triumphant over the shadows of earthly struggle, and at the same time a tribute to the divinity of the creative powers within Man the artist.

Finally, in 1669, the last year of his life, Rembrandt gave his final accounting of himself. The portrait in The Hague is at first a little comic. A fancy gold-cloth beret perches atop the pudgy pink face. But this is a tragic face. The eyes are lustreless, the expression slack, vacuous. It is as though the great Dutch humanist, who in the years of light with Saskia saw the godhead in the humblest crone, now grasps the opportunity to write his testament, to paint this pitiful figure of failure just as he was and yet, as the shadows crowd in, to touch his brow with that golden light that was his symbol of man's immortal soul. It is hard to imagine another work in which the tragic discrepancy between Man the mortal animal and Man the death-spanning creator is expressed in such moving personal terms as it is here in this work, at once the record of Rembrandt's physical decay and the evidence of the undiminished greatness of his artistic powers.

So Rembrandt took his leave. In addition to his paintings, he left a large body of drawings and etchings. No artist has ever approached his mastery of the etching. His scenes around Amsterdam and his life of Christ series are the finest achievements in this medium. And Rembrandt's drawings are among the greatest works of art. Like Shakespeare's songs, they are only of a different magnitude from his major works. Yet if certainty in capturing an impression with the utmost speed and economy is a hallmark of great art, the leaping lines and soft sepia washes of Rembrandt's many drawings are matched in expressiveness only by the drawings of Wu Chên, Sesshu, Hokusai, and other oriental masters. With a few strokes and a stain of watered ink he could make even a shed in the monotony of the lowlands vibrant with interest. But the greatness of Rembrandt's drawings, etchings, and paintings lies ultimately in the way in which his mastery of technique reveals his sense of life and his compassion for his fellow men.

PAUL CÉZANNE, THE PHYSICIST OF ART

How does modern art hold up a looking glass to our times? The greatest of modern artists is unquestionably Paul Cézanne (1839–1906). What moved this solitary, intense, questing genius but the scientific spirit of his age? There is no sentiment in Cézanne—emotion but not sentiment. His tremendous achievement lies in his divorcement from sentiment arising either from any form of myth or from any romantic involvement with the subject. In fact he said, "There is no such thing as subject." His portraits of his wife are solutions to technical problems, no less so than his studies of fruit or his rocky landscapes. The clumsy nudes he occasionally attempted are cylinders like the trees about them.

Cézanne is the physicist of painters. Pissarro, Monet, Renoir, and the other Impressionists, but particularly the older Pissarro, taught Cézanne to get out of the studio into the open air and paint in a scientific spirit. They stopped when they captured in dappled colors the appearance of surfaces reflecting the light at a specific moment. Cézanne went beyond optics. He spent forty years doing research, his own word, in how to use his colors to seize on the essential form of objects, to convey a sense of their

volume and weight, and to anchor them in the planes they oc-
cupy at different distances in space. In his indifference to the
charm of the accidental, the anecdotal, or the subjective, Cézanne
intellectualizes the visible world. His passionate preoccupation
with the nature of matter is an expression of the greatest force of
his times, the exploration of space by Rutherford, Planck, Einstein, and a host of other scientists who reshaped the Newtonic
universe. Cézanne exhibits the same disciplined concern for the
abstract that has led to the creation of all of the mathematical
miracles of our times from the Brooklyn Bridge to Sputnik. By
the same token he is also father of cubistic, nonobjective, and
other impersonal forms of art.

Cézanne's scientific detachment is present in his landscapes,
portraits, and still lifes. He is one of the few great artists to
achieve equal stature in all three fields. Cézanne's still lifes are de-
void of domesticity, and his landscapes are empty of human
beings and of human accomplishments. The paradoxical expression "still life" applies to his landscapes and portraits as aptly as
to his geometric fruits. Card players, his wife, his gardener, the
boy in the red vest, himself, matriarchal Mont-Sainte-Victoire,
houses like diced carrots, bare-trunked trees slanting up from
among huge rocks—all are vibrantly alive, yet all are still, brooding. It might seem that Cézanne must propitiate the struggle
within him by creating works in which the tensions are so cunningly opposed that his world becomes one of apparent repose. It
is safer to say that the shy Paul Cézanne, returning to his parents'
estate in Provence after learning what he needed in Paris, painted
those scenes and objects that lent themselves to his slow methods
and agonizing dislike of personal encounter.

One of Cézanne's most famous paintings is "The Card Players"
in the Louvre. It is the final version of several preliminary studies
and paintings. Two countrymen sit immobile, studying the cards
in their hands on the table between them. Their bodies and arms
in profile with a tall bottle of wine just between their hands make
a locked W design. The competition of the game is carried out
in a witty counterpoint of drawing and color. The man on the

left is thin, hollow cheeked, sharp nosed. The man on the right is rugged, pink cheeked, snub nosed. The man on the left wears a high hard round-crowned derby hat with down-turned brim. The man on the right wears a soft crushed hat with up-turned brim. Left wears a dark coat and light pants; Right reverses the combination. Left smokes a white clay pipe, and his cards are white. The only white on Right is his shirt. All of Left and his chair is visible; the back of Right and his chair are cut off. But this thrust rightward is countered by Right's hunching over his cards and by his light coat, hat, and unshadowed face. The most intense color is the burnt sienna and yellow ochre of the tablecloth and table that unite the players and move them into the frontal plane. In the background the horizontal movement of a reddish screen ends with two uprights that cooperate with the table legs to keep the player at the right from being shoved out of the scene. Swarming over the entire design are violet shadows and transitional purples to create a world without finite space, a world without time in which the card players remain forever lost in contemplation.

Paul Cézanne's innovation lay in making the act of painting solely the record of an esthetic experience. That is, he responded only to the intrinsic qualities of things, their physical sensations, without recognition of their traditional significance or the unique feelings they might arouse in him. The esthetic emotion has nothing necessarily to do with what ordinarily passes for the beautiful. In fact, it is impossible to say more than that Cézanne found certain arrangements, forms, and colors stimulating enough to paint. Then no matter how keen his delight in what he saw, he became absorbed in a wholly new set of sensations growing out of the paint he brushed onto two or three feet of canvas.

First, however, Cézanne, a studious admirer of the great painters of the past, is a master of architectonic composition. Then using blue, violet, green, and ochre with red, yellow, and white for dramatic passages, he gives volume and depth and vibrancy to the forms and surfaces within the composition by moving the colors about over the whole design according to a logic of his own. Thus Cézanne turns commonplace subjects—a scattering of peaches and apples on an ugly deal table, an abandoned quarry in a forest, or a boy in a red vest posing before heavy draperies—into masterpieces of immense structural strength and chamber-music harmonies of color.

PICASSO'S PRISMS

The most noted of living artists, the Spaniard Pablo Picasso (b.1881), has kept a link with the past because he has never separated his paintings, drawings, lithographs, and ceramics from the world of objects. Nor have most of his older contemporaries such as Matisse, Rouault, Chagall, Léger, Ensor, Modigliani, Vlaminck, Derain, Delaunay, Kokoschka, Beckmann, Hofer, Chirico, Marin, Sheeler, Hopper, Burchfield, Shahn, and Albright. But in our present inquiry Picasso has more interest to us than any of his contemporaries. You may find him less ingratiating than many others—charm is not one of his strong points. But if your concern goes beyond whether or not you like his work, you will find Picasso the most illuminating of contemporary artists.

Picasso's significant work begins conveniently in 1900. His "Blue Period" of despairing, starved-looking figures and his "Pink Period" of melancholy strolling players present symbolically modern man's joyless alienation from his world. Picasso's is a much more thoughtful statement than any his predecessors had put down. Like Cézanne, Pissarro, Renoir, Manet, Monet, Degas, and the other Impressionists had ignored the negative state of things. They found a healthy reality in the play of light on buxom nudes, ballet dancers, horse races, quiet water scenes, flowers, family sitting rooms, and similar non-upsetting subjects. Only the Expressionists Van Gogh, Toulouse-Lautrec, Ensor, and Munch among his older contemporaries had anticipated Picasso's intensity of feeling for the dispossessed.

African masks led Picasso to prismatic distortions of the face. This departure from naturalism, aided by Cézanne's experiments, led to the comprehensive distortion of Cubism. With Georges Braque and Juan Gris, Picasso created not merely a new technique but a new way of looking at reality. The application of theories of perspective about 1500 imposed a mechanistic logic on painting that in the long run is at variance with the creative imagination. Indeed, the whole wooden business of eye level and lines converging at a vanishing point is pseudo-scientific. Lines do not converge; objects at a distance are not smaller—they only seem so. Artistically, perspective serves no useful purpose whatever. The pity is that it is still being used by teachers to kill children's natural creativeness. Cézanne renounced perspective in his scientist's search for a truer way to represent reality, but he remained faithful to the image before him.

Picasso and his colleagues in successive stages of Cubism attacked the whole rationalistic system of art. Not only did they reduce forms to cubes; they adopted multiple points of view and intersecting planes. For several centuries the artist had accepted the premise that the reality of a subject, a person, say, was what the artist saw from a particular point at a certain moment. But think of someone you know well. Is it not almost impossible to hold to any such arrested image? So Picasso and his followers brought about a revolution in the way the plastic artist looked at his world, a way that emancipated him from simple representation and permitted unlimited complexities of psychological vision. Picasso has adopted several styles in the half century since he invented Cubism, but he has not returned to academic literalism. For instance, the famous "Guernica" (1937) in the Museum of Modern Art, New York, includes a number of two-eyed profiles.

It is a tremendous accomplishment to bring about a revolution in taste, to be the leaders—as Cézanne and Picasso were—in changing the entire direction of the plastic arts. But this does not in itself make them great painters. For instance, Picasso's "Guernica" is often called great. To me it seems hardly more than a huge political cartoon in paint. Esthetically, that is, it seems far below the source of its inspiration, Goya's etched "Disasters of War." As social criticism, however, it rates high. The mural, nearly 12 feet x 26 feet, is a bitter memorial to the men, women, and children slaughtered by the Fascists in an air raid on the

Basque city of Guernica during the Spanish Civil War. The bull, the horse, the dismembered bodies, and the rest of the violent design form a cry of rage and pain at the bestiality of war. The emotional impact may outweigh esthetics.

OUR TIMES

One clear conclusion about art as the mirror of the spirit of the age is that it reflects the divisiveness of our times. No artist has been able to project an encompassing image of the twentieth century, only of aspects and problems. The drafting-board style of Feininger and Nicholson and the sanitary colored rectangles of Mondrian are closely related to the bone-bare functional architecture that is probably the most accurate symbol of our depersonalized industrial culture. But as reaction against the loss of footing in a world of meaning we have the turbulences of Vlaminck, Kokoschka, and Soutine; the compassionate icons of Rouault; the fantasies of Ensor, Rousseau, Dali, Tanguy, and Chagall; and the private hieroglyphics of Klee and Miro. In sculpture we have a good deal of pseudo-primitivism, the womb-like abstractions of Brancusi, Arp, and Moore, and the anguished metal emblems of Roszak and Giacometti.

Finally there are the painters who wish not only to represent no objects, not even abstractly, but also no static structural patterns such as Mondrian's—painters variously called tachists, abstract expressionists, and action painters. They can be divided according to whether their cosmos seems one of orderly housekeeping or of disorder. The work of Afro, Santomaso, Gorky, Wols, Fautrier, Riopelle, Hofmann, and De Kooning is full of tension, strife, and sometimes chaos. But other painters who are supposed to wear the same school tie—Albers, De Staël, Bissiere, Vieira da Silva, Winter, Nay, Pollock, Tobey, Tomlin, and Rothko —betray in their work an underlying tidiness. Indeed, notwithstanding the rich gurgle of recent art criticism, the work of some contemporary painters seems static, variations on the patterns of Persian rugs and other forms of Islamic decoration. It is possible that anxiety has driven them into nerveless ornamentation as a form of escape.

In our tragic century the artist has pictured the unhappy condition of modern man by various means and in differing moods. Utrillo, Vlaminck, and Chirico have symbolized it in streets and plazas empty of human life. Van Gogh has made his own haunted face a symbol. The split anatomies of Picasso and the Cubists admirably suit the allegory of the divided soul. And the further developments in abstraction and two-dimensional representation, as in Picasso's latest work, suggest man's diminishing individuality and substance, until in a vast amount of painting today he has vanished—only paint in angry swirls or tranquil ripples mark where he went down.

10

MUSIC, THE IMMORTAL DISCOURSE

Music is the most difficult of the arts to talk about; yet the easiest for you to enjoy. Unfortunately, even persons who have studied music often stop their appreciation with obvious melodies and fail to grant themselves the richer pleasure of great masterpieces. This does not mean that you should not take pleasure in a simple folk song like "Greensleeves" or in Strauss's "Emperor Waltz" before—and after—you find yourself sitting through Brahms' first symphony with delight. The point is that the greatest music *is* delightful, something to seek out eagerly, not to shy away from. You can probably reach keen enjoyment of Brahms' Symphony No. 1 sooner than you can *Hamlet* or a Cézanne still life.

My first exposure to music beyond "Humoresque" and "Barcarolle" from *Tales of Hoffman* came in my freshman year at Columbia. My German professor took me to my first symphony. As the good man closed his eyes and drank in what to him must have been the long familiar notes—of the Brahms' First, as likely as not—to my skeptical country-boy eye he seemed to be putting on an act. I doubted that anyone could make sense of those storms of sound. Not very much later I remember sitting under a midsummer moon in the Lewisohn Stadium in uptown New York listening entranced to Strauss's tone-poem "Also sprach Zarathustra." Now it seems obvious, and I fidget till it ends. You can be sure that your taste will change with exposure to great music.

Because music is a formal arrangement of sounds following strict systems of composition, you may feel guilty about enjoying it without technical knowledge of its structure. Certainly if you acquire such knowledge, it should sharpen your appreciation. It is especially desirable to be able to identify a *theme* and to follow its elaborations through a composition. You are more comfortable if you can hear the *melody* and trace its horizontal progression and be aware of the *harmony*, the vertical combination of sounds at one time. The music then emerges through the *rhythm*, the length and stress of the sounds. And of course the voices and instruments give it its special quality.

TECHNIQUE AND TASTE

Many leading authorities decry having the layman go beyond these basic elements to learn the shoptalk of the musician. A painter chooses among cobalt, cerulean, Prussian, ultramarine, and thalo blue with exquisite discrimination, but he does not expect anyone else except a fellow painter to recognize the blue chosen, only the effect it creates. So with music. The technical devices at the command of a modern composer are as awesome as those of a nuclear physicist. But they are the composer's business. He wishes you to respond to the effects he creates. And this you can do in only one way—by listening. The comforting fact is that in time you become clearly aware of subtleties of technique without knowing how they are contrived.

Many persons who have had a considerable amount of musical instruction seem not to be discriminating in their musical taste. They are more likely to inflict on their students and friends tricky pieces such as Khachaturian's "Saber Dance" than to encourage a taste for Mozart sonatas. During their student years they have had to practice intensively showy pieces, such as Rachmaninoff's Prelude in C Sharp Minor and Schubert's Impromptus, in order to develop technique. Then they abruptly give up serious study either to do something altogether different or to make a living teaching. In the shuffle they have little time for much thought about music beyond the technical proficiency of the performance.

This cult of the performer does a great deal to distort public response to music. First, it has all but driven the amateur out of the field. Listening to the professional has taken the place of music made in the home by family and friends. It leads to forgetfulness that in the first place the music is the creation of the composer, and second that it is the important thing, not the personality or the skill of the person who interprets it. The glorification of the performer also leads to emphasis on solo pieces for voice, violin, and piano. With the abundance of recordings now available, however, you can correct the lopsided impression of a composer's works you might get from concert choices, and become acquainted with his larger and more complex works.

Only those of us who are full-fledged members of advanced industrial societies do not naturally create music. All the leading composers from Bach to Bartók have delighted in jigs, gypsy dances, peasant songs, and other folk music and have used folk themes in their serious works. Here we are up against another of the mysteries of art—the magic of the songs and dances that anonymous composers, unblessed with any written system of musical notation, have passed down the memories of generations of their peoples. Today a vast body of the folk literature of all countries has been recorded and is available from the Library of Congress and other catalogued sources. It is a spine-tingling experience to hear the voices and instruments straight from a village in the African bush, an Eskimo hall, or the Malayan archipelago. Instrumental groups and singers, such as Burl Ives and Richard Dyer-Bennett, specialize in American and Western European folk music. If you wish to get your bearings in music, to make a fresh start in a field that is sure to open up exciting new vistas, try exploring folk music.

DOES MUSIC HAVE MEANING?

Before going on, let me add a few words to the opening remark. Music is difficult to talk about because words can give no specific sense of the sound of a particular passage of music. The problem is further complicated because most musicians abhor talking about music as anything but sound in organized forms. They like to say music is pure form. They grant that biographical and technical talk is legitimate. But they object strenuously to the "literary" interpretation of music—finding in it any "meaning" whatever. We have seen that artists and even some poets take much the same position, and we respect their sensibilities. It is true: All that you can say for sure about a landscape by Constable is that it is paint applied in certain arrangements of color. So the only reality of Rachmaninoff's C Sharp Minor Prelude is the sounds made by a piano when a particular person plays the piece. The sounds, like the look and fragrance of a rose, *are* the experience. Just as flowers evoke strong emotional responses whether you are a botanist or not, so does music.

But a great deal of music has another aspect. Singing is music, and the words have meaning. The music for songs, dances, and marches is not independent form. Of course, opera music "says something"—it is paralleling and reinforcing the libretto. There is religious music. Handel's "Messiah" is an eloquent statement of the Christ story in musical terms. The music for masses and the Jewish religious observances have "literary" association. Then there is "program music": Gershwin's "An American in Paris," Respighi's "Pines of Rome," Debussy's "Afternoon of a Faun," MacDowell's "To a Wild Rose," Strauss's "Til Eulenspiegel," Grieg's "Peer Gynt Suite," and a thousand similar works. They are music, and they were written to say something. We are left with symphonies, chamber music, and a large body of instrumental pieces that usually seem to have no apparent "program" content. This substantial body of music is what musicians really are talking about when they say that music is pure form.

We might make one or two additional observations. First, discussion of a piece of music when it is free of overt associative content does not necessarily involve bald statements of "It means this" or "Haydn here is saying thus." It seems legitimate to say "It suggests this to me," "It makes me feel like this," "Haydn seems to have this effect in mind," "Haydn said he had this effect in mind," "Mozart said this about this work of Haydn's." To the expert musician such commentary may be a waste of time. But possibly it may help the non-musician to listen to great works with some sharpening of awareness.

The sum of the matter is this: Music is expressive. Even at its most abstract it has an emotional quality. In its obvious forms it may go so far as to mimic natural sounds—"the sobbing of the violins"; in its subtler forms it merely suggests a general mood—sadness, for instance. This expressiveness, obvious or not, is the only meaning that music has. Behind this meaning is the form itself—the written notes, their relationships, and their progression—and the sounds that spring from them when they are sung or played. Bach's Cantata No. 131, "Aus der Tiefe," is greater than Victor Herbert's "Ah, Sweet Mystery of Life" in the estimation of experienced judges, not because it is sadder or happier or prettier, but because it has ever so much more variety and complexity of form that, incidentally, evoke feelings of far greater depth and delicacy.

In music as in any other art, the listener's reactions are a reality of *his* experience, and his experience has its own integrity, just as the composer, the score, and the performer have theirs. But this fact does not justify the boorishness of dismissing masterpieces of music after sitting through one or two performances with your mind unprepared and unfocused. Do not announce, "I don't like chamber music"—or Bach or modern music or whatever. On the other hand, do not fake a pleasure you have not had. Just keep listening.

JOHANN SEBASTIAN BACH, ENCOUNTER WITH GREATNESS

One of the simplest observations about unquestioned greatness in the arts as in science is that it is the product of a lifetime of intense industry. One of the greatest of creative forces in human guise, Johann Sebastian Bach (1685–1750), put in a long working career at poorly paid labor. Most of his works were composed for immediate occasions that dictated exacting conditions of form, voices and instruments, mood, length, and time of completion. Many were done as exercises, for fun, as compliments, or for the instruction of his children, with little thought of their being heard outside the family circle. That family was extensive. It reached back through two centuries of musicians. It included two wives. Of twenty children, two—Carl Philipp Emanuel and Johann Christian—became more esteemed in their day than their father. At his death, Johann Sebastian Bach was known to the music public solely as one of the greatest of performers on the organ and clavier. Like Shakespeare he never tried to enhance his reputation as a composer through publication. The manuscripts of his great works were divided among his sons, and many were lost, a loss comparable to that of the scores of plays by the Greek dramatists.

Bach was left an orphan at the age of ten to be brought up by an older brother. A story has it that the boy Sebastian damaged his eyesight—he went blind before he died—by copying a Buxtehude organ work by moonlight because his brother kept it from him. Copying whatever works of Palestrina, Couperin, Buxtehude, and other predecessors that fell into his hands was Bach's main form of instruction. His brother died when he was fifteen, and he became a choirboy. At nineteen he was an organist at Arnstadt near Lübeck, where he was scolded for allowing a "stranger-maiden" to sing in the church unchaperoned. Doubtless she is the cousin he married in 1707, after getting his second job as organist at Mülhausen. There he wrote the first of his great cantatas and began to be famed as an organist. In 1714, aged twenty-nine, he was appointed Concert Master to the Duke of Weimar, where musicians doubled as footmen. From 1717 to 1723 he was Chapel Master of the Duke of Anhalt-Cöthen. The duke was a violinist and singer and a member of a sect that did not believe in having music with religious service. Therefore Bach concentrated on secular music and wrote his finest instrumental works at Cöthen. The duke married a woman who had no taste for music, and Bach moved on. After the death of his first wife, Bach married again and added thirteen children to the seven born earlier. He wrote many arias for his second wife's soprano voice, and she helped him by making fair copies of his manuscripts.

THE CANTOR OF THOMASSCHULE

After 1723 for the twenty-seven years of the remainder of his life Bach was cantor of the Thomasschule in Leipzig associated with St. Thomas' Church. As cantor, Bach was responsible for the music in the five churches of the city and for civic and university occasions. His responsibilities also included instruction of the fifty-five "Thomaner" foundation scholars in singing, playing instruments, and Latin. Feeble administration, divided authority, and poor finances brought about a state of low musical standards.

Proud, obstinate, and contentious, Bach was involved in endless bickering. He complained bitterly that the school funds were too pinched to attract boys adequate to fulfill the assignments given him. Only half the boys had even passable voices, and all were dirty and disorderly. It is appalling to think that Johann Sebastian Bach ever had to lead a raggle-taggle band of boys out to serenade alumni at New Year's and to beg in the wet winter streets—or that he should be driven to worry about good weather because then his fees from funerals dropped off! Like Rembrandt before him, Bach was caught on an ebb tide: The Thomasschule and schools like it were the pathway to the university, and for generations music had been an important part of the curriculum. Now with the humanist passion for learning running strong, citizens, masters, and students were begrudging the time spent in music lessons, rehearsals, and church services. Musical talent was beginning to count less heavily in bestowing scholarships.

BACH'S MUSIC

It seems impossible that Bach wrote music of such grandeur to the tight specifications of whatever voices and instruments he could round up on the day of performance. Yet he wrote five complete annual series of fifty-nine cantatas—295 in all, new arias and recitatives for every Sunday, and oratorios, motets, masses, and passions for special religious occasions. And during the Leipzig years he went on heaping up secular songs and instrumental works to add to the treasures of his Anhalt-Cöthen years.

But the tide was running swiftly against Bach. First, the polyphonic style was on its way out. Second, the operatic sacred musical drama, into which, Apollo-like, Bach breathed life, was doomed from the start. Banned by Roman Catholic and Calvinist, it was much too opulent, baroque, catholic to survive even in the church founded by Martin Luther, who had marched up and down tootling on his flute melodies to fit his first hymns, melodies often borrowed from soldiers and lovers and topers; for, he said, "The devil does not need all the good tunes for himself." When singing in the Protestant churches became limited to hymns by the congregation, Bach gave way to banality.

For a century Bach was forgotten. Then it was the Methodist Wesley in England and the Jew Mendelssohn in Germany who recognized his greatness as a composer, something he had not noticed himself. Though much of Bach's work is lost, the scholarly society that in 1850 began editing and publishing his extant manuscripts, took fifty years to complete its task. Perhaps the simplest tribute to Bach is that every great composer since his time—Mozart, Beethoven, Brahms, Wagner, Schumann, Liszt, and every other one—has immediately recognized his greatness and called him master.

Bach's greatness must rest primarily on his religious music. He is one of the last great artists to devote his life and his art to the service of the church. By their sheer volume and variety his cantatas are his main achievement, with his oratorios and passions as pendants. His Mass in B Minor is generally regarded as one of the supreme works of man, in spite of the fact that he did not create it as an entity and never heard it performed.

Bach's secular instrumental works—concerti, suites, fantasias, variations, partitas, preludes, fugues, sonatas, toccatas—are also among the glories of human civilization, some of the evidence that there is a "fleck of divinity in the eye of the beast." Only mechanic performers, pedants, and the dull in spirit have contributed to the nonsense that Bach is difficult to understand, cold, stuffy, or monotonous. Just listen to the four Bach suites, the sort of chamber music he wrote at Cöthen for Prince Leopold and his small orchestra to play and that he used to conduct on Friday nights at Zimmermann's coffee house in Leipzig. Listen to Suite No. 3 in D. Its grave "air" for strings is surely one of the most palpably beautiful creations in the whole literature of music, as it is one of the most loved. Yet it is followed by three dances that wind up in a rollicking "gigue" that would make a cigar-store Indian kick up his heels. A few of Bach's works are severe, especially those meant as technical demonstrations. But even so uncompromising a work as the monumental "Art of the Fugue" yields deep delight with each hearing.

THE "ST. MATTHEW PASSION"

In the whole realm of art Bach's "St. Matthew Passion" of 1729 stands among the most wonderful single achievements. No matter how valid the case for pure music, here direct illustration of the text is part of the composer's intent and of the listener's response. Bach is putting into music the world's greatest drama, the trial and death of Christ. For centuries the Passion story had been familiar to everyone in Christendom, even the unlettered. The events are at the heart of the deepest beliefs of every Christian. Every detail of the incidents was known from recitation in church and from graphic representation in stained glass, painting, sculpture, engraving, and woodcuts. The simplicity, tautness, and vividness of the accounts by Matthew, Mark, John, and Luke gave the public possession of the subject to a degree shared by no other theme.

By an accident of history, Bach came to his task at a time when the Italian opera, invented in 1500, was becoming influential in Germany. His early cantatas reflect this influence in their arias, recitatives, and choruses. But the operatic treatment of religious themes reaches a high point when in 1727, Bach revises his earlier "St. John Passion," partly based on a text by Brockes, the first German poet to have the audacity to retell in a verse drama the events leading to the Crucifixion. The "St. John Passion" is

236 THE CULTIVATED MIND

a great work, but it also provided a rare opportunity for a master to try to improve on himself. In the "St. Matthew Passion," Bach did.

One Christian Friedrich Henrici wrote this verse drama, sandwiching the lapidary verses of chapters 26 and 27 of Matthew between his own emotional elaborations and Lutheran hymns, or chorales. Thus the story develops in a psychologically complex way. Holding to the Biblical text, the Evangelist narrates what takes place, in the not-quite-singing recitative style; Jesus, Judas, Peter, and others speak for themselves; and two boys' choruses, like the chorus in a Greek play, utter the lines of the Disciples and the crowd. The four solo voices—soprano, alto, tenor, and bass—representing the Christian soul, sing a commentary on the action with fervid intimacy. The chorales, supposedly sung by the congregation, offer a more removed reaction, the voice of all the faithful. The two choruses, the second originally made up of the less able of Bach's boys, supplement both the solos and the chorales and sing their own sweet commentaries.

To fulfill his routine duty of supplying the music for the Good Friday service of St. Thomas' Church on April 15, 1729, therefore, Cantor Bach had both the most profound theme known to Western man and a format and text that encouraged a dramatic intensity congenial to his mystic soul. Bach's music rises far above the banality of Henrici's verse—although that is not as miserable as the Drinker English translation makes it seem—because his text was not really the words but the events they deal with, events to which his spirit responded with a cello-like vibration.

The "Passion" opens with a breath-takingly lovely chorale prelude of instruments, double chorus of boys' voices, and a soprano, Henrici's Woman of Zion. Their intertwined tender grieving establishes the ambivalent mood that arises from the situation and permeates the entire work. This opening section laments Christ's death but ends beseeching, "Have pity on us, O Jesus." After this the tenor narration of Matthew gives the drama unified movement, but the portentous bass of Jesus is the emotional center. The Last Supper, Jesus' prophecies of what is to take place, the betrayal by Judas, the trial, the denial of Peter, the scourging, and the Crucifixion are projected in terse recitative that often descends in chilling steps as the episodes reach their grim climaxes. The instruments build celestial bridges between the recitatives and the commentaries. These choruses, arias, and chorales surround the tense unfolding of Christ's ordeal with compassionate meditation and bathe the dark events in a luminous aura.

The richness of this contrasting development is overwhelming. It contains ethereal arias such as "Blute nur, du liebes Herz" ("Yea, bleed, Thou beloved heart"), "Ich will bei meinen Jesu wachen" ("I will watch by my Jesus") with its oboe accompaniment like a bluebird in flight, the haunting "Erbarme dich, mein Gott" ("Have mercy, Lord"), and the lovely flute-accompanied "Aus Liebe will mein Heiland sterben" ("Because of love will my Savior die"). These are offset by choruses that are syncopated and strident, sometimes jazz-like to represent the impatient, callous crowd. In contrast the chorales are compassionate, brooding, prayerful. They include "Ich bin's; ich sollte büssen" ("I am the one; I should atone)," "O Haupt voll Blut und Wunden" ("O Head, all bloody and wounded"), all richly beautiful and reverential.

The climax of the "Passion" comes with Jesus' cry from the Cross: "Eli, Eli, lama, lama asabthani?" and the Evangelist's translation: "My God, my God, why hast thou forsaken me?" From this tense point, with only the Evangelist and the commentators left, the "Passion" becomes a requiem and sweeps like a great Pacific wave to its quiet end. The moving chorale "Wenn ich einmal soll scheiden" ("When I must sometime depart") is followed by the exalted double chorus "Wahrlich, dieser ist Gottes Sohn gewesen" ("Truly, this was the Son of God"), the peaceful bass recitative, "Am Abend, da es kühle war" ("At evening, when it was cool"), the touching farewell by the second boys' chorus, "Mein Jesu, gute Nacht," ("My Jesus, good night"), and the withdrawing final double chorus threaded with the spiritualized lullaby, "Ruhe sanfte, sanfte Ruh'!" ("Rest gently, gently rest").

MOZART, THE PRINCE OF CHARM

No music has more charm than Mozart's, and no musical career is sadder than his. Born in 1756 in the small Austrian city of Salzburg six years after Bach's death, Wolfgang Amadeus Mozart spent the last ten years of his short life in the gay and musical Austrian capital of Vienna. He died in 1791, aged only thirty-five; yet he had composed over 600 works. Had the powers that are so kind to mediocrity been half as kind to him, he might have lived to write 600 more wonderful works.

The bitter part of Mozart's story is that he did not lack recognition. From the time he was being dragged around Europe as a child prodigy by his musician father, authorities hailed his genius as a composer and as a performer on the harpsichord, pianoforte, organ, and violin. When he was fourteen, on a visit to Italy he composed an opera that ran twenty nights, he was given an honorary title by the Pope, and he was elected to an academy of composers. Musical triumphs studded thirty years of incredible creativeness—he habitually carried whole scores in his head and then wrote them down at the last minute at breakneck speed. Yet he never had steady dignified employment commensurate with his talents.

Mozart and his wife, the inconstant Constanze, were a happy-go-lucky pair, unfitted to cope with practical affairs. On the other hand the jealousy of rivals was an unending cause of Mozart's ill luck. Today the main cause seems that, like a business-school senior being screened by a corporation, Wolfgang Amadeus Mozart flunked the personnel test. He was small, he had a big nose, and though he was gay, lovable, and eager to please, he was a genius and would not tolerate being treated like a servant, as musicians were. So for thirty years he received applause, trinkets, and irregular commissions, but never a post that would keep his family from want or allow him to create without harassment the great music he knew was his to write.

Mozart is the ideal composer to introduce you to classical music, if you are at all intimidated by it. He was born with faultless taste. Whatever he wrote has a certain enchantment about it, like a flight of goldfinches in a field of great mullein, all dazzle and innocence and delight. Much of Mozart's music is deeply serious—even as a boy he wrote religious pieces. Yet even when his music is most serious, it is stamped with ineffable grace. No one else has ever been so successful in finding musical expression for laughter and love and what might be called the conversation of civilized society. Unless you are repelled by the smell of roses, the song of a thrush, the play of children on a windy day, and all other exquisite experiences, you cannot fail to be captivated by Mozart's charm.

K FOR KÖCHEL

Composers are often best known for their least important works, usually pieces used as piano exercises. Mozart in his deepest misery dashed off dances and other trifles to earn a few dollars —and to be remembered by the multitude for the tinkling of "In an Eighteenth-Century Drawing Room." But you will not go wrong if you use Schwann's Record Catalog as your guide to his works. These are, of course, the most commonly played pieces. After the title of each composition you will see the letter K followed by a number. The K stands for Köchel, Dr. Ludwig, Ritter von Köchel, a musician, botanist, and mineralogist, who catalogued Mozart's works, a great feat of musicology and devotion. Six hundred and twenty-six works, a lifetime of listening, though half are rarely played and have never been recorded. The thought of how much music by the masters one will never hear is maddening. Yet if you become familiar with sixty of Mozart's works, a mere tenth, you will fill countless hours with delight. Which sixty? The pleasure is all yours to decide.

One of the chief attractions of Mozart is that he wrote in about every form for every combination of instruments. He even wrote a quintet for glass harmonica, flute, oboe, viola, and cello. Like Bach and Haydn, he often wrote for particular occasions and persons. He wrote for the piano alone and the piano with one or two other instruments; for strings alone and in various instrumental combinations; quartets and quintets; full orchestral works including about fifty symphonic works; concertos, a form that he perfected; vocal works, of which the masses are major achievements; and operas. It is idle to do more than urge that your enjoyment of Mozart not stop with the piano pieces, many and matchless as they are. You might be sure to include the following: piano and violin—K. 304, 379, 481; trios—K. 496, 502, 548; quartets—K. 387, 421, 428, 458, 464, 465, 499, 575, 589, 590; quintets —K. 452, 515, 516, 581, 593; divertimenti, etc.—K. 361, 525, 563; symphonies—K. 543, 550, 551; concertos—violin, K. 207, 208, 218; piano, K. 459, 466; clarinet, K. 622; masses, K. 427, 626.

Master as he was in every other musical form, Mozart's major preoccupation was opera. It is sad to think how much the world lost because writing operas was not his occupation. Of the operas he wrote, three are masterpieces, among the greatest of human achievements—among those works of man that the Western world might at this time in history take the trouble to save from future holocausts or to export to the frontiers of space. The three great Mozart operas are the *Marriage of Figaro* (1786), *Don Giovanni* (1787), and in the last tragic year of his life *The Magic Flute* (1791). *Così fan tutte* (*All Women Are like That*, or *The School for Lovers*) (1790) is generally given a somewhat lower rank, but it contains some of Mozart's loveliest arias.

Figaro is comic. The libretto, written by Lorenzo da Ponte, was borrowed from the successful French play by Beaumarchais. *Don Giovanni,* put together by Da Ponte, is comic with a serious ending. *Così fan tutte,* also by Da Ponte, is comic. *The Magic Flute* is a romantic fantasy with a comic element and a serious background of Freemasonry. Da Ponte, a wandering Italian poet, spent his last years in New York, where he was a failure as a distiller and not much of a success as a teacher of Italian or as the entrepreneur of the first Italian opera house in America. The old adventurer, whose teaching included a tenuous connection with King's College, now Columbia, is solemnly memorialized by the Da Ponte Professorship of Italian at that institution.

Only Mozart's genius could infuse such comic material with greatness. Like John Keats, that other young genius who died young, Mozart had an exuberant sense of fun. He reveled in life and love and laughter, and opera gave his talent freedom for dramatic expression in musical terms. Probably because he had scant formal education, he was not dismayed by the absurdities on which he lavished his talents. He was happy to have a commission to write an opera, and so, like the milkmaid's swain, he was able to transmute the source of his inspiration into a thing of the utmost beauty and gaiety.

THE MARRIAGE OF FIGARO

The Marriage of Figaro is technically the best libretto Mozart had to work with. It has unity of tone and action. It is comic throughout, and it develops consistently from its basic situation to its happy ending. Figaro was the Barber in Rossini's opera *The Barber of Seville,* based on an earlier comedy by Beaumarchais. Now Figaro is about to be married to Suzanna. They are personal servants to Count Almaviva and the Countess Rosina. Though the Count has recently announced the abolition of the *droit du seigneur,* the medieval right of the master to enjoy the bride first, he wishes to make an exception in the instance of Suzanna.

The events of the opera cover the stratagems employed in the course of one day by the Count to try to secure his end and by Figaro and Suzanna to balk him, together with Figaro's escape from marrying an older woman and the Countess' winning back the love of the straying Count. A side curiosity of Beaumarchais' play is that, though Louis XVI reluctantly approved its performance, it is a milepost on the road to the bloody French Revolution. Comedy or no, it published the triumph of the servant over the master. But Da Ponte and Mozart ignored the political overtones.

Mozart had a refined sense of comic character and situation and in his music reflects the nuances of both with delicious aptness. He can clown drolly as he does in the opening scene when Figaro, as yet untormented by jealousy, fatuously rejoices that he and Suzanna may sleep in a room between those of their master and mistress. Then she can hear the Countess' bell—"din, din!" —and he the Count's—"don, don!" When Suzanna opens his eyes, he brags in the swaggering aria "Se vuol ballare, signor contino" that if the little count wants to dance, he will play the tune. Witty recitatives, duets, and arabesques of several voices are punctuated by arias as rollicking as "Non piu andrai," in which Figaro mocks Cherubino, the amorous page, about the deprivations of army life; as moving as the Countess' "Porgi, amor" imploring the restoration of the Count's love; as playful as Suzanna's "Venite, inginocchiatevi" while she dresses Cherubino in her clothes; and as lovely as the "rose aria," "Deh vieni, non tardar, o gioia bella," Suzanna's invitation to love, addressed to the jealous Figaro, who thinks it is inspired by the Count. Exquisite but subordinate instrumental music folds the opera together to produce what is much rarer than great tragedy, a masterpiece of the comic spirit, a marriage of laughter and grace on the same high pinnacle of art as Shakespeare's comedies.

DON GIOVANNI

Music historians consider *Don Giovanni* one of the supreme achievements among operas and indeed among all the arts. This is remarkable because the story zigzags from tragedy to comedy to melodrama. Don Giovanni—the great lover Don Juan of Spain —starts out by killing Don Pedro, the Commandant of Seville, as he tries to defend his daughter, Donna Anna, from the libertine. Donna Anna and her fiancé Ottavio swear to avenge her father. Unfortunately in the dark she did not see her attacker. Unremorseful, Don Giovanni with the aid of his rascally servant Leporello lives only for feminine conquests. Simultaneously he tries to throw Donna Anna and Ottavio off his track, flimflam Donna Elvira, who still loves him though he has deserted her, lay siege to a pretty country flirt, Zerlina, on the eve of her marriage, outwit her bellicose fiancé Masetto, and find fresh diversions. The farcical bustle of disguises, assignations, concealments, and disclosures abruptly turns into a serious final episode. The stone statue of Donna Anna's father comes to dinner and brings the Don to judgment. His hand clutched in the icy grasp of the statue, Don Giovanni disdains to reform and meets his doom in a blast of smoke and flame.

This is the story as it had come down from Spain in many

literary versions, including an Italian opera of 1787. Don Juan had become a universal legend. Molière had put it on the stage, and later Byron transformed it into the wittiest poem in English. In Da Ponte's treatment Don Giovanni does not hold steady. Sometimes he is a charming rascal; at others a cold-blooded scoundrel. He is equally engaged with Zerlina, a light comedy character, and with Donna Anna and Donna Elvira, who are serious and pathetic, if not quite tragic. Add the solemn tone of the absurd stone statue business at the end, and the question is: Is not the claim of greatness compromised by this mixture of values?

Are we supposed to despise Don Giovanni, admire him, be amused by him, or what? One answer is that it does not matter —in opera the story is only an excuse for the music. A more complex one is that this is an eighteenth-century, pre-romantic view of life. Don Giovanni is to be regarded seriously but not sympathetically. His never-satisfied pursuit of women is an analogue of man's unsuccessful pursuit of happiness. In the unsentimental eighteenth century he is what has happened to the tragic hero. Don Giovanni's compulsive quest of beauty, his humor, his relish of good living, his cruelty, his courage, and his unrepentant spirit are all of a piece. The tragic sense being philosophically unsuited to a libertine hero, the only tenable serious position to take is ironic. This is largely our position today.

The ironic stance was a congenial one for Mozart, whose own love of pretty women and fun had been tempered amid the gaiety and the bitterness of Vienna. Mozart wrote the music at the happiest time of his life—after the great success of *Figaro* in Prague. The score was finished outside of Prague in a party atmosphere at the estate of the gay and easy Josefa Duschek, an opera singer fallen on lucky times. The sophisticated Don Juan theme called forth all of the worldliness and all of the musical mastery that Mozart had acquired with such intensity in his swift lifetime.

In the rake's progress of Don Giovanni, Mozart saw drama and color unsensed by Hogarth in his pitiless engravings. The many-leveled play of personalities—Leporello's earthy humor and peasant concern for his own skin, Donna Anna's vengeful piety, Donna Elvira's hate-love conflict, Zerlina's temptation, the frustrations of the faithful fiancés Ottavio and Masetto, and Don Giovanni's mocking of virtue and his courage—yielded Mozart a range of emotion far greater than that in *Figaro, Così fan tutte,* or *The Magic Flute.* With wonderful expressiveness but without nineteenth-century sentimentality, Mozart endowed his seven lead roles with the richest of arias, duets, and recitatives. But his triumph lies in the way he holds this great variety of feeling within the range of sardonic humor and beauty. The point of view is always sophisticated, but the music is always beautiful.

THE MAGIC FLUTE AND THE "REQUIEM"

Toward the end of the eighteenth century an interest in magic and orientalism was sweeping Europe. Emanuel Schikaneder, who ran an amusement park on the outskirts of Vienna, decided to capitalize on the fad by means of an opera. Unhampered by talent or taste, Schikaneder threw together for Mozart an olla-podrida of fantastic characters and incidents. Prince Tamino, Papageno, a bird-catcher, Princess Pamina, the daughter of the Queen of the Night, Sarastro, High Priest of Isis and Osiris, and Monostatos, an evil dwarf, engage in a series of incidents impossible to remember. Schikaneder gave himself the fat comic part of Papageno and introduced novelties such as a maiden disclosed as the leaves of a giant artichoke unfold—and of course a magic golden flute. During the writing Schikaneder or Mozart turned the whole thing into an allegory of Freemasonry with veiled references to the Emperor, the Empress, and Jesuits.

Beaten in his ten-year struggle to establish himself in the musical circles of Vienna, harassed by debts, exhausted, Mozart had been swept into the backwaters of the city and into the company of unfashionable people like Schikaneder. With Constanze away enjoying a "cure" and the taste of death in his mouth, Mozart turned Schikaneder's fantasies into a score more truly magical than anything in the book. With his impeccable taste he clothed them in music of pure delight and, ardent Freemason that he was, added a solemn quality of great beauty.

A presentiment of death had come vividly to Mozart while he was writing *The Magic Flute*. A tall stranger dressed all in gray mysteriously commissioned him to write a requiem mass. Mozart took his fee but would not set a delivery date. So he was often visited by the lugubrious gray stranger. With the success of *The Magic Flute* and the failure of an opera in Prague crowding him, Mozart turned to the high seriousness of the requiem he knew he was writing for himself. On his death bed—he had typhus—he fought to keep his bargain. With a brilliant assist from a devoted student, after his death he did. The final irony is that the "Requiem" was first performed as the work of Count von Walsegg, the master of the mysterious stranger, as a memorial for his dead spouse—truly a pious fraud. But though Mozart was buried in a pauper's grave, the story was soon out, and the "Requiem" became a noble monument to his memory.

LUDWIG VAN BEETHOVEN, ROMANTIC PROMETHEUS

The conjunction of a great artist and his age has rarely been timed as well as the arrival of Beethoven on the European scene. The American and French revolutions had shattered the static balance of the aristocracy-dominated society to which Bach, Handel, Haydn, and Mozart had been attuned. The emergence of political democracy and the bloody vindication of the worth of the common man had ironically been followed by idolatry of the conqueror Napoleon Bonaparte. In the *Sturm und Drang* of German plays and poetry, the painting of William Blake, and the verse dramas of Byron and Shelley there was celebrated, not the good citizen enjoying his new-won share in the advance of civilization, but the untypical man pitted against society. Anti-social behavior, violence, and passion are characteristic of the romantic hero.

Ludwig van Beethoven (1770–1827), the son of a drunken musician of Bonn, seemed to have far greater odds against him than Mozart had in the struggle for worldly success in their adopted city of Vienna. He was undersized, ugly, uncouth, ill-mannered, suspicious, intolerant, self-centered, grasping, and on occasion dishonest. His boorishness was often heightened by rages. Since much of his obnoxious behavior was directed at benefactors, it would seem that he would have suffered Mozart's ill luck with interest. Instead, from his teens Beethoven enjoyed critical recognition, social adulation, publication, financial support from noble patrons, advance payments for works, and public performances. But Beethoven could be self-critical, contrite, and lavishly generous, and he must have had an attractive side to inspire so much tolerance and loyalty. He brought a good deal of grief on himself by his excessive affection for his nephew and his muddleheaded effort to be a father to him. Like a number of great creative persons, he was ill most of the time; for the last twenty-five years of his life he suffered the onset and then the catastrophe of deafness.

No doubt Beethoven dramatized himself as the man of genius above the conventions of the crowd, the superman that later in the century his countryman Nietzsche exalted in flatulent rhetoric. His life was crowded with the drama of an unhappy childhood, lofty ambitions, passionate loves unconsummated by marriage, amazing creative vitality crowned by tremendous successes, and tragedy. The times permitted him to play the role of genius flouting the rules with impunity. The catch is that he was a genius. His personality and behavior are to us of no consequence, except as they contributed to the creation of his music. About this mystery of his creativeness, it is possible to say only that his rebelliousness and egocentricism encouraged him to aspire to create great works in new shapes, to be a one-man revolution. But suffering and defeats must have led him to extract solace from the beauty and order of the musical universe, as certainly they brought him to brood over the riddles of human destiny.

Beethoven, like Mozart, wrote every form of music: songs, piano, violin, and other instrumental solos, quartets and works for other groups of instruments, concertos, music for the theater, religious music, opera, and symphonies. Circumstances fell so that he wrote only one religious work to compare with Bach's, the great "Missa Solemnis," and only one opera, *Fidelio. Fidelio* never fully satisfied him; yet its subtitle, "Conjugal Love," and its serious dungeon melodrama of a disguised wife rescuing her imprisoned husband indicate how far in his first try he pushed opera beyond his beloved *Magic Flute* into the full tide of romanticism. As we have noted, Bach explained his achievements by saying simply that he worked hard. The notebooks of Beethoven are illuminating evidence how hard genius does work —the slow groping from the first sketchy notions through numerous revisions to the final score that seems so inevitable and "inspired." Beethoven enlarged the scope of every musical form from the piano sonata on, introduced daring technical innovations, and added an emotional range and intensity not dreamt of before. He left his special imprint on the symphony and the quartet.

THE HEROIC FORM

Beethoven's greatness might easily rest on his symphonies alone. Greatness has a quantitative aspect as well as a qualitative one. Chopin's etudes, preludes, and impromptus do not have the weight of greatness. Beethoven's nine symphonies have this weight. To join the elect, a creative artist, like a scientist, must also move his medium ahead—either by new inventions or by carrying the work of his predecessors to new heights. Bach did the latter. In symphonic music Beethoven did both. He took the symphonic form where Haydn and Mozart had left it, and turned it into the noblest expression of the spirit of his age that exists in any form.

Haydn wrote over one hundred symphonies and Mozart wrote thirty-nine. Before Haydn and during his earlier years the symphony was not the large serious affair that we are accustomed to. It was conceived mainly as instrumental diversion in the salons of the nobility, was circumscribed in size and unadventurous in structure, and was primarily agreeable in nature. Mozart had written one when he was eight. His 1778 symphony (K.297) and his last great three added to the stature of the form, and Haydn followed him in his last twelve.

Beethoven was thirty when in 1800 he got round to emulating

the two other great masters of Vienna. Not till his third effort, the "Eroica" of 1804 did he make the form fully his own. Then the symphony was reborn in all its might and amplitude. Of his nine symphonies the Third, Fifth, and Seventh are the most familiar, the Sixth (the "Pastorale") the most delightful, and the Ninth the most tremendous. Because the Fourth and Eighth are not performed as often as the others, they sometimes seem fresher.

The symphony is the musical form most expressive of certain important aspects of the new romanticism that was in the air Beethoven breathed. Restraint, structure, elegance were characteristic of eighteenth-century art. The forces that had liberated the American colonies and France drew the artist about 1800 to give precedence to freedom, feeling, and sincerity. The great universal themes of man's destiny in the universe once more troubled poets like Goethe, Schiller, Blake, Wordsworth, and Shelley. Rebellion against oppression and convention was sanctioned everywhere.

By taking on himself the philosophic concern for the fate of mankind assumed by the poets and by enlarging the dimensions of the customary three movements to accommodate the emotional burden he put on them, Beethoven made the symphony the leading vehicle of serious music. The passion and grandeur that Beethoven evoked made necessary permanent changes—larger orchestras, a wider variety of instruments such as the trombone, and a bold use of the whole orchestra as an instrument. The result might be crudely simplified by saying that along with greater seriousness Beethoven introduced more noise and more contrasts. More significantly, Beethoven imposed an emotional dominance over structure and gave the symphony an organic development —that is, he takes a handful of notes as a theme and makes them grow, branch, bud, and foliate until his symphony, like a huge pasture elm, spreads to majestic heights. His suffering, believing soul led Beethoven to a progression, as in the Promethean Ninth Symphony, from the probing statement of a problem, through doubt and sadness, to final victory and exultation. If you have any doubt about what music has to say to you, try listening to the Ninth. Of course, it will mean much more to you if you too have suffered than if you have not.

THE ENCHANTMENT OF CHAMBER MUSIC

It is curious that so many people are willing, even eager, to say that they find chamber music intimidating. The main reason, of course, is that they hear so little and then in the mortuary atmosphere of a concert hall rather than in the intimacy of a music lover's living room for which it is intended. Another reason is that the talk of chamber music buffs, like that of golf, jazz, and horse-racing fans, seems to the uninitiated to be forbiddingly technical and pretentious. But as we have already agreed, you do not have to be a jockey, a trainer, or a veterinarian to enjoy a horse race.

To experience the special excitement of chamber music, you have to do nothing more than sit still and listen. (It should be a misdemeanor punishable by fine to cough during a symphony or opera and a penal offense to talk, but only capital punishment seems suitable for persons who talk during chamber music.) The special appeal of a quartet arises from the exquisite balance of the four voices—first violin, second violin, viola, and cello. In the works of the masters these four voices talk together sociably, whisper, debate, challenge, laugh, mourn, and unite to pronounce the most dignified, droll, or dramatic judgments.

This fine balance seems to me thrown off by the omission of one voice in a trio or by the addition of the bullying piano or an alien wind instrument in a quintet. You may not share my bigotry. I will not quarrel with you, so long as you make an effort to understand why many of us are exasperated by the canard that the enchantment of chamber music is reserved only for the few. Denied the monopolistic advantage of solos or the theatricality of the full orchestra, the instruments do not acknowledge the audience even by facing it but speak with one another in the most intimate preoccupation. The special balance of opportunity and limitation offered by the quartet has made it a form of discourse peculiarly fitted for some of the greatest composers to make their most profound personal statements.

Beethoven wrote sixteen quartets. He came to the quartet even later than to the symphony. Haydn had written over seventy-five and Mozart twenty-six. Haydn had slowly disengaged chamber

music from its casual nature and its subservience to the harpsichord. His mature quartets set Mozart afire and led him to write
the great six compositions that he dedicated to Haydn. They in
turn inspired Haydn to greater heights. In his six earliest efforts,
as in his first two symphonies, Beethoven respectfully, but brilliantly, explores the quartet as his two masters had shaped it.
They had established its form and suffused it with exquisite
charm. If you have any reservations about chamber music, expose yourself to Haydn's and Mozart's. Their intent was to entertain intimate audiences. They often wrote parts for titled
amateurs—Haydn wrote 126 trios alone for his employer, Prince
Nicholas Esterházy, who played an instrument called a "baryton."
Their works are still the delight of amateur chamber music
groups, though the last compositions of both stiffen the demands
on the players.

Beethoven accepted support from wealthy nobles, but he wrote
only at the command of that inner voice that possessed him, as
head down he walked furiously through sun and rain about the
Vienna streets or the country fields nearby. From the outset until
the end Beethoven had the good fortune to have capable musicians under the devoted Schuppanzigh at hand to play his
chamber music. It was well that he had, for his later works
were at first incomprehensible to his contemporaries—they even
thought he was joking, so far from eighteenth-century custom
had he moved. But the technicalities of Beethoven's chamber
music—he wrote about three dozen other pieces of chamber
music besides the sixteen quartets—are the professional problems of musicians, not ours.

Five years after the six quartets of 1801 Beethoven wrote the
three of Opus 59 that have come to be referred to by the name
of Count Rasoumovsky, the Russian ambassador to Austria who
commissioned them. In 1809, Beethoven wrote Opus 74, the
"Harp," and in 1810 Opus 95, the "Serioso." The three Opus 59
Rasoumovsky quartets are among the most completely satisfying
of musical works. Their good humor, graceful invention, and
serene seriousness show their kinship to Haydn and Mozart. But
their passages of deeper emotional tone mark the emergence of

a new form of musical discourse. Chamber music now takes on "significance": in the mysterious way of art it must transmute the composer's insights into musical expression that, while obeying the strict discipline of the form, adds to our comprehension of those aspects of existence, such as joy, love, grief, and reverence, that we find words inadequate to express.

THE GREAT LAST QUARTETS

Fourteen years after the "Serioso," having reached the pinnacle of his powers in the "Missa Solemnis," the Ninth Symphony, and many a lesser work, Beethoven turned once more to quartets. That he did so because he was in financial straits, and had generous English and Russian commissions to cheer him, does not lessen the sense that in these last quartets genius met perfect fulfillment. Beethoven had tested his powers on every known form and had mastered them all. He was one with Rembrandt of the "Family Group" of Brunswick and Shakespeare of *The Tempest*—so completely in control of his technique that he could command it to express whatever musical thoughts he had, with no doubts about the execution. What were those thoughts? Here the mystery of the essence of art baffles us again. But you cannot listen to these noble works without the conviction that Beethoven puts into the language of music some of the most profound reflections on human destiny that have ever floated to the still surface of a man's reverie.

In this sequence of works, one following the other in one sustained burst of creative energy, Beethoven found in the reticences and eloquences of the four voices of the strings the perfect mode for expressing his deepest feelings about life. In his symphonies Beethoven speaks in oracular language to the world about universal themes. In his solos he takes the audience into his confidence much as a lyric poet does. In the last great quartets he seems to forget the audience, to be listening to the conversation of the four voices, his own voice, even as sleepless in the dark all of us, bewildered, defenseless, living on the edge of tragedy, listen to ourselves wonder about life, ask questions, weigh answers, doubt, despair, acquiesce. The difference is that, even in half-sleep, our feelings turn to thoughts and they to banal words. In these quartets they turn to immortal sounds.

Like the early quartets (Opus 18) and the Rasoumovsky (Opus 59), the last quartets have been recorded together and can be heard as one unique experience. In this unity you will find much diversity. No. 127 should induce you to shake off the "respectful apprehension" that, as Roger Ficke says, used to be accorded these works. Its grave second movement is in itself so beautiful that it engenders something of that shivery reaction that Wordsworth must have had in mind when he wrote about "thoughts that do often lie too deep for tears." The adagio Cavatina is Beethoven's Christlike benediction on all who bear the burden of the world's sadness, a short movement so tender, poignant, and lovely that Beethoven wept as he wrote it.

You must not think that these five quartets are unrelievedly somber. They contain energy and gaiety, even dance tunes. But it is always as though Beethoven is summing up life, that his nearly total deafness forces him to *remember* the bustle and laughter at a distance, just as he seems in the two slow movements in Opus 127 and Opus 130 and in the brooding serious passages of the great Opus 131—his greatest quartet, he thought—to be moved not by sadness but by pity. Thus Beethoven, mightiest of romanticists, arrives at the same complex vision of reality and the same pervasive compassion that make him one with Euripides, Dante, Shakespeare, Cervantes, Milton, Rembrandt, Bach, and the other great spirits who have made their art a source of pleasure, an acknowledgment of man's tragic entrapment, and a revelation of his essential nobility.

EPILOGUE

No Restoration or eighteenth-century play was complete without an epilogue, a short speech to the audience wittily defending the play and disposing of criticism—and critics—in advance. Now at the end of this confrontation with greatness in philosophy, science, literature, and the arts, to be either humorous or critical is unseemly. True, when I think of my effrontery in electing myself your guide in this journey among masterpieces, I am seized with the same nervous desire to laugh one feels in places like Grant's Tomb. And no critic is likely to help me to realize any more acutely than I do now that not a single page of this book does justice to its subject. I am appalled at how little I have managed to say and at how much I have not said anything about at all.

But my mission has been a modest one. It has not been to propagate my preferences, which are of course debatable; my aim has been to bring you into the company of great and stimulating spirits with whom possibly you have not been fully acquainted before or from whom you may even have thought you had little to learn. During the course of this introduction, my conversation, like that of a marriage broker, has been largely irrelevant. Only what happens between you and the person under consideration matters. Like an honest broker, though, on one point I must insist—the enthusiasms I register, the reactions I report, have all been experienced afresh while I was writing.

Neither you nor I will ever have a cultivated mind in an absolute sense. Only a limited mind would seriously harbor the possibility. In the relative sense discussed in the first chapter we can both be hopeful. You can see, therefore, why it does not matter so much how many works of art I have discussed or you can identify. The only matter of significance is the quality of the effect sustained exposure to the Great Teachers has on you. It is my passionate conviction that you will discover this effect to be an almost unbelievable enlargement of the intellectual and imaginative resources on which you rely to give your life meaning and order and joy.

We have not had space to emphasize how the concern with all of the liberal arts gives to the cultivated mind a sense of placement, an ability to make fruitful connections among apparently unrelated phenomena. We could demonstrate the force of this proposition in reverse simply by giving thought to how profound must be our ignorance if we are unable to place a phenomenon—an event occurring at a certain date, 1535, let us say—against a background of contemporary architecture, agriculture, history, law, and religion. Yet in this book we have hardly set foot in any of these wide provinces of human activity. We must not be dismayed. The farther we push our inquiries, the more eager we are to go on. At this time, for instance, how urgent it is to know Africa. How exciting it must be for those young Americans who are beginning to know the geology, geography, anthropology, ecology, economics, language, art, and all the other ways of comprehending this continent as its peoples emerge from millennia of tribal darkness.

But the most important discovery to be made in an exploration of philosophy, science, biography, fiction, drama, poetry, painting, and music is that the stubborn struggle for clarity, unity, and beauty underlying all of the forms is applicable to your own life. Through the ages cruelty, ugliness, misery, and fear have dominated human existence, and still do in most parts of the earth. Only the forces of reason, imagination, and love, manifest in science, religions and other social systems, and the arts, have prevailed against the destructive energies of nature and the animality of man. The individual today faces an extraordinary paradox: He is being deprived of both his sense of personal identity and, except in war, any sense of a common purpose deeply shared with his fellow man; yet he is rapidly being blessed by both leisure and longevity beyond the dreams of his ancestors. As you draw inspiration from the company of the great creative spirits, you will strengthen both the uniqueness of your individuality and the bonds of your relatedness to others.

APPENDIX

A PROGRAM FOR GROWTH

All of us grow. We vary in degree and in the direction our growth takes. But all of us can cultivate our minds more, just as we can lose weight, if we seriously try. It is necessary, of course, to have reasonable ideas about how much growth is possible. The great creative minds should be our constant inspiration. But it is idle to talk about "culture" as though it were some exotic power which, like solid fuel, might propel us into fellowship with Newton and Leonardo. Rather, we are concerned with a conceivable increase in habitual attitudes and behavior that will make us more productive, more aware, and more interesting.

It is well to recognize at the outset three of the chief reasons why we usually do not measure up to our full potential. First, most of us are held back by inhibitions of one kind or another. In our security- and comfort-oriented society, parents and teachers rarely encourage creative thinking and actions because they lead to change and this constitutes an attack on the status quo— that is, on *them*. Thus by the time most of us begin our adult careers, we are conditioned to living within the norms of thought and behavior prescribed by others—just as Bacon said long ago. So we stop growing.

Second, many of us find ourselves inhibited by our environment, particularly by our superiors and associates wherever we work. Or so we believe. Supervisors and fellow workers often show a lamentable lack of enthusiasm for new ideas. Often the sense of rebuff, especially when we are young, arises from inexperience, failure to understand others, and lack of tact in presenting new ideas. At any rate, we stop growing.

The third, and main, reason that most of us have not the cultivated minds we would like to have is that we do not make the effort that has to be made. To a considerable degree, we are not sure how to go about making such an effort. In *The Cultivated Mind*, I have tried to give a background and motivation for that effort. Now in this Appendix I will offer some suggestions for what might be a broad and sustained growth program.

CREATIVE GROWTH

What is this growth we are talking about? It is many things. It cannot be the same for you and anyone else, since your goal is the fulfilling of *your* potential. You may find in the study of astronomy a partial remedy to your lack of understanding of the physical universe. Your wife may be a serious student of the piano and your son of Russia. You have no need to match the intensity of their studies, nor they yours. Much of your program for growth must therefore be a pursuit of those experiences that hold a deep interest for you. It will also include wide exploration beyond the interests you already have, in order to find new ones. Yet equally important is your need to enter into meaningful discourse with others, to have a just appreciation of their interests and in so doing to increase your appreciation of them as individuals. By reading books about music and Russia, by listening to music, by intelligent conversation, you can forge new links of understanding with your wife and son and others. At the same time you will be learning—which has the same relation to personal development as eating has to physical growth.

Developing a cultivated mind is not the result merely of a few years of formal study. It is partly the result of a lifetime of study, and it is no less the product of a lifetime of practice, preferably within a hospitable environment. Most of us now have ample opportunity to continue our formal education from wherever it left off. Continuing education at school, college, and graduate level is available in most communities. Business, civic, and social organizations sponsor courses, short programs, and lectures in bewildering profusion. The miraculous advances in the techniques of reproducing sounds and images, coupled with advances in literacy and economic well-being, have brought the best of music, drama, art, and literature into our homes. And these manifestations of the human spirit at its noblest are available to a respectable degree in the libraries, little theaters, concerts, and museums of towns of modest size. In addition, the great riches of Chicago, Washington, Boston, New York, and the other large cities are today much closer than they used to be.

Some of the suggestions in this Appendix will not fit your needs or circumstances, but few will be too difficult for you to carry out. Lack of resources is hardly likely to be a serious handicap. Almost anywhere you live, cultural riches are available to you with almost no effort and at little or no cost. All that you have to do is to say to yourself, I honestly do want to make the liberal arts a living part of my daily life; to this end I will follow a permanent growth program of my own. The rest is sheer pleasure.

Once you have made intellectual growth an objective, it becomes a way of life. It is impossible to limit it, as though it were a trivial hobby like collecting match folders. It goes on in one guise or other during hours of work and of leisure. The result of your efforts will be a sense of aliveness, an eagerness to learn, and a thankfulness that you have resources with which to meet the needs of everyday living and to satisfy the more imperious demands of the spirit.

STUDYING WITH OTHERS

You will make conscious efforts to extend your interests in two general ways. You will study, and you will do. Your study may be in a formal course, in an informal group, or alone. A formal course usually gives assurance of acquaintance with essentials in the shortest time. It also provides fellowship and criticism. If you cannot go to a regular class, you might find a home-study course given by a university a satisfactory substitute. A Great Books Program is an alternative that you should consider. Your librarian can tell you whether or not one is active in your community. If it is not, you might form a group. The virtues of the Great Books Program are that you confront great writings in all fields and that you develop your reactions by means of teacherless discussion.

Do not register for a course unless you can do the reading assigned. Listening to someone talk about books that you have not read is a fraud. If you do the reading in advance, the lectures and the discussion will help you to clarify your reactions to what you have read. Otherwise, the time you spend going to hear a lecture—say one evening a week—might better be spent reading at home or in the public library. The same is true of a study group. The value of the usual literary club report or paper is nil because too often the members listen to judgments about something they have not experienced.

A book club worth belonging to might run according to the following ground rules: All members will read the same books and do equal assignments. Any member unable to keep up with the reading will drop out. No minutes will be kept. No food will be served. One or two members will act as discussion leaders at each meeting. This responsibility will rotate. Members will bring their books with them. (Paperbacks are indicated.) One will give a succinct summary in no more than five minutes. In accordance with the type of book, the summary will identify the author, the background, what happens, and the main ideas. The discussion might start by trying to secure agreement on the theme and key issues raised. These should be explored with concrete reference to the book. Members of groups too often ignore the specifics of books and spend their time debating large social problems. The other main aspect of the discussion might concern the quality of the writing and might be illustrated by reading brief passages of special effectiveness. A quick final evaluation is desirable. Rigid procedures are undesirable in a friendly group, but aimless expression of likes and dislikes is juvenile. An underlying plan such as the one suggested can make a literary club a lively intellectual experience instead of the waste of time most of them are.

STUDYING ALONE

You may decide to go it alone, as indeed you must most of the time. Courses and study groups are only beginnings. No mind ever becomes cultivated except through its own effort. The major part of this effort is reading. The simple reason that so few of us, including those of us who are college graduates, have minds that can be called cultivated, is that we read little and what we read is light. We starve our minds on a low-protein diet of newspapers, magazines, and chance book selections. To grow, you have to have the nourishment of solid books. You need a steady diet of hours of serious, extensive reading every week. On the shelves of the library you help to support are enough of the right books to keep you in good mental health for life. What your library does not have, it can get for you on loan.

Owning books, having them at hand when you want them, and rereading them provide a strong incentive to master their contents and to build your interest around them. Reference books are a scholar's best friend. The *Encylopaedia Britannica*, for example, is the starting place for inquiry about any subject, and it is a great arouser of respect for the wide world of knowledge. The articles are authoritative, and the bibliography at the end of each sends you on to the next step in an investigation. According to your own interests, you will find other reference books indispensable in saving your time by giving you accurate information when you want it. Of course, a great deal of anyone's education must come from diligent use of a good dictionary; an unabridged dictionary makes excellent reading.

It is a truism of education that you learn by doing. Doing, in terms of what we have been talking about, has three meanings: You think about what you read and otherwise experience; you formulate your thoughts in writing or speech; and possibly you engage in similar activity. One aid to thinking is note-taking. In your own books you might use the margins and blank pages. If you are gathering facts and ideas from different sources, 3" x 5" cards are useful. They are easy to carry, and they can be filed and rearranged rapidly. Talking about your intellectual interests is one of the best ways to make sure of what you know and to contribute something besides your presence and platitudes to conversations. Doing something creative on your own may be the most satisfying reward you get from any study. This might take the form of research on the ecology of your backyard, just as well as painting pictures or writing a play.

READING AND DOING

In the course of reading the previous chapters of this book, you will presumably examine the works discussed. Beyond that you do not need any elaborate reading list to guide you. Just follow the radiating pattern of the ripples after a pebble is thrown into a pool. At the center is the person or work discussed. The first work under Biography is *Plutarch's Lives*. If you wish to become better acquainted with this famous book, you might start by reading the life of Pericles. Then you can radiate out by reading the other lives, about Plutarch, other studies of Pericles, histories of Greece and Rome, and so on. After following this procedure as your interest dictates, you can explore for yourself in the wide and wonderful field of biography, autobiography, essays, diaries, and letters. You will find the same simple radiating pattern applies to all your reading—after *Hamlet* there are more plays by Shakespeare; after Shakespeare there are other Elizabethan playwrights; and so on.

By all means read the works themselves, not just books about them. Deciding which of a number of books on the same subject you should read is a problem that in time you will not find difficult. In addition to what you can learn from outside sources about an author and his book, every book offers clues as to its worth—the tone of the title, the date, the publisher, the typography, and the jacket write-up. You will find published reading lists and reference librarians both helpful. But the best way to make up your mind about which books to read carefully is to browse among them in the stacks, sample passages as you stand at the shelves, take an armload home, read.

What you might *do* about biography, philosophy, and other social studies depends on your inclinations. Autobiographies, family histories, and regional biographies and histories offer the challenge of available material. They need not be tedious. Amateur efforts at writing on philosophy, sociology, or economics run the danger of being naïve. If you are not experienced in writing, I would suggest that you start in this area by keeping a journal after the fashion of Emerson's. Try each day to enter some fresh thought or observation in a few compact and colorful sentences. In the long run, of course, ability to express yourself well in writing is one of the marks of a cultivated mind. That ability comes only from practice.

Science offers fascinating possibilities for active interests, even for someone ungrounded in any scientific field. Without reaching even the status of a member of the Audubon Society, I have derived great pleasure from increasing acquaintance with birds. In appropriate surroundings all you need are a handbook or two, feeding stations, woods and fields to walk in, and someone to swap anecdotes with. The first time you see a pileated woodpecker or a wood-duck are memorable occasions. You grow more sophisticated when a sparrow is no longer a sparrow but a white-crowned, white-throated, song, field, lark, vesper, or other member of the family. Gradually, as you observe, read, attend lectures, and come in contact with the disciplined unsentimental work of professional ornithologists, you begin to appreciate the elegance of scientific method and to marvel at the intricate interdependency of bird, bug, flower, and tree.

Wildflowers offer a parallel edification. A garden does the same, and adds exercise, too. Mushrooms are an exact science—you should know exactly which are which before eating them. Collecting stones, shells, and butterflies leads into similar discovery of the methods and materials of science. Astronomy, geology, and archaeology have always been attractive fields for amateurs. If you have a desire to investigate chemistry, physics, biology, or any other laboratory science, you should start with competent instruction before experimenting with amines or arachnids in the bathroom.

RECORDINGS AND READING ALOUD

In the chapter on poetry I emphasized reading aloud because this is an intrinsic part of experiencing poetry. Since some verse is especially appealing to read, you might borrow my *Poems to Read Aloud* from the library. Take advantage of any opportunity to talk to reputable poets—and all other creative artists—about their work. But if poetry has been literally a closed book for you, as it is for most, the multitude of splendid recordings now available in libraries and record shops should open up its riches for you. Start with Dylan Thomas reading his own poems and keep listening. Read aloud the same poems after you have heard them.

Recordings of plays have also become abundant. You can hear some plays that you may never have a chance to see in a theater —Shakespeare's *Measure for Measure* and Dylan Thomas' *Under Milk Wood,* for instance. But since plays are meant to be seen as well as read and heard, you should make every effort to see as many serious plays as you can. Keep track of what is being offered in your area, particularly at universities. They usually put on classics and significant new drama. If you can possibly do so, plan ahead to see the best of the season in New York, off Broadway as well as on.

The best way to experience a play fully is to take part in an actual production as an actor or director. If you cannot join a theater group, make believe—read every play as though you are going to direct a performance. Almost any line, you will see at once, can be read in several ways. How you would guide an actor in reading any one speech and tell him and the other actors what to do at that moment depends on your grasp of the tone and meaning of the entire play and thus the relation of this part to the whole. You will find this approach to play reading much more illuminating than reading along just "to see what happens." Your understanding and pleasure will be intensified several times over if you read aloud with a group. Such a reading before seeing a play in the theater will sharpen your reactions to the performance.

CREATIVE WRITING

Your insight into novels, short stories, essays, poetry, and plays will be enhanced by writing some—one of each, say. This is a tall order and can be disregarded without guilt. Yet it is probably a sign of the immaturity of our culture that American businessmen, bankers, lawyers, engineers, scientists, or doctors rarely engage in serious creative writing. Such a combination is fairly common in Europe. Success in selling furniture or removing cysts should not be a bar to writing a sonnet or a novel. Perhaps after studying contemporary verse, let us say, you write something of the same sort in rimeless or off-rime verse; you may discover a serious lifelong avocation. Or perhaps you translate some of the moral dilemmas of a modern business executive into novel or play terms; you may become another C. P. Snow.

THE PLASTIC ARTS

For consistency of discussion, I limited my remarks to painting in Chapter 9. You need not limit yourself so drastically. Your investigation should include prints, sculpture, ceramics, architecture, and allied art forms. You might, for instance, take an interest in printing. It is a fine art with a humanistic history, learned conventions, and subtle charm. Because painting seems an easier art form to understand than most persons realize and is the least rigorous to practice, I will make somewhat extensive suggestions about this part of your growth program.

Visit all of the art museums and galleries easily accessible to you. Go often for one hour and try to *see* a few works thoroughly. Listen to gallery talks. Do not overlook shows at universities, commercial art galleries, and department stores or any private collection that may be seen by appointment. Collect whatever information about the exhibitions that you can and then find out more about the artists and their works. Museums publish books, pamphlets, photographs, and prints. Try to know something about the most famous works in a distant museum before you go there. Do not wander idly about a museum. Study what you see, and leave before you are exhausted.

Watch for announcements of current art shows and talks in your area. Occasionally a special exhibition will bring within your reach works that you will never have another chance to see. Museums and libraries usually have loan services that enable you to borrow framed reproductions, prints, replicas of sculpture, and even original works. You might join your local art association or "friends of the museum," as it may be called. You then have special privileges such as private showings with gallery talks and meetings with artists and critics. If your community has no art activities, why not help start some?

Become an art collector. This need not be an ambitious or expensive undertaking. You can start by cutting reproductions from magazines. You can buy prints in second-hand shops; an interest such as law or wildflowers or political caricature can be your focal point. I have enjoyed collecting English illustrated books in a modest way. Original paintings and other works by established artists are expensive enough to be looked on as investments. But every community of 25,000 or more has competent artists, some of whose paintings, prints, ceramics, or sculpture you can buy for five to one hundred dollars. You can then have live art about you for enjoyment and stimulation. Do not be timid. You will probably outgrow your first purchases. As you become more knowing, your purchases may well increase in value.

A good many persons have tried their hand at art with discouraging results. One trouble is that they take an academic course without enough serious interest to get them over the hurdle of learning basic techniques. One answer, therefore, is to be serious and to take the time to master these skills. Beginners invariably tackle much too difficult technical problems. Drawing is a mechanical skill, but it is not learned quickly. To do an accurate drawing of a face or a flower takes patient apprenticeship. In addition, to try to capture the colors observed, particularly in watercolors, is an extraordinarily difficult feat. Oils have a great advantage—you can paint out your errors.

If you have tried to paint without success, try doing nonrepresentational designs. They require none of the hand skill needed for representing objects. They allow you to let yourself go and spread paint on canvas, or on cheaper masonite or cloth-covered cardboard panels. Yet they will help you grasp some of the basic problems of art quickly. Imitate but do not copy the work of several of the nonrepresentational painters, such as Mondrian, Nicholson, Soulages, Poliakoff, and Tapiès. For more original exercises you may find inspiration in the patterns of rocks and shadows. In the end you will find that when you do not have the image of a real object or scene to check against, handling form and color and their relationships is a challenging game. You will be exhilarated when you finally produce something interesting enough to frame.

Among the various other arts and crafts, you may find working with the new polymers has special appeal. But if all else fails, I recommend what, inaccurately, I call driftwood sculpture. It consists simply in mounting a small piece of driftwood on another piece as a base. My rule is not to polish or paint the beautiful weathered surfaces. Selecting two pieces of driftwood that are interesting and harmonious in shape, texture, and color is an excellent creative exercise.

MUSIC TO GROW BY

Music surrounds us without effort on our part. It is easy to flatter ourselves that it is more a part of our lives than it is. Perhaps a self-analysis would be helpful: (a) What has your musical experience been—performing? study of musical appreciation? attendance at concerts? ownership of records or tapes? listening to FM broadcasts? (b) What types of music do you like and dislike? What is the degree of your understanding? Who are the composers whose works you can identify? (c) Keep programs and other records of your musical experiences for the next six months. Then ask yourself the questions in (b). What have you learned?

A course in musical appreciation is a standard offering in adult education programs and in organizations such as the Association of American University Women. Some FM stations offer splendid programs of classical music with intelligent comment and restrained commercials. They list their programs in advance. If listening to the radio is especially convenient for you, buy an FM radio or a tuner to plug into your hi-fi set. You probably have a high-fidelity record player. If you are not sure about its quality, a technician or a hi-fi enthusiast among your friends will check it for you. Tape recorders have advantages that might appeal to you. How representative is your record collection? Check over the Schwann catalog to see what major composers and forms you lack. Buy steadily to fill the gaps. Records borrowed from a library or a friend will help you decide which ones you want to own.

The best way to make sure you hear live music in sufficient amounts is to subscribe for series of concerts. You would have to live in a remote area not to have some sort of concert series or musical organization within driving distance. Small colleges often have excellent musical groups, and large universities offer a wealth of student, faculty, and guest recitals and concerts. Evenings at home wholly devoted to music, whether live or recorded, with no talking allowed except between pieces, are a part of a civilized existence.

If you have any musical ability at all, try to find a way to exercise it. Take lessons. Join a choir, orchestra, or chamber music group. If you want to start on something less difficult than a standard instrument, try a recorder. An ensemble for recorders is a delightful family activity. If you have no one to play with, playing a part along with a phonograph recording is a possibility. Composing your own works, of course, has the same need for disciplined learning that creative activity in any other art form has, but it must give deep satisfaction.

Finally let me say that wonderful experiences wait for you in the music before and after Bach, Mozart, and Beethoven. Scarlatti, Brahms, Berlioz, Mendelssohn, Schumann, Liszt, Chopin, Wagner, Tchaikovsky, Dvořák, Debussy, Ravel, Stravinsky, Bartók—the list is not inexhaustible because genius is rare. You will have to explore for yourself to discover what finally interests you. You will almost certainly find modern music bewildering at first. I must confess that I am only in the process of getting acquainted. My knowledgable musical friends say, "Try Bartók." So I listen to Bartók. I remember him as a sad-faced refugee who rode up and down with me in the same elevator at Columbia. His music is discordant to the point of intolerability. But I have long since come to feel at ease among the discordances of contemporary poetry and painting. I have only to be patient and keep listening to the works of Bartók, Bloch, Honegger, Hindemith, Berg, and the other contemporaries, I am confident, and they will become at least accessible to me. You can have no greater handicap in this exploration than I have.

I would not have you think that these suggestions are meant to comprise a systematic or exhaustive program. They are meant to encourage you to take specific action to break through any barriers that you feel are between you and those concrete experiences which, accumulating day by day through the years, make up the amenities of the cultivated mind.

INDEX

Voyage of the "Beagle," (Darwin), 69

Way of the World, The (Congreve), 172

Webster, John, 194

Wild Duck, The, (Ibsen), 174

"Words in Time" (MacLeish), 185

Wordsworth, William, 67, 195

Writing, creative, 265

Yeats, William Butler, 126, 195

ABOUT THE AUTHOR

Born on Long Island, N. Y., EDWARD HODNETT attended Columbia University, where he received his A.B. and Ph.D. degrees. He taught English and held an administrative post at Columbia, where he also served as an editor of the Columbia University Press and editor of the *Columbia University Quarterly.*

Dr. Hodnett has had wide experience in university affairs, having served as dean at the University of Newark (now a part of Rutgers); vice-president at the University of Massachusetts; president of Fenn College in Cleveland; and professor of English at Ohio University. He is currently assistant to the president of the Dow Corning Corporation in Midland, Michigan.

He is the author of *Industry-College Relations, The Art of Problem Solving, The Art of Working With People, Which College for You?,* and *So You Want to Go Into Industry.*

Format by Gayle A. Jaeger
Set in Linotype Caledonia
Composed, printed and bound by The Haddon Craftsmen, Inc.
HARPER & ROW, PUBLISHERS, INCORPORATED